The Ecstatic World
of
JOHN COWPER POWYS

Also by H. W. Fawkner

*Animation and Reification in Dickens's Vision of the
Life-Denying Society* (1977)

The Timescapes of John Fowles (1984)

The Ecstatic World
of
JOHN COWPER
POWYS

H. W. Fawkner

RUTHERFORD • MADISON • TEANECK
FAIRLEIGH DICKINSON UNIVERSITY PRESS
LONDON AND TORONTO: ASSOCIATED UNIVERSITY PRESSES

© 1986 by Associated University Presses, Inc.

Associated University Presses
440 Forsgate Drive
Cranbury, NJ 08512

Associated University Presses
25 Sicilian Avenue
London WC1A 2QH, England

Associated University Presses
2133 Royal Windsor Drive
Unit 1
Mississauga, Ontario
Canada L5J 1K5

The paper used in this publication meets the minimum requirements of the American National Standard for Permanence of Paper for Printed Library Materials Z39.48-1984.

Library of Congress Cataloging-in-Publication Data

Fawkner, Harald William, 1946–
    The ecstatic world of John Cowper Powys.

    Bibliography: p.
    Includes index.
    1. Powys, John Cowper, 1872–1963—Criticism and
interpretation.   I. Title.
PR6031.O867Z716   1986   828'.91209   84-48690
ISBN 0-8386-3249-1 (alk. paper)

Printed in the United States of America

For my son
ROBIN FAWKNER

And would it not be reasonable to affirm that what is essentially eternal and divine also knows all things in a divine manner, but what is human in a human manner, and that the undivided already indivisibly contains even the divided; the eternal, in a manner beyond time, even the temporal; and the rational reasonably even the irrational? It is clear from this that both gods and spirits will know both the intermediate determinately and the unstable stably and firmly.

Proclus, Alcibiades I

Thus it becomes quite definite for consciousness how its perceiving is essentially constituted, viz. that it is not a simple pure apprehension, but *in its apprehension* is at the same time *reflected out of the True and into itself.* This return of consciousness into itself which is directly *mingled* with the pure apprehension [of the object]—for this return into itself has shown itself to be essential to perception—alters the truth. Consciousness at once recognizes this aspect as its own and takes responsibility for it; by doing so it will obtain the true object in its purity.

Hegel, Phenomenology of Spirit

As soon as we admit spacing both as "interval" or difference and as openness upon the outside, there can no longer be any absolute inside, for the "outside" has insinuated itself into the movement by which the inside of the nonspatial, which is called "time," appears, is constituted, is "presented." Space is "in" time; it is time's pure leaving-itself; it is the "outside-itself" as the self-relation of time. The externality of space, externality as space, does not overtake time; rather, it opens as pure "outside" "within" the movement of temporalization.

Derrida, Speech and Phenomena

Now although it would be very foolish to see in the phenomena of animal magnetism an elevation of mind above even Reason with its ability to comprehend, and to expect from this state a higher knowledge of the eternal than that imparted by philosophy, and although the fact is that the magnetic state must be declared pathological and a degradation of mind below the level even of ordinary consciousness in so far as in that state mind surrenders its thinking as an activity creative of specific distinctions, as an activity contradistinguished from Nature: yet, on the other hand, in the visible liberation of mind in those magnetic phenomena from the limitations of space and time and from all finite associations, there is something akin to philosophy, something which, as brute fact, defies the scepticism of the abstractive intellect and so necessitates the advance from ordinary psychology to the comprehension afforded by speculative philosophy for which alone animal magnetism is not an incomprehensible miracle.

Hegel, Philosophy of Spirit

And when you gaze long into an abyss the abyss also gazes into you.

Nietzsche, Beyond Good and Evil

CONTENTS

ACKNOWLEDGMENTS

I wish to thank Laurence Pollinger Ltd. and the Estate of John Cowper Powys for permission to quote from Powys's works. Mr. Thomas Yoseloff first supported the publication of this book. I extend special gratitude to him and to Professor C. Schaar, who read the first manuscript and inspired theoretical innovation in general. Miss Katharine Turok most helpfully clarified various editorial issues, and Ms. Beth Gianfagna provided valuable assistance in the ultimate stages of editing and typesetting. Finally, I would like to establish my cordial gratitude to Carolyn Sylvander, University of Wisconsin, Whitewater, who, like Denis Lane of the Powys Society of North America, was instrumental in bringing the text to its definitive form. Grateful acknowledgment is also made to Prentice-Hall, Inc. for quotations from Arthur L. Blumenthal, *The Process of Cognition* © 1977, pp. 19, 20, 21 (reprinted by permission of Prentice-Hall, Inc., Englewood Cliffs, N.J.); to Academic Press for "Time and Consciousness" by Richard A. Block, in *Aspects of Consciousness*, volume 1.

WORKS BY JOHN COWPER POWYS
(1872–1963)

Wood and Stone	1915
Rodmoor	1916
Confessions of Two Brothers	1916
After My Fashion	posthumous
The Complex Vision	1920
Ducdame	1925
Wolf Solent	1929
The Meaning of Culture	1929
In Defence of Sensuality	1930
A Glastonbury Romance	1932
A Philosophy of Solitude	1933
Autobiography	1934
Weymouth Sands	1934
The Art of Happiness	1935
Maiden Castle	1936
Morwyn	1937
Owen Glendower	1940
Mortal Strife	1942
The Art of Growing Old	1944
Porius	1951
The Inmates	1952
In Spite Of	1953
Atlantis	1954
The Brazen Head	1956
Up and Out	1957
All or Nothing	1960

The original editions have been used in quoting from the works of John Cowper Powys, except in the following cases. The Picador editions have been used for *Autobiography, The Brazen Head, A Glastonbury Romance, Maiden Castle, Owen Glendower,* and *Weymouth Sands.* The Village Press editions have been used for *The Complex Vision, Ducdame, Mortal Strife, The Meaning of Culture,* and *Wood and Stone.* Quotations in *Confessions of Two Brothers* refer to the Sinclair Brown edition, in *Morwyn* to the Sphere Books edition, in *Rodmoor* to the Macdonald/Colgate edition, and in *Wolf Solent* to the Penguin edition.

ABBREVIATIONS

WeS	*Weymouth Sands*
WoS	*Wolf Solent*
WS	*Wood and Stone*

Each quotation is followed by a chapter and page reference, except in cases where the quotation is taken from the same page as the one given in one or several preceding quotations. Abbreviations have been omitted wherever the reference is obvious from the context. It is to be observed that there are two works by Powys called *The Art of Happiness*. In this study, I refer throughout to the *book* with this title (first published in 1935) not to the *booklet* (first published in 1923). It should also be noted that different versions of *The Meaning of Culture* have different paginations. Finally, one must point out that critics are still waiting for the full version of *Porius*. When this appears, the novel will no doubt deserve a more generous treatment than the one given here.

INTRODUCTION

As I stand back from the written past of this completed study and look for some supplementary notions that could suggest its place within the overarching concerns of modern critical thinking, I am struck by what seems to be the synchronic bias of my project—its lack of emphasis on the temporal background that shapes the particular literary achievement. This leaning away from the diachronic toward the synchronic is, however, quite illusory. Indeed, were I to challenge certain existing criticisms of John Cowper Powys—there are several finely written ones—I would base such a challenge on their tendency to be ahistorical. Much depends here, of course, on what we mean by the history of a work. For some people, the intellectual past of a novel is thinkable in terms of literary influences, biographical data, and so forth. For me, however, the temporal-intellectual dimension means much more than this—means so much more, indeed, that these "facts" that seem to be formative in the conception of the work look quite trivial and unimportant. They are not unimportant in themselves, or unimportant for scholarship; but they certainly are insignificant in relation to other, much wider forces. This is particularly so when these wider forces are left unexplained, or when their presence is not even felt.

The historical dimension of a literary work, in the broader sense, can only be suggested through an awareness of the larger sweeps of history. If history, for us, is simply such and such a decade, this or that particular period that immediately preceded the publication of the work, or even the three recent centuries in which novels have been written, then we are likely to miss the most crucial points that can be made about Powys's work from a diachronic point of view. For, in fact, Powys's thought questions the tacit assumptions of the entire post-Cartesian era; and when criticism does not give itself (historical) elbowroom sufficient to throw that era into a critical light, it is likely to become blind to its own belonging to Cartesian thought.

Commonsensical, unselfconscious criticism takes for granted precisely the post-Cartesian epistemology that John Cowper Powys did not take for granted. The shift to first person perspective in metaphysics initiated by Descartes led to a line of thought in Western philosophy that totally contradicts Powys's views by seeking to purify subjectivity—indeed, to rid us of subjectivity. This movement climaxed in Kant's (fallacious) notion of the thing-in-itself, a notion that quickly infected aesthetics through Schiller's notion of the *aesthetic* thing-in-itself. In fact, this spurious notion that the work of imagination is an object of some kind— thus open to investigation as objects are open to investigation—has completely dominated criticism for centuries. It is rooted, essentially, in a single work of German idealism, Schiller's *On the Aesthetic Education of Man.* Out of Cartesianism springs "scientific" man—that is, unscientific man. He is a man, who, through a sleight of hand, thinks he can do away with subjectivity by purifying it and making it absolutely transparent. Having performed this trick, "scientific" man sets out to study a *thing,* something he believes has certain fixed, inert, autonomous properties, all liberated from the subjectivity of consciousness and self-consciousness. The result of this sleight of hand is the unselfconscious observer, the one who has converted his ignorance of the mechanisms of (his own) awareness into a facile notion of objectivity.

Against this type of creature fights dialectical man, fights John Cowper Powys. Cartesian man has of course his own (naive) idea of dialecticity. He thinks one thing is "here," another "there;" and then he posits some "dialectics" between these two fixed and inert givens. Descartes, like Fichte and Husserl, believes that man has an immediate intuition of himself. First there is himself, then there is the world that becomes discoverable to this self. For Cartesian man, knowledge is thus a relation between me and the world, between a knower and the known. Nearly all Western philosophers believe in this model. The greatest of them all, however, does not: in a famous section of his *Phenomenology of Spirit* (§§178–96), Hegel shows that the idea of a *Cogito* as an intuitive given is fallacious; subjectivity is a result, not a beginning; consciousness-of precedes consciousness. Jacques Derrida, probably the most important—and certainly the most influential—thinker of our time, has introduced this Hegelian concept into the field of literary criticism, thus finally overthrowing the facile notions of objectivity formerly used to promote Schillerian aestheticism. Dialectical man does not believe that there is *first* a subject and *then* an object (for consciousness)—and that some kind of "dialectic" follows upon this. No, dialectical man believes that there is always already dialectic. Dialectical man believes that the study of our (self-)awareness *is* the study of the objective world. This does not at all mean (as Cartesian man tends to believe in his misunderstanding of Hegelian idealism) that "everything is in the mind." The Hegelian theory does not at all cause dialectical man to find truth in subjectivity, untruth in objectivity; nor does it in any way cause him to believe that truth is the dialectical "interaction" between subjectivity and objectivity. The theory means, in fact, that there is always some kind of dialecticity *before* any given entity can come into being at all: whether physically or psychically. Dialectics precedes the subject, precedes the object. Common sense cannot understand this at all. Common sense (whether in popular consciousness or in Cartesian scientism) counts "One-two-three-four-five-six-seven," and so on—and so does dialectical man. But there is one crucial difference. Dialectical man suggests that the world only makes sense if we add a "Two" *before* the first "One:" giving "Two-one-two-three-four-five-six-seven," and so on. This notion does not imply that you suddenly discover that you have two dollars, when you have spent your last dollar; it is a metaphysical notion of ontological suggestibility, implying that unity fails to make sense without duality, that duality in some sense must "precede" monality. If this were not the case, there would be no becoming, no difference, no fluidity, no movement in the cosmos—no creation becoming created.

I am suggesting, then, that if John Cowper Powys is to be understood diachronically, what we first need is not information about certain *events* in the past immediately preceding this or that work, this or that phase of his intellectual development; what we first need is an understanding of his (historical) place within the overall patternings of Western thought.

What is this place? There are two ways of viewing the issue. The first is to look upon Powys as a man writing within a very ancient tradition—a tradition, indeed, which has roots in Vedantism and ancient oriental schools of thought, most of them seeking truth through the enhancement of self-awareness. More directly Powys's thought is related to the thought of the late Stoics in Rome, in which emphasis is given to withdrawal from the world and indifference to its frustrations (Seneca, Epictetus, Marcus Aurelius). Self-awareness, here, is not simply a metaphysical notion—Aristotle's "thought thinking itself"—but an autonomous domain offering absolute freedom, a divine world where all events can be controlled because they are interiorized. This tradition of Stoicism is related to that of Skepticism. In the fourth and third centuries B.C., the great Skeptic Pyrrho returned from India to preach a doctrine of human happiness through a life of quietude, simplicity, silence, and anti-intellectualism. Like Gurdjieff in our own century, Pyrrho had a student

(Sextus Empiricus) who committed the master's purely oral teachings to writing. There are significant similarities between a work such as Powys's *The Art of Happiness* and Sextus Empiricus's *Outlines of Pyrrhonism.*

There is, however, a second way of viewing Powys's place in Western thought, and this alternative way, I submit, is far more important. The major problem for philosophy has been to explain how God, who must be the One, can be reconciled with the world, which is the many. How can the harmonious ideality of the godhead ultimately become reconciled with the chaotic diversification of lived reality? How, in other words, does the cosmos produce difference and still remain cosmos—that is, order? The only viable answer to this question has been given by a few great thinkers who have chosen to break with the entire central tradition of Western metaphysics—notably, Hegel, Nietzsche, and Derrida (possibly also Heidegger). The answer is to be found in a refusal to accept the premises of the question. *The cosmos does not produce difference; difference produces the cosmos.* Although this at first looks like a quite simple idea (indeed a truism that we immediately grasp), it is in fact extremely complex and contradicts the commonsensicality with which we normally conceptualize reality. Thus we take for granted what we ultimately must refuse to take for granted: the self-unity of a thing, the self-identity of a consciousness, the primordial selfsameness of any given entity that we innocently believe has some autonomous stability as a fixed given in a world of fixed givens. The idea that Two gives One (replacing the idea that One gives Two) is so explosive—if we begin to apply it rigorously and universally—that we begin to live in a metaphysically inverted world, a world, indeed, that completely erases and surmounts the commonsensical world. It annihilates a naturalistically conceived world of "things"—but also an idealistically conceived world of Platonic forms, or fixed Ideas. These two worlds, the materialist and the Platonic, are conceived, Derrida would say, by the "metaphysics of presence"—that is, by the notion of selfsameness (without self-repulsion) that Hegel so successfully attacked. So odd, so uncanny, does the (Hegelian) inverted world become that language seems to refuse to mediate a vision of it. It is significant that the thinkers who have troubled to fight against the metaphysics of presence have found themselves trapped in language itself: so that their metaphysical ventures have become linguistic ventures, efforts to use language in order to avoid being used by *it.* One thinks of the immense obscurity of Hegel's rhetoric, its teasing convolutions; one thinks of Nietzsche's extravagance, his high-pitched hysteria, his violence; one thinks of Derrida's absolute excess, his obscene elusiveness. Insofar as John Cowper Powys is himself odd, awkward, tortuous, self-complicating, this to a large extent reflects the characteristic desire to escape from the conventional conceptualizations and (linguistic-imagistic) compartmentalizations of traditional thought. Just as a Hegel, a Nietzsche, a Heidegger, a Derrida, can be dismissed as a windy crackpot, a charlatan wrapped in euphemisms, so John Cowper can be dismissed as a pretentious fool—an interesting but ultimately unsystematic thinker. My purpose, in this book, is to refute that view.

It may be objected, at this point, that my thesis is contradicted by Powys himself. Does he not consistently warn us against the "in-sucking vortex of this final development of the Hegelian Universe" (*MS*, XIV, 231)? Is he not, in fact, the very opposite of a Hegelian? Indeed, does not Derrida himself (the father of poststructuralist criticism) warn us against Hegel, constantly suggest a cosmos that escapes the final Hegelian *Aufhebung* (surmounting of difference)?

These questions and the answer I shall give to them suggest my reasons for sticking (within the limited scope of this work) to the synchronic and the psychological—leaving the diachronic and the philosophical aside for the moment. If you *are* going to bring in Hegel into the actual business of analyzing a text, you cannot do this in a halfhearted way. *The Phenomenology of Spirit*, probably the greatest intellectual achievement of Western man, is an immensely complex work; moreover, it is difficult throughout, frequently unreadable. The most radical of all Hegel's notions is the principle of the identity of opposites: identity, he says *is* difference, and vice versa. But this principle applies also to Hegel himself; Hegel is not Hegel. Hegel, in other words, is not a selfsameness; he is, just like the identities he discusses, in a state of self-repulsion. Hegel is Hegel versus Hegel. Thus, it is common knowledge among philosophers that it is possible to distinguish a first, conventional, monistic Hegel as well as a "second" Hegel—a totally different Hegel, who is much more radical and audacious in his thinking. It is this "second" Hegel, largely, that inspires Derrida. Because of this internal rift within Hegel, the most Hegelian of all philosophers—Derrida—can define his venture as anti-Hegelian. It is extremely important for us to understand this tension within Hegel, not only because Hegel is the thinker closest to John Cowper Powys and because Derrida is the chief force behind modern critical theory, but also because this tension between Hegel and Hegel has an exact equivalent in Powys himself. This is the tension that he gradually begins to work out as the conflict between the universe and the multiverse. What he ultimately keeps saying is this: the cosmos is a universe-multiverse. Yet this does not make sense; for in the universe unity finally always overcomes diversification, and in the multiverse diversification finally always triumphs over unity. One side submits that there is finally synthesis; the other side submits that there is finally no synthesis at all.

Clearly, an over-synthesis between this synthesis (championed by monism) and this non-synthesis (championed by anti-monism) is rather absurd, perhaps theoretically nonsensical. The tension soon becomes unbearable—and it is out of this immense strain that the intellectual venture is born. Needless to say, perhaps, it will manifest itself in terms of a gigantic self-contradictoriness. Yet this (as in the cases of Hegel, Nietzsche, Heidegger, and Derrida) is the beauty and strength of that venture, not its weakness.

Is John Cowper a monist?—no, he is far too obsessed with difference, displacement, contingency (H, 20). Is he an anti-monist?—no, he is far too obsessed with finding some cosmic clue that would bring endless diversification under the supervising control of a sovereign formula. Is he then something between a monist and an anti-monist?—certainly not, such a hybrid is ridiculous, less valid that the two first options. We are left, then, with only one possibility, and this is that there must be some fourth option. The fact that this fourth option is inconceivable from the viewpoint of classical ontology is not something that will obstruct the intellectual project; on the contrary, it will be the very driving force behind it.

In summary, then, there is cleavage in the world, permitting us to be guilty with our left hand and innocent with our right (LLW, 216). In addition, this polarity is a double polarity, for one of our hands itself clutches polarity, whereas the other rejects or ignores polarity. G. Wilson Knight has argued that there is some central lack in criticism, since a full and comprehensive theory of criticism ought to be able to come to terms with the richness of John Cowper Powys's literary achievement. I am in absolute agreement with this view. Moreover, I think the theoretical supplementations for which we are looking are discoverable within the thinking of Powys himself.

John Cowper's favorite element was water; Hegel, *contra* Plato, believed that the Absolute was fluid. I think there is a significant connection. Water, the ocean, is at one and the same time something fully selfsame to itself and something fully nonselfsame to itself. It is absolutely itself; yet it can only achieve this absolute self-identity through a (fluid) process of self-repulsion, of visible self-effacement and metamorphosis. The ocean, as Derrida would say, *is not.* Its identity *is* its nonidentity. Water distinguishes itself from itself through a zero-distinction, what Hegel in the *Phenomenology* calls "a distinction which is none" (§258). A moving liquid surface, a heaving massive fluidity, is continually suspending its own being. Its being *is* its nonbeing. The ocean is not a thing—not something that first *is* and then happens to have movement added to this "is-ness;" on the contrary, the sea is unthinkable (qua sea) without motion (of some kind). Motion precedes nonmotion—a metaphysical notion that runs back, in the West, to Heraclitus. Strictly speaking, then, it is naive to think of the world in terms of *things* (§236). Ontologically, fluidity precedes thing-ness. The self-movement that is explicit in the ocean is in fact (implicitly) present even in the apparently most fixed and inert "objects." According to naive realism, the world is just "there" (*AFU*, 10). For a Russell, reality is given through the atomic facts of sense data; but against such a view stands the more subtle one that knowing presupposes the universals that we use to pick out atomic particulars. This red pen I am holding seems to be something that my atomic (that is, monadic) subjectivity immediately and intuitively grasps as that which it is. This immediacy, however (this atomic selfsameness of myself, this atomic selfsameness of my red pen) is an illusion. The individual "thing" (whether the self or the red pen) presupposes a system of differentiation, or infinite difference. The redness of my pen can only be given to me (as redness) in a world where all the other colors in the world *precede* it—not experientially, but logically, ontologically. A baby can smile at the redness of a pen without first having knowledge of any other colors; but the point is that she could not do this in a world that did not *already* include all other colors. First you have all colors, then you have one color; first you have difference, then you have atomic givens: facts, things, individuals, sensations. Strictly speaking, the only thing that actually *is* is difference (§235); but we do not "see" it; it is perfectly transparent. The red pen *is not*, because it is (implicitly) also a blue pen, a green pen, a yellow pen, a pink pen, a gray pen, a black pen, and so on. The red pen only knows itself as such through the secret workings of otherness within it. Ontologically, in fact, the red pen is fluid: it rests peacefully in my left hand; yet, really, it acquires this stability only through a tremulation, only through a self-movement that is invisible to me because of its enormity.

There is a crucial passage (to be discussed later) in *Wolf Solent*, where the protagonist rejects ontological self-identity (*WoS*, VII, 153). The face of the miserable man he has seen outside Waterloo Station (I, 15) represents infinite unhappiness. But Wolf comes to see that this unhappiness *is not*. Because this unhappiness is infinite and absolute, it turns over into its opposite. Powys does not only say that this (experientially) absolute misery is something relative in a world that knows both misery and felicity; he also says that this suffering *is* happiness. This, obviously, is no psychologically relevant statement—it is an ontological statement. Powys is not saying that there is some kind of infinite pleasure in being infinitely uncomfortable; he is saying that the opposite of misery is (implicitly) at work within misery itself. In the *Phenomenology*, Hegel advances the idea that each thing is its own opposite:

> We have to think pure change, or *think antithesis within the antithesis itself*, or *contradiction*. For in the difference which is an inner difference, the opposite is not merely *one of two*—if it were, it would simply *be*, without being an opposite—but it is the opposite of an opposite, or the other is itself immediately present in it. Certainly, I put the "opposite" here, and the "other" of which it is the opposite, there; the "opposite," then, is on one side, is in and for itself without the "other." But just because I have the "opposite" here in and for itself, it is the opposite of itself, or it has, in fact, the "other" immediately present in it. (§160)

Now any schoolboy can understand that a black and a white ball next to one another are polar antagonists. He can also easily grasp that the black ball is still an "opposite" when the white ball is removed or made invisible. What he is not likely to grasp, however, is that the black ball is the opposite of itself. Even if there were no white balls around anywhere in the world, there would still be a white ball (implicitly) present "within" the black ball. If this were not the case, the black ball could not gather itself into itself as "black ball." Identity is always subverted and erased by nonidentity. Identity, in other words, is a secondary phenomenon—is a result.

I mention these metaphysical notions in order to make it absolutely clear that this book, while seeming to be a purely psychological study of John Cowper Powys's work, in fact is (implicitly) an ontological inquiry into them. Or, to be more exact: the psychological venture, in examining situations where the self paradigmatically shoots out of itself, itself moves out of itself—so that psychology as such slides over into ontology.

The psychological mechanism we are about to study is ecstasy. "Ecstasy" is a word of Greek origin and means standing-out. Standing-out from what? From the self. Or, as I shall argue, from one "I" into another "I." But this shift from "I" to "I" (or in my terminology, from Ego to Self), while *manifesting* itself as a psychological event, can in fact be seen in terms of an ontological displacement. This is why I have mentioned Hegel's concept of the Absolute as fluidity. If the Absolute slides in some way (away from itself, or into itself, or both at once), then ec-stasy is the only event in our mind that fully brings us into intuitive alignment with this sliding. When, in other words, we "stand out" of ourselves in ecstasy, we stand "into" Being. Why? Because Being itself is a standing-out. This notion that I have called a sliding has been glimpsed and evoked by most great thinkers, and the choice of imagery used to suggest it is ultimately a matter of taste—Hegel speaks of a lifting-up, Heidegger of a falling-in, Derrida of a spreading-apart *(differance)* and so forth.

Why is it important to understand this ontological dimension in John Cowper Powys? Because it is the only idea that gives insight into the writer's special attitude to sensuality. If I have called John *Cowper's* multiverse-universe the *Cowperverse*, I have done this primarily to suggest its magnificent idiosyncrasy. Cow*perverse*, however, also suggests the notion of a topsy-turvy world, a world that is not only inverted, but doubly inverted. In order to escape, like Powys, from naturalism as well as from Platonism, from materialism as well as from (primitive) idealism, Hegel developed the idea of a doubly inverted world *(die verkehrte Welt*, §§157–65). In the *Republic,* Plato posits an absolute world of real Forms outside the cave where the prisoners are trapped in the phenomenal world of sensory certitude. The philosopher, here, fallaciously imagines some fixed ideality that is supposed to spawn "appearances." This notion of a fixed ideality survives, it can easily be argued, in Kant's notion of the thing-in-itself, in Husserl's idea of pure intuition—even in Heidegger's concept of authentic Being. Like Powys, however, Hegel believed in a conceptual world that was dynamic, not static; fluid, not fixed *(AFU,* 7). This conceptual world, moreover, was not really divorced from the sensual and objective world of appearances. The difference between the two was, again, a difference which is "none." The difference between the thing (in its corporeality) and the thing-in-itself (in its conceptual ideality) is, so to speak, a difference within the thing itself: it is the very difference that permits the thing to be distanced from itself as an entity requiring space and time.

I shall now explain why it is essential to grasp the ontological status of an object in this odd, perverse, topsy-turvy, absurd, *verkehrte,* inverted world. Powys is immensely fascinated by things. Yet he is not fascinated by things qua things; he is fascinated by objects insofar as objects suggest a world of fluid ideality. But this fluid ideality, far from being a Platonic overworld, is an ideality that is, as it were, "inside" the thing. The curious subject-object interaction that characterizes Powysian awareness can only come into being in a world where both subject and object are in a state of self-repulsion. The subject is a subject-subject (is fluid), and the object is an object-object (is equally fluid). Because he is much more open to the ontological instability of all entities than the average writer, Powys comes to define a world in which objects are neither things sensually enjoyed by self-refining hedonism, nor mere symbols representing an ideal overworld fundamentally divorced from their objective actuality. He does not achieve his greatest effects through descriptions of the thing qua thing (for this is often trivial, common, plain, indeed vulgar); instead, he gives intensity to the act of perception by suggesting that particular state in which we all, at one time or another, have glimpsed the divineness of Being in the mysterious factualness of ordinary things. The Powys world, it will be seen, is neither a world of material objects naturalistically described, nor a world of floating idealities devoid of sensual substance. Least of all is it a world in between these two alternatives. Thus, in *Wolf Solent,* chapter XVII climaxes in Wolf's ecstatic enjoyment of Gerda's blackbird song (in itself an event of ontological significance, suggesting a sliding between the human and the subhuman, so that in Wolf's inability to differentiate Gerda's voice from that of a real blackbird, a vibrant indeterminancy is given to the singing itself); but when Wolf returns home, after this ecstatic experience, Powys does not have to give any special twist to his description of the objects in the building. He lets us understand that Wolf is still in an altered state of consciousness; and because he has so skillfully convinced us of the reality of this state, Powys only has to enumerate the objects seen by Wolf to achieve the effect he wants:

> A blackbird was whistling above his head! Faint and low at first, each liquid flute-note went sailing away upon the wind . . .
> Then the notes changed, varied, overlapped, grew charged with some secret intention, some burden of immeasurable happiness, of sadness sweeter than happiness.
> Rising still, freer, stronger, fuller, they began to gather to themselves the resonant volume of some incredible challenge, a challenge from the throat of life itself to all that obstructed it. Tossed forth upon the darkness, wild and sweet and free, this whistled bird-song, answering the voice of the rising wind, took to itself something that was at once so jocund and so wistful, that it seemed to him as though all the defiant acceptance of fate that he had ever found in green grass, in cool-rooted plants, in the valiant bodies of beasts and birds and fishes . . . had been distilled, by some miracle, in this one human mouth.
> The whistling sank into silence at the very moment when its power over Wolf's soul was at the flood. But without one single second of delay, when the last note had died, Gerda came scrambling down, laughing, rustling the leaves, and giving vent to petulant little outcries as her clothes impeded her descent. Wolf, when she finally fell, all panting and tremulous with wild gaiety, into his arms, felt that it was difficult to believe that this was the same Gerda whom he had watched, that very noon, asleep on the summit of Poll's Camp.
> As they returned hand in hand to their house door, a queer, abashed sense came over him that all the events of this turbulent day had been a sort of feverish delirium. What *was* his mind that it should go through

such agitation and remain unaltered—remain the same "I am I" of Wolf
Solent?

But once again his self-knowledge received a shock. For no sooner
were they inside their small domicile, no sooner had he glanced at the
linoleum on the staircase, the wooden clock in the parlour, the familiar
kitchen-table, than all these little objects hit his consciousness with a
delicious thrilling sense of happy security, as if he had come back to
them from some great voyage over desolate and forlorn seas, . . . his
hands wounded by tarred ropes! His mind may have remained unaltered by all this but it had at any rate been washed very clean!

Upon every tiniest and least-important object he looked, that night,
with a purged simplicity, a spontaneous satisfaction. The pine-wood
boarding at the edge of the linoleum stair-carpet, the pegs where their
coats hung, the handles of the dresser drawers, the rows of balanced
plates, the cups suspended from the little hooks, the metal knobs at the
end of their bed, Gerda's comb and brush, the candlestick still covered
with grease, and two exposed soap-dishes on the washing-stand, one
containing a small piece of Pears' soap and one containing a square
lump of common yellow soap—all these things thrilled him, fascinated
him, threw him into an ecstasy of well-being. (XVII, 372–74)

Am I suggesting, then, that John Cowper Powys is "influenced" by
Hegel? Am I suggesting that Powys, equipped with Hegelian wisdom,
shapes his imaginative universe in terms of a fixed and elaborate metaphysical scheme? Certainly not. The novelist has, to be sure, read much
of Hegel's work (A, X, 478, 518), but he is also familiar with numerous
other philosophies. Moreover, he is so individualistic that he only brings
into his own overall schemes certain select fragments from the various
systems of thought that he encounters. These he absorbs into his unique
and individual awareness. Why, then, need we involve Hegel? As I have
suggested, a writer is not a universe but a multiverse—a notion I shall
develop as we come to discuss the phenomenon of multiple personality.
When I claim that Powys is *ultimately* closest to Hegel in Western thinking, I am considering a very complex Powys and a very complex Hegel.
Just as there are all kinds of statements in Hegel that contradict the
highest insights of Hegel (which are ontological insights), so there are all
kinds of statements in Powys that contradict (or seem to contradict)
Powys. The first great task that criticism must set up for itself—whether
in Hegel criticism or Powys criticism—is that of defining subsystems
within the intellectual multiverse of the individual thinker. Once certain
clusters of ideas have been clarified, there follows the task of establishing
some kind of hierarchy. Which ideas are central, crucial? Which ideas are
of marginal significance? If the critic believes that the writer has a single,

selfsame "I" without internal rifts and displacements, he will fall into the enormous error of imagining that all the statements and ideas of the writer belong to one single, unified field of discourse. He will then think that ideas that contradict one another (in the writer's work) actually cancel one another.

In reality, however, the ideational world of a great writer is hierarchically structured. Sometimes, he is writing with a slack hand; at other times, he is writing in a white heat. In this way, the inner world of the writer is an intellectual landscape with fairly autonomous regions of intellection—each with its own color, rhythm, strategy, and level of intensity. When I claim that John Cowper Powys's thought is akin to Hegel's, indeed sometimes almost coextensive with it, I am not at all thinking in terms of "influence." I am suggesting, instead, that the most intense regions of intellectual awareness in the two writers come to deal with one and the same nucleus of insight. This nucleus of insight—also penetrated by Shakespeare's texts—is a sphere with a logic that we are still only beginning to understand. It may be that, in our efforts to approach this sphere, we are in fact removing ourselves from it.

The Ecstatic World
of
JOHN COWPER POWYS

1
THE COWPERVERSE

1.1 Ego and Self

The intelligent exploration of the world of John Cowper Powys immediately involves subtle questions of psychology. In *Weymouth Sands,* Dr. Daniel Brush suddenly does away with the old psychoanalytical theories with which he has been professionally concerned as leading psychiatrist for Hell's Museum. He arrives at "a totally new perspective in scientific psychology" (XIV, 505). The subsequent presentation of a radically innovative model of the mind is part of John Cowper Powys's sustained campaign against reductionist behaviorism and reductionist Freudianism. He does not turn instead to any alternative psychology that flourished at this time. Instead, he develops a quite intricate model of his own. The reader who takes the trouble to explore most of Powys's nonfictional works will find that his model is remarkably similar to those developed by today's cognitive scientists.[1]

The difference between the first and second psychologies of Dr. Brush suggests the difference between the old-fashioned psychology that literary criticism usually relies on and the psychology that is outlined in this book. Freudianism posits an *equator line* dividing the mind into an Above and a Below, whereas contemporary cognitive science sees a *fall line* separating the sinistral from the dextral. This latter cleavage is not to be thought of simplistically as the physiological rift between the two lobes of the brain. Nevertheless, functional brain asymmetry plays enough of a role to warrant the preference of right/left dualisms over above/below dualisms.[2] The present study will use terms derived from modern neuroscience rather than from "psychoanalysis." While *sinistral thinking* and *dextral thinking* will be easily misunderstood by naïve adherents of bicameral psychologism, I find these words to be more scientifically precise and critically suggestive for an analysis of the Powys world than the old *unconscious, subconscious, ego, id, superego,* and so forth. These terms have not only been exhausted through use and misuse—they no longer have any true scientific value even in the purity of their virginal form as conceived by Freud and others.

In *Weymouth Sands,* Powys informs us that Dr. Brush had come to a sudden new insight: "The breaking up of that mysterious 'equator-line' between Conscious and Unconscious and the merging of these two worlds into one equally fantastical continent began to lead to the spasmodic introduction of new methods in the psychiatry of Hell's Museum" (XIV, 507). Intense inner dislocations are no longer explained in terms of an upstairs/downstairs antinomy:

> In his old system these volcanic neuroses were resident in an entirely subliminal region, a permanent underworld of the human ego from which they broke forth to cause unhappiness and anguish. This region was out of reach, and possessed locked, adamantine gates, as far as our ordinary processes of mental introspection went. . . . Daniel Brush's new theory, on the other hand, abolished this distinction between conscious, and sub-conscious as arbitrary and dogmatic, and, in place of this hard-and-fast division, regarded the whole ocean of human experience,[3] with all its maddest and most unspeakable delusions, as *always open* to flashes of intelligent exploitation by minds that cared to dive into that deep sea. . . .
>
> One of these clue-thoughts that came to the Doctor . . was that not only from the surface of that sea within us *but from all levels and depths of it* we have the power of coming into contact with one another. . . . It was the unequalled objectivity of Daniel Brush's mind that was the cause of this mental "volte-face." (XIV, 505–6)

It is crucial to understand the difference between the Freudian equator line and the Powysian fall line because John Cowper Powys has centered his whole literary effort on the *altered state of consciousness,* what we shall here call *ecstasy* (a shorter and more manageable term); and this phenomenon of the altered state of consciousness is precisely what Freud never comes to terms with and never can come to terms with. For this reason, Freudianism downgrades ecstasy, writing it off, with daydreaming,[4] as an aberration. Ecstasy, daydreaming, and ecstatic daydreaming are looked upon as atavistic forms of mental life. There is said to be a regression to "primary-process" thinking.[5] Today cognitive science is building toward a totally different analysis and evaluation of these phenomena. It is likely that they play a centermost role in the mental world.[6] Far from dismissing ecstasy and daydream to the periphery, we shall place them at center stage. As we follow the thought of John Cowper Powys, we shall notice that he is continually stressing ecstasy and daydream as keys to the riddle of consciousness. I shall call the universe/multiverse of John Cowper Powys the *Cowperverse:*[7] a world in which ecstasy is both entrance and exit. It is entrance because Powys manages to gear himself into a non-drug–induced ecstasy in order to achieve the extraordinary creative mood out of which his best works spring. It is exit because no sophisticated reader can avoid being contaminated by this special mood. John Cowper Powys alters consciousness.[8]

Bypassing the whole issue of ecstatic daydream and the altered state of consciousness (both of which I refer to as *dextral thinking*), Freudianism and post-Freudianism have seemed to demystify the mind. In fact, however, the opposite has happened. Freudianism is mystification. The more psychology rejects the idea of the altered state of consciousness as a primary faculty of intellection, the more absurd become its attempts to account for the significant displacements that ecstasy creates. The problem can be understood historically too. Ecstasy has always been the fuel of faith and mysticism. In its efforts to get away from myth and superstition, science also made sure to get away from ecstasy.[9] Indeed this is perhaps the thing it most of all wanted to get rid of. The logic of this is simple but nevertheless spurious: science is the opposite of superstition; superstition springs from ecstasy; therefore, ecstasy must be the opposite of science. This kind of thinking still runs as an invisible undercurrent among those scientists who have not yet been illuminated by the "third revolution," or "cognitive revolution."[10] The fear of ecstasy is the hallmark of the lesser scientists. Criticism has not been entirely free from this fear.

I mention these issues first because they are essential in an understanding of a writer who is so intimately concerned with mystification, demystification, myth, mythology, and mystery; second, because they are of chief significance in determining what mode of procedure will be most suitable and profitable for the exploration of the Powys world. This is also a matter of scientific-academic respectability. I do not believe that a straightforward, commonsensical, positivistic approach to John Cowper Powys will do him justice. Nor do I believe in magical insight through the tracing of literary or mythological "influences." I do not think Powys can be "explained" quite that simply. He himself warns against both procedures:

The pedant's point of view is the strictly explanatory one. What in every least detail were the opinions of Aristotle, of Hegel, of Spinoza? As to the living application of these doctrines to his own stream of consciousness—that is another matter. The typical philistine, on the contrary, labours under the illusion that all these early systems are steps forward in a steady line of progression. Philosophy, to the Philistine, is an evolutionary process, watched over by some sort of brisk dynamic Providence, and culminating in the supreme insight of modern thought. (*MofC*, I, 19)

Like various other Powys critics, I do not believe that a clarification of the structure of different myths, used by Powys in his novels, clarifies anything central in the structure of the novels themselves. Indeed, I think the very opposite. The novelist is quite explicit on this matter, as can be seen from his advice to the reader of Dante's *Inferno,* in *The Meaning of Culture:* "Slide lightly . . . over the historical allusions. Dodge the theological problems" (III, 55). I believe that the knowledge currently emerging about the workings of the mind explains more than "source" research explains. This view may upset some people, but it would not upset John Cowper Powys himself:

> There are book-lovers, of course, who are so bookish as to find every sort of reality detestable; unless it can be given a sort of literary twist, or can be made to remind them, in some detail or other, of a favourite author. . . . What they mean when they talk of "life" is something that belongs to the pressure of the practical world. . . . But there is, in reality, no such thing as this practical "life," opposed to literature and free from any tinge of literature. (II, 24; 41; 42)

While I would be the first to acknowledge the poststructuralist view that any single text is made up of an endless number of invisible subtexts, displacing it endlessly from itself, I also feel that (precisely because this is the case) the determination of such an ever-receding genealogy or intertextuality is the least profitable of all critical enterprises. In *The Meaning of Culture,* Powys distinguishes between the merely educated man and the cultured man. However learned, the educated man cannot be called cultured while there is "an unbridged gap between his reading and his life" (I, 22). My general outlook is in alignment with this distinction. While attempting to expand and solidify documentation as far as possible, I do not think that such investigation per se really leads anywhere. Thus, critically, there would seem to be a difference between an educated view of John Cowper Powys and a cultured view of him. This book does not claim to offer the latter, but it certainly articulates the need and desire to move in that direction.

This strategy also has aesthetic implications. Powys saw literature as art, but he also saw it as something much greater than art (*PL*, 8). From a purely literary-artistic point of view, critics will debate the way in which

certain sections of a Powys novel are aesthetically "successful" or not. I
will not be doing this. A reason for this (if there is one: my disinclination
for this approach being intuitive rather than premeditated) may be the
sense of a larger aestheticism that overrides narrowly conceived ideas of
purely technical or artisanal perfection. This issue is again one perceived
by Powys and articulated in *The Meaning of Culture* as the difference
between the "beautiful" and the "poetic" (IV, 62).

Not only does such a differentiation largely disqualify certain types of
critical approach, it also calls attention to the very special demands that
the Powys text makes on the reader. A certain type of critical mind seems
to be eternally removed from Powys criticism. This aesthetic or critical
issue is related to the Ego-versus-Self polarity that will presently be outlined. Powys is himself conscious of these two diverging reader stances
(*AGO*, IX, 144), and so are several of the Powys critics.[11] Basically, this
polarization has to do with the different speeds or work rates of Ego and
Self. The cultured, writes Powys, makes a lot out of a little; the uncul-
tured makes a little out of a lot (*MofC*, IX, 176). As a mental system
formed by sensory overload rather than sensory deprivation, the Ego will
tend to apply upspeeded, masculine-aggressive scanning or skimming
habits to a kind of text that requires afterthought rather than thought,
empathy rather than sympathy. Bluntly, the reader only faintly in touch
with a personal Self of his own or her own is not likely to feel the aesthetic
texture of the Cowperverse at all. In a certain sense the novels have been
written in an invisible writing. This does not mean that they are supernatural or paranormal, requiring interpretative esotericism. It merely implies that, at the receiving end, the reader will have to summon a form of
overall sensitivity that somehow matches that of the writer-creator.
Writer and reader must in one way or another come to share a common
wavelength or frequency. Take the first page of *A Glastonbury Romance:*
If you are "inside" the range of this frequency you are already expanding,
as recipient, from the first words onward. A special atmosphere is
created, distinctly and uniquely the atmosphere that John Cowper Powys
is able to create. Within this special mood, the whole conception of a
fiery orb extending its personality down through space into the consciousness of a human individual will appear as the most natural of
events—one that we accept with the same breadth of mind and lack of
narrow vigilance with which we accept the reality of the three witches at
the beginning of *Macbeth.* They just have to be there, to give us the
adequate sense of infinitude. But outside this special mood the whole
thing is a bit ludicrous and almost ridiculously inflated. The same applies
to the reader of Dickens: if you do not allow yourself to work *with* him,
but remain aloof from the special understanding of the world he is per-

mitting you to share, everything looks strained and artificial. The new vision of reality, given for instance on the first page of *Bleak House,* or *Little Dorrit,* merely becomes rhetoric, a kind of endless verbal meandering. This issue has precious little to do with being subjective rather than objective, sympathetic rather than unsympathetic. It has to do with the altered state of consciousness and the vast expanses that it opens in the human mind. It is easy to deny oneself a vision, but in doing so one must always remember that it is oneself that is denied, not the vision.

There seems to be a dividing line in criticism, and particularly in Powys criticism. This line is formed by the willingness or the unwillingness to debase the intensity of the original reading experience—by the willingness or unwillingness to find critical criteria that will explain rather than dismiss the validity of that intensity. The work of criticism comes to function in one of two opposite ways: either it intervenes between reader and writer, or else it communicates between them; either it intervenes between the literary ecstasy and the literary-critical understanding of that ecstasy, or else it establishes a vital rapport between ecstasy and knowledge.[12] This also means that the Powys interpreter must ultimately come to a contemporary insight corresponding to that which Coleridge once developed from German transcendentalism and which has never really been allowed to achieve a rounded completion within the tradition of Anglo-American literary theory. This, if you will, is a romantic position. It is simply based on the willingness to center rather than bracket the altered state of consciousness. Since this state is a reality and not some concoction of fantasy,[13] such romanticism is ultimately realism—a realism with a more vital thrust than a realism that fences off ecstasy by deploying an elaborate system of intellectual taboos.

Through its peculiarly ecstatic-poetic impact, the Powys world forces us to consider and reconsider the validity of the whole theory of the novel as it is today actualized in the standard mode of interpretative awareness. This Powys world also asks more profound questions, affecting the ideas of academic respectability mentioned above. How is the sober, essentially nonecstatic world of professional scholarship to come to terms with the ecstatic world of the hallucinatory vision? Is the scholar to descend from that prolonged hypnotic trance in which literature is felt as a total experience? Is the critic to remove and alienate himself from the first ecstatic reading, so that with repeated readings the vision cools, evaporates? Or is in fact the ecstatic to be seen as an integral part of the literary experience and therefore as an integral aspect of the theory of criticism, of the act of criticism? A commonsensical view of the commonsensical makes sense, but a commonsensical view of the ecstatic does not make sense at all. This is the dilemma. How to avoid a trivialization of John Cowper Powys.

In his 1967 introduction to Powys's *Autobiography*, J. B. Priestley
claims that the most able writers do not belong to the Powys type of
personality and that most people who do happen to belong to this type
cannot write anything whatsoever. There is, in a very special sense, some
truth in this. Yet, as I see it, there is a danger here of missing a much more
important point. This is that ecstasy is a universal phenomenon, and that
the writer's superb ability to describe altered awareness should not make
us think that he is radically different from the rest of us. Scientific investigations suggest that ecstasy is a near-universal human experience. The
same goes for the phenomenon of extensive daydreaming. It is like sleep.
All people dream. The difference is that some people remember their
dreams intensely and in great detail, while others will forget their dreams
or even actually deny that they have dreams. Among the former group, in
addition, there will be those who will be able to understand the peculiar
significance of their recurrent dreamings, while others will tend merely to
dismiss the whole phenomenology of dreaming as something nonsensical—an area of pure fantasy disconnected from the more profound
aspects of living. The same goes for ecstasy, daydream, and ecstatic daydreaming. The fact that John Cowper Powys was able to develop an
extraordinary self-consciousness allowed him to observe the peculiar
quality of the ecstatic daydream as it unfolded itself in his daily life. That
he is exceptional in his intense self-observation should not lead us to
think that he is all that terribly exceptional *as daydreamer.* Thus the
general reader can come to the Powys novel with profit and recognize the
intensity of his own or her own ecstasies and daydreams. The Powys
world does not intensify our daydreams or our ecstasies, it intensifies our
awareness of them. John Cowper Powys realizes that the superficial interpreter will view him as peculiar, when he is really at his most normal
and significantly universal:

> I know perfectly well that everybody born into the world has the
> feelings I am describing, is visited by these indescribable and appar-
> ently causeless transports. I am not in the least suggesting that I am
> peculiar in this. But why, in the Devil's name, then, do we go on
> making a cult of everything else except these? . . . A time will come
> when these feelings will no longer be the monopoly of women and
> babies and lovers and saints and mystics and idiots! (*A*, V, 194)

The question I am raising here is the vital one of whether John Cowper
Powys is centric or eccentric. In my view, he is centric: "My poetry deals
with those elemental feelings that the race has always had. My *earth soul*
is not a bit different from Wordsworth's earth soul or Virgil's either, or

Plato's for the matter of that" (XVII, 221). These are the words of Richard Storm in *After My Fashion*, but they are also very much the words of the writer himself.

In the early part of the twentieth century, science stood at an extreme low-water mark with respect to the whole structure of daydream and ecstasy. (This region of consciousness I shall call *dextral awareness*.) It is not strange, therefore, that the writer should turn in desperation to foreign schools of wisdom in his attempt to confirm the reality of those internal processes he knew were real and ultrasignificant events. It is easy to misunderstand why Powys turns away from the psychic models of his time. First, this can be misunderstood as a movement from center to periphery, from the normal to the abnormal. Second, it can be misunderstood as a rejection of reason and science in favor of the irrational or anti-intellectual. It is crucial to realize, however, that it is only because science had a narrow and limited view of human consciousness that Powys moved in this direction. He reads Colonel Sinnett's *Esoteric Buddhism* or Mrs. Besant's *Seven Principles of Man* (A, VII, 252); he is attracted to Celtic and oriental mythology, to Taliessin and Kwang-Tze (X, 454), to Tarot card diviners, Cabbalists, Thaumaturgists, and Taoists (X, 465, 498; XII, 642). Far from suggesting escapism or antirationalism, this dalliance with occultism and theosophical doctrines (V, 186) reflects dissatisfaction with the taboos and dogmas that were dominating reductionist paradigms for science at this time. The writer looked around for *some* acknowledgment in science for what he felt to be the centermost human experience. Finding nothing but "psychoanalysis,"[14] a theory that was intellectually very confused on the whole issue of ecstatic daydreaming, it is natural that Powys turned to far-distant systems of thought in the hope that somewhere the dextral capacities had been fully centered rather than comfortably dismissed. Mainly, therefore, we must see the writer as being fenced in on both sides by the dogma of church and by the dogma of reductionist science. It is evident that Powys never fully embraced any of the esoteric systems which he explored as a third alternative to science and church dogma. Restlessly, he moves from system to system. In the novels, this does not come across as a sustained half-distance vis-à-vis the esoteric or occult. Instead the skepticism activates itself through a two-phase strategy involving first a total identification with the esoteric system and then, at a later stage, a denial of that identification. This denial is quite as complete as the initial affirmation, and thus a double vision is forced upon the reader. The first pages of *A Glastonbury Romance* seem to suggest the presence of an extravagantly occult narrator or pseudo-author. The naïvistic reader is likely to miss the tongue-in-cheek grandeur of Powys's irony. Yet even the reader who applies a face-value interpretation to the work will find plenty of sections in the novel where the occult scheme is ruthlessly undermined by the most savage materialism, foreshadowing that coldbloodedness in which Powys finally accepted the nakedness of things.[15] John Cowper Powys is esoteric rather than eccentric. He belongs to the circle of life itself, not to some peripheral area in which only the quaint and extravagantly fanciful can find a home:

> What is wrong with so many clever people to-day is the fatal distrust lodged in their minds—and lodged there by a superstitious awe in the presence of transitory scientific theories—of the power in their own souls. What we need—and the key to it lies in ourselves—is a bold return to the *magical* view of life . . . to that kind of faith in the potentialities of the ego, with which all great poetry and all great philosophy has been concerned. That feeling of exultant liberation from the immediate pressure of practical life. (A, XII, 626)

John Cowper Powys, then, is an esotericist. The esoteric stresses the center; it rejects the circumference, because it sees that circumference as an outer shell, a dogma, or reified collection of statements and external knowledges. The esoteric has in all times been concerned with the same central issues, the same central insights. These insights have passed from generation to generation and from system to system, often "surviving" as the secret center of some apparently futile or rigidly doctrinaire ideology or myth. As an esotericist, John Cowper Powys is attracted to Christianity, but only to the esoteric center of Christianity. In the novels, this esotericism is often reflected as an affirmation of Christ and a rejection of God. Christ, for Powys, is essentially a symbol of the correct interpretation and evaluation of dextral capacities: "If there was ever a saying of any sage that pierced to the heart of things it was that word of Jesus that we must become as children to enter heaven" (II, 60). Powys can accept the word "God" only if it is interpreted supratheologically as something suggesting the universal dextral capacities: "That they called this power, welling up from inside themselves by the name of 'God' had an historical justification which is lacking to-day. But *that* is no reason for deserting the living well-spring of mysterious magic within us. Never mind the name" (VIII, 361). Similarly, the writer is willing to embrace Taoism, but only as an esotericist, concerned with the center of Taoism: "A Taoist is what I really am; but a Taoist uninfluenced by that later Buddhistic element, that indifference to pleasure and pain" (XII, 642).

John Cowper Powys is consistent here. He refuses to surrender the center of insight to the periphery of external dogma. From the nonesoteric point of view he looks very inconsistent, for he will shift from dogma to dogma, moving freely within various systems in a way that is bewildering for those who do not realize that ostensibly antagonistic systems can contain the same core of interior wisdom. This phenomenon can be studied not only in the writer's attitude to mythologies and systems of faith, but also in his flexible relationship to socio-political ideologies. Here again, one must penetrate the surface in order to determine the driving force behind the particular system.

The Powys world is of course mysterious. The esoteric is in itself mysterious. But this is not so because the "object of study" is mysterious. It is so because man is mysteriously removed from a facile rationalization of the dextral capacities. There is nothing really mysterious about ecstasy itself. The mystery lies in the veil that consciousness places between ourselves and ecstasy once the transport is over. Ecstasy becomes the other, and it is this estrangement that creates a sense of mystery.

The dextral faculties produce what Powys calls "a blind eternity of feelings beyond any analysis" (*AMF*, XVII, 219).[16] Far from being surrounded with the vague mystique that belongs to the post-Coleridgean notion of "imagination," such mental capacities are today nakedly reviewed by the most coldblooded psychologists as realities of the inner world. From the standpoint of a neodissociative theory of the mind,[17] I shall define Ego and Self as two personae essential to an understanding of the works of John Cowper Powys. My thesis is that ignorance of this Ego/Self dichotomy severely restricts our ability to perceive the various nuances of the Powys novel. For this reason, my definitions of Ego and Self will have to be fairly rigorous. These terms are not arbitrarily imposed on the literature in question or lightheartedly transposed from current psychology in a quasi-scientific fashion. I have chosen them for their simplicity. My use of Ego and Self roughly corresponds to Roland Fischer's use of "I" and "Self" in his cartography of the ecstatic.[18] Because the word "I" can be ambiguous, however, I have used "Ego" instead. The resulting Ego/Self antinomy can also be found in *The Double Helix of the Mind* (1980)—a controversial book by Stan Gooch on dual thinking and the cerebral hemispheres.[19]

The present theory does not visualize a homunculus (Ego) squatting in the left brain and a homunculus (Self) squatting in the right brain. But the theory does recognize a central cleavage in human awareness and, in accordance with current scientific knowledge, relates the two main personae emerging from that cleavage to subtle shifts in dominance between the left brain and the right brain.[20] Since John Cowper Powys spent most of his life trying to clarify the difference between these two subper-

sonalities, it may be worth looking at the professional psychologist's view
of this polarity:

> The separateness of subject and object during the daily routine levels of
> arousal (in the "I"-state) has been elaborated in our customary, ra-
> tional, Aristotelian logic and language—a two-valued (either-or, true-
> false) logic that discounts the interaction between observer (subject)
> and observed (object). . . .
>   But when we depart . . . from the "I" toward the "Self," the sepa-
> rateness of object and subject gradually disappears and their interaction
> becomes the principal content of the experience. . . . During the "Self"-
> state . . . meaning can no longer be expressed in dualistic terms, since
> the experience of unity is born from the integration of interpretive
> (cortical) and interpreted (subcortical) structures. Since this intense
> meaning is devoid of specificities, the only way to communicate its
> intensity is the metaphor; hence only through the transformation of
> objective sign into subjective symbol in art, literature, and religion can
> the increasing integration of cortical and subcortical activity be com-
> municated.[21]

Schematically, we have a fall line. For the sake of symbolic clarity, we
can imagine this line running straight down the middle of the skull,
separating the two cerebral lobes. To the left of this line we have the
center of the Ego, to the right of it, the center of the Self. "All souls,"
Powys writes in *Mortal Strife*, "are, so to speak, *amphibious*" (X, 169).
As both Ego and Self, "we are, and have always been, *on both sides of the
barrier*" (XIV, 231). What the writer conceives in *Morwyn* as the struggle
"to loosen the ultimate knot of the cosmos" (V, 236) concerns the development of our ability to comprehend what I am calling the dextral
faculties of the Self. Dextral awareness is to be understood as a heightening and intensifying of the intellect, not as a departure from intellection,
and it has been given a variety of names by different scientists in our
century: B-cognition (Maslow); parallel processing (Neisser); trans-
schematic experience (Schactel); diffuse thinking (Semmes); nonlineal
thinking (Lee); preconscious processing (Kubie); acausal thinking (Jung);
divergent thinking (Taylor); blind thinking (Wertheimer); fringe perception (James); unreflected cognition (Husserl),[22] and so forth. Distinctions
tend to be fuzzy on account of the complexity of these inner processes.
  An over-elaborate review of the various properties of Ego and Self
seems uncalled for at this point, since it is our exploration of the Powys
world that must counterdefine these personae. A preliminary outline
must, however, be given. Broadly, the Ego has those "masculine" features

that are today associated with the left brain and (what I call) "sinistral" thinking. The Ego thus has a tendency toward the lineal and therefore also toward the temporal as well as the verbal, since in their simplest form time and language are conceived sequentially: the linear flow of minutes and seconds, the linear flow of words and letters on the printed page. In complex ways, this patterning is related to the location of the verbal center in the left cerebral hemisphere of most adults. The Ego also tends to be intimately linked up with the mathematical, the analytical, and the causal (cause-and-effect being in itself a form of the lineal, or genealogical). The Self, by contrast, favors aspects of awareness considered to be centered in the right brain. These include spatial and visual components, and, generally speaking, those complex and integrative operations required, for instance, within the higher reaches of art and science. Here the creative and holistic supersede the purely lineal-analytical. In fact, ecstasy, daydreaming, and altered states of consciousness seem to play a crucial role in forming those innovative intellectual configurations that distinguish genius from mediocrity.[23]

A more sophisticated model will perhaps also have to acknowledge that real intellectual innovation always involves the ability to interconnect certain cognitive mechanisms that are normally held apart on either side of the fall line. As early as *After My Fashion*, Powys shows an awareness of this dichotomy and of the need to dissolve it. Here, in a crude form, Ego is associated with science, Self with art. The sinistral consciousness of the Russian materialist Karmakoff is made to clash with the dextral faculties of Elise, an expert dancer. In New York, Richard Storm sees "this great city of marble and iron as some huge Colosseum, in the arena of which the art of Elise wrestled with the science of Karmakoff" (XIV, 195). Rather than seeing this struggle as a one-sided affair in which Self conquers Ego, the writer envisions a dialectic, moving toward a state of synthesis and harmonization: "He felt vaguely and obscurely that the mind which could bring these two tremendous forces into some vital relation with one another would be the mind that would dominate the world." This state of harmony between the "masculine" and the "feminine" is also a prerequisite for the aesthetic success of the artifact. It is quite clear that a sudden condition of creative poise was established in John Cowper Powys sometime near the period of *Wolf Solent*, published in 1929. This period lasts for about fifteen years, and nearly all the works produced in this period have a certain overall balance, favoring the aesthetic concrescence of astoundingly heterogenous material. Put simply, the antecedent period of Powys's creativity is unsuccessful because of its pure masculinity, the succeeding period because of its pure femininity. I refer to the awkward Byronic elements of the early novels and to the embarrassing slackness of the last works.

Seeking an overview of Powys's thought, the intelligent reader must first of all turn to two chief sources: *A Philosophy of Solitude* (1933) and *In Defence of Sensuality* (1930). These two nonfictional works give the best and fullest treatment of the intellectual structures that form the metastructures of the great novels. They do not provide simple clues: none of the nonfictional works do this; but they give a rounded and complete account of the metaphysical and psychological stance of the writer at the time of his richest composition. In balance and clarity they differ radically from earlier and more confused works, such as *Confessions of Two Brothers* (1920), and from later books, like *In Spite Of* (1953). Several other works, of somewhat weaker impact, are in overall agreement with these two key books: *The Complex Vision* (1920), *The Art of Happiness* (1935), *The Art of Growing Old* (1944), and *Mortal Strife* (1942). Personally, I find a psychological subtlety and existential wisdom in this last work exceeding anything Powys achieved elsewhere—yet this sophistication is caused by a very special intellectual twist and not by the central clarity achieved earlier. Both in content and form, all these books have much in common with the teachings of G. I. Gurdjieff as they have been recorded in numerous works by P. D. Ouspensky.[24] In order to convey the exact quality of the esoteric insight, this type of work tends to restate, seemingly ad infinitum, what is a very simple idea, if not a truism. Accordingly, such literature is quite tiresome for anyone not finely attuned to the sophisticated and complex intentionality behind it. Read with full empathy and afterthought, however, these books will disclose insights into self-awareness that are quite remarkable.

As the first in this series, *The Complex Vision* is a crucial work for the Powys scholar because it offers a primal account of John Cowper Powys's ideological centering of the altered state of consciousness. To begin with, the author emphasizes the mental duality that I have called the conflict between Ego and Self. The rhetoric here is quite Hegelian. The "soul itself finds itself divided against itself in an eternal contradiction which may be compared to the positive and negative pole of electricity" (VII, 161). Powys's thought is also in agreement with the current neuro-psychological theory of a conflict between the sinistrality of the verbal and the dextrality of ecstasy. We "cannot avoid asking ourselves the curious question whether it may not be that language, which is so dependent upon the peculiarly masculine attributes of reason and sensation, has not become an inadequate medium for the expression of what might be called the feminine vision of the world" (IV, 89). The altered state of consciousness is "the culminating ecstasy of the art of life" (III, 59). It has been referred to as "religion," but Powys sees it from the viewpoint of his secular mysticism. The altered state of consciousness is an "apex-thought" in what he calls "the complex vision." Always, he returns to "the ecstasy in the heart of the complex vision."

As I have suggested, John Cowper Powys has a two-sided attitude toward the altered state of consciousness. In this state, he concedes, we lose our normal grasp of time and space so as to enter a primitively timeless and spaceless reality. Yet we can look at ecstasy in a more profound way, according to which we gain (rather than lose) a special sense of time and space—a sense, if you will, of hypertime and superspace. Powys transcends this contradiction: he rejects a nonecstatic vision of the world, a vision that downgrades the altered state of consciousness, dismissing it as superstition or atavism; yet at the same time he also rejects an ecstatic experience that fails to somehow stay in contact with the nonecstatic:

> There are indeed certain ecstatic moments when the soul feels as if such a power of liberation from the bodily senses were actually within its grasp; but it will inevitably be found, when the great rhythmic concentration of the apex-thought is brought to bear upon such a feeling as this, that it either melts completely away, or is relegated to unimportance and insignificance. (IV, 77)

In the complex vision, ecstasy is fully acknowledged as the apex moment of consciousness, but it is never allowed to control consciousness, to take over and wipe out the normal state of intellectual awareness. The Powys world always moves toward a marriage of ecstasy and nonecstasy; moreover, ecstasy is believed to be of human-practical value only when it becomes a thing that can be manipulated through the controlling will-power of the individual. Will controls ecstasy; ecstasy never controls will. This notion is what makes the Powys world a "demonic" world. The crucial implication here is that a traditional male/female, occidental/oriental duality is broken up and destroyed. The demonically *will*ful rejects the dehydrated world of the nonecstatic, of will without ecstasy. At the same time, the demonic rejects a surrender to ecstasy, a world of ecstasy without will—a world, precisely, where ecstasy comes into being through the cancellation of will. In *Confessions*, this fear of a total surrender to ecstasy is preeminent, resulting in sections of hysterical overreaction. In *The Complex Vision*, however, Powys is working toward his mature and unique vision of a life in which ecstasy can be brought under control. This means that in the swoon of ecstasy our normal feeling of the infinitude of space and the fluidity of time should not give way entirely to the sense of timelessness and divine self-presence:

> At its great illuminated moments the complex vision reduces the limitlessness of space to a realizable sensation of liberty, and the "flowingness" of time to an eternal now; but even at these moments it is conscious of an unfathomable back-ground, one aspect of which is the immensity of space and the other the flowingness of time. (IV, 85)

The attitude toward ecstasy is quiet complex here. Ecstasy is the great life moment, but it seems to threaten the autonomy of the will and the uniqueness of personality. For a person like Powys, who cherishes the sense of release as well as the sense of power, this release must be brought under the control of power, must *become* power—*his* power. *The Complex Vision*, then, contains a double message. Like most of the nonfictional works, it is bewildering as a metaphysical statement. The ecstatic moment is said to be a crowning achievement of human awareness, yet through "the passion of identity" (IV, 93), it threatens to dissolve individuality: "If the 'ecstasy of identity,' as the unbalanced attribute of intuition forces itself upon us, were in very truth the purpose of life, how grotesque a thing life would be! It would then be the purpose of life to create personality, only in order to drown it in the impersonal" (IV, 94). Antagonistically facing this denial of ecstasy stands the central idea of *The Complex Vision*. This is the idea that the altered state of consciousness is the key to consciousness in general, that the supranormal or abnormal is the key to the normal. Ecstasy is not self-referential. It is the only road to the whole. The complex vision

> is not the normal vision of the human soul. The philosophy of the complex vision rejects the normal vision of the human soul on behalf of the abnormal vision of the human soul. Its point of view, in this matter, is that the human soul only arrives at the secret of the universe in those exalted, heightened, exceptional and rare moments, when all the multiform activities of the soul's life achieve a musical consummation. (Conclusion, 340–41)

It is important to understand the significance of this idea. It is maintained throughout *The Complex Vision* and throughout the other works that I have listed as belonging to this group of texts. Furthermore, it forms the central thrust of the novelist's personal approach to criticism and literature: Powys comes to share Croce's view that a full aesthetic appreciation of an artifact requires a participation in the creative vision of the artist equal to the "living ecstasy" of its most intense original actualization (VII, 178).

According to Powys's theory of life, and according to the present theory of criticism, it is in the extraordinary moment (in life, in text) that we glimpse the overall meanings and structures supporting the whole. The Ego is a mental formation that springs out of the common state of consciousness. The Self is a mental formation that springs out of the altered state of consciousness. Without some vital linking up of ecstasy with ecstasy there will be no Self: there will just be Ego, the persona tailored to cope with our survival routines in everyday existence. The Self is aware of how the mock supremacy of the Ego only becomes possible through a rigid denial of ecstasy. The rejection of the altered state of consciousness is the very basis of the Ego's existence. For the Ego, ecstasy is death:

> The test of any philosophy is not that it should appeal immediately and directly to what is called "common-sense," for common-sense is no better than a crude and premature synthesis of superficial experiences; a synthesis from which the supreme and culminating experiences of a person's life have been excluded. (V, 102)

> The pragmatic philosophy judges the value of any "truth" by its effective application to ordinary moments. The philosophy of the complex vision judges the value of any "truth" by its relation to that rare and difficult harmony which can be obtained only in extraordinary moments. (VI, 157)

These statements prove beyond a shadow of doubt that John Cowper Powys was concerned with the difference between common and altered states of consciousness. My thesis is that current scientific theories on the altered state of consciousness uncover a complex phenomenology identical with that suggested by the Powys novel. Moreover, my selection of relevant material from the novels is based precisely on this idea of the heightened significance of the extraordinary moment. To move across the territory of the Powys novel is to come suddenly upon vertiginous peaks affording superior panoramic vision. It is my belief that a peak-to-peak strategy offers the most spectacular and economic line of progress through the Powys world. In this respect, the chosen *haute-route* avoids a mode of progression that the novelist himself saw as the foundation of a false philosophy:

> To be an "interpretation of life" a philosophical theory cannot afford to disregard the whole turbulent desperate-dramatic content of emo-

tional experience. It cannot disregard the fact, for instance, that certain moments of our lives bring to us certain reconciliations and revelations that change the whole perspective of our days. To "interpret life" from the material offered by the uninspired unconcentrated unrhythmical "average" moods of the soul is like trying to interpret the play of "Hamlet" from a version out of which every one of Hamlet's own speeches have been carefully removed. (VI, 159)

A Philosophy of Solitude provides us with John Cowper Powys's most succinct statements on this central issue of ecstasy and daydreaming. Like *The Complex Vision*, it posits a fundamental duality in the human psyche, a notion that is related to the thought of Heraclitus (I, 23–24). The dextral capacities are seen in *A Philosophy of Solitude* as "the master-currents of our nature" (I, 41). Here, "primal ecstasy" is the central experience of that delicious daydreaming mood which the author believes can only take place in a life of sustained solitude. Powys claims that the Ego fights the enjoyment of ecstatic reverie in two principal ways. The first of these defense mechanisms is a cynical sense of humor. This hardens the Ego, causing it to look upon the daydreaming Self as something sloppy, effeminate, or sentimental (IV, 117). The second defensive mechanism is intellectual. The ancient religions placed the dextral capacities in a transcendental overworld; replacing religion, psychoanalysis brings in a new superstition, confining the dextral faculties to an obscure underworld. In alignment with theories of ecstatic daydreaming that have emerged after his death,[25] Powys's model claims that the simplistic above/below antinomy of post-Freudian thinking is inadequate for an understanding of the special function and significance of the altered state of consciousness:

> Modern psychology, by its tiresome trick of giving morbid and disparaging names to the most powerful gestures of the mind, would seek to fix some label upon what you are now doing; a label which would turn this gesture of spiritual authority into a grimace of weak insanity. (IV, 117)

> Psycho-analysis insists that we subject our most sacred feelings . . . to its particular set of ready-made categories, its division of our soul into "conscious" and "unconscious," into mental rationalizing on the one hand, the dark impulses of the sea-serpent "Libido" on the other. (V, 146)

These remarks bring us to a crucial insight within the thought of John Cowper Powys: first, there must be a reversal of Freudianism's tendency to place the altered state of consciousness below the common state of consciousness; second, the ecstasy-versus-nonecstasy conflict is not to be naïvistically conceived as an emotion-versus-logic duality; third, the erotic is not something dark and repressed that pops up now and then when we are off guard—instead, it is luminous and all-pervasive, saturating thought itself. There is no moment and no scene devoid of eroticism. There is erotic space and erotic time, not space with regions of sex, not nonsexual time interrupted by sexual time.

We now see that the Powys world is largely a world that describes the inner landscape of *reverie*—a word that I shall henceforth use to designate *ecstatic* daydreaming, mentation directly or indirectly related to the altered state of consciousness.

The most significant thing about this reverie is that it is no minor function in the psyche: "Most men, and nearly all women,[26] spend a considerable part of their conscious life, when they are not engaged in any absorbing work, in vague, brooding thoughts, that have little to do either with the rationalizing brain or with any dark 'Libido' " (V, 160). This is an important point, and it concerns what was recently said about the eccentric and the esoteric. The mind does not consist of one part rational consciousness and one part irrational subconsciousness: "This natural and normal stream of human consciousness . . . is by no means a mere meeting place of clear-cut rationalism and dark, mysterious, sinister subconsciousness." Reverie is a broad and wide mental landscape, a central plateau in consciousness—not some slender strip, squeezed to narrowness by logic and libido. Had it been such a narrow strip, the Powys novel would have belonged to the quaint and extraordinary. Knowing the size, volume, and centricity of reverie, we can now come to a more accurate and generous evaluation of the true dimensions of John Cowper Powys's achievement.

1.2 The Fall Line

The chief significance of *A Philosophy of Solitude* lies in its delineation of John Cowper Powys's effort to work out a system that turns the randomness of ecstasy into the control of ecstasy. The great mystics ultimately fail us because "their ecstasies come by chance" (IV, 111). They record their altered states of consciousness and make these a starting point for a new conception of reality; but since they only achieve the ecstatic illumination a few times during an entire lifetime, their schemes really evaporate.

Powys looks with a certain contempt on this inability to control ecstasy. He believes that the human ability to develop a power to unite the will with the altered state of consciousness will trigger the next phase in the evolution of man. The universe that has become so malleable to exterior masculine-aggressive manipulation through action must become malleable through thought (VII, 213). The demonic masculinity of the will must penetrate the femininity of ecstasy, and not only the femininity of the earth. The author defines the *"premeditated ecstasy"* (III, 88) as the "dominant clue-gesture" to a new form of controlled consciousness. This gesture can no longer take place in the ritualized form of church worship. Thus Powys defines a difference between the formalization of ecstasy in the Black Mass of organized religion and the triggering of ecstasy in the "Green Mass" of his own cult (III, 95). This triggering he calls the "machinery of the ecstasy-release" (III, 93). Such a device will enhance the quality of daily life by multiplying the number of experienced ecstasies. At the same time, however, there will be disappointing moments when the trick does not work. Yet far from throwing the individual into total dejection, such a moment of failure is in itself exhilarating. This is so because of the soaring feeling of mental control that comes from the effort to achieve such an intensified mode of awareness: "The willing towards this ecstasy does much in itself, even if the desired consummation never comes, to enrich and heighten our interior life." Powys was to develop this existential strategy in his own life, and the fact that the same propaganda for this mental gesture is fed to the reader much later, for instance in *Mortal Strife,* suggests that it is no whimsical fancy of purely theoretical value, but a practical and consciously refined inversion of normal, semi-automatic thought processes. There is no reason to doubt that the writer actualized this particular strategy in his daily life and writing. In *A Philosophy of Solitude* it is largely conceived also as an evolution gesture, affording release from the confined modes of consciousness prevailing in the current phase of human development:

> It is astonishing to think how long humanity has existed, and yet how little we have advanced in gaining control over our thoughts. To control your thoughts—that is the most important thing you can do; far more important than to control your children or your food or your drink or your wife or your husband or your business or your work or your reputation. He who can control his thoughts is at the key-position of the Cosmos. (III, 82)

The altered state of consciousness gives us a feeling "for which at present human language has no name" (IV, 113). This is also the problem of the Powys critic, who can neither use the saplessly general terms of everyday language ("emotion," "intuition," and so on), nor the more specific jargon of cognitive science or neuroscience. I am aware, even now, that the word "ecstasy" will carry transcendental-magical connotations for the more coldbloodedly scientific reader, while "dextral capacities" will meet with a corresponding reserve from those generally hostile toward rigorous psychological determinacy in criticism. This problem also shows up in Powys's own nonfictional writing. While "Ego" and "Self" have been defined as closely as possible here, words like "ego," "egoism," "egotism," "self," and "selfishness" are used by Powys indiscriminately throughout the psychological or quasi-metaphysical sections of his work. This, however, should not lead us to imagine that Powys is unaware of the various subtle differentiations that exist between qualitatively shifting forms of altered consciousness. There are "many measures, levels, gradations, in this premeditated ecstasy" (IV, 122), and it is precisely because the writer is aware of this that he can turn the structures of ecstasy into the skeletal core of an entire literary achievement.

The ecstasy that is "attainable at any moment and in any mood" (IV, 112) is a tremendous thing, "some sort of entire reversal of human thought" (IV, 126); yet at the same time, it grows out of the ultranegative and out of the ultradiminutive. It grows out of the negative in the sense that only "under some tremendous disappointment or under some spiritual shock" (IV, 119) will the Ego break down in such a way that the Self can take over as a projector of interconnected ecstasies. The premeditated ecstasy emerges from the ultradiminutive in the sense that it in no way requires the extraordinary or magnificent as a trigger. If there is complete control over the mind, man can achieve the ecstatic even in the least favorable conditions. With such a mental command, even the confined prisoner will be able to move into a delicious trance by staring at a single fragment of a windowsill (III, 97). Indeed, one sometimes feels that there is a strong ascetic bent in John Cowper Powys. It is as if such narrow and meager life conditions were actually favorable to the achievement of tranced reverie:

A person may know that he is advancing, for example, in the true direction when he can get as great a thrill from walking along a muddy or a dusty road as from walking over soft green grass; when he can get as much happiness from seeing a tuft of waving grass-blades reflected on a bare stone, as from a woodland glade that is like the sky itself by reason of its masses of bluebells. (VII, 215)

Two important things can be said about the Powys novel in the light of these remarks. First, it contains numerous astounding evocations of ecstasy. Second, it contains two main types of ecstasies: those related to that which in itself is poetic-ecstatic (magnificent landscapes, weathers, lovemakings) and those related to that which we normally think of as supremely nonpoetic and nonecstatic. While the latter phenomenon is given full literary development in Dickens and the French naturalists, it is nevertheless remarkable in Powys not only through the superior and unequaled intensity with which he brings this art to perfection, but also through the way in which it becomes connected with that very different art of celebrating the naturally and effortlessly poetic. This means that the lyrical appreciation of the ecstatic qualities inherently belonging to nature is made to fuse with the willed trance that transforms the nonecstatic into the ecstatic. In this way, the world that we conceive as poetic is felt to exist on exactly the same level as the nonpoetic dimension of life. Out of this synthesis, a special Powysian vision emerges. It is a vision of the world as hologram, of a multiverse (with seams and dislocations) magically turned into universe through ecstasy. This faith in the infinite power of ecstasy, and in the infinite power of the mind to produce ecstasy, permits the writer to move with unprecedented abruptness from pastoral grandeur to the most trivial aspect of the seamy and colorless: "When I say I had an ecstasy in the entrance of this forlorn shanty at the back of Hove Station . . . I am not exaggerating" (A, VI, 219). Here in *Autobiography* (1934), this emphasis on the ecstatic perception of reality is outlined from the very beginning in the account of how John Cowper came to view his father's shoes. This experience forms his first memory of the altered state of consciousness. These boots, with their enormously thick soles, acquire a significance that is inexplicable in the context of their workaday reality:

> If I could capture now the real significance of the soles of my father's boots I should be master of one of the great clues to the secret of the cosmos. Was it purely a matter of the wonder of contrasted size—the difference between the thickness of *my* boots and those of my father— that so enraptured me? No, there was something else! Those great boot-soles as I saw them in a row in a little back room near the kitchen must, I really believe, have become significant to me, in that mysterious way in which all through my life certain inanimate objects have become significant, by gathering into themselves that element in life that might be called *inscrutable ecstasy.* (I, 5)

This passage introduces one of the macrotensions in the Cowperverse: that between the inanimate and the animate. This tension could very well be focused as a central organizing principle in the Powys world, with the device of animation as a shaping force—skidding into pantheism, cosmogonization, fetishism, and so forth. Such a macrotension, however, coexists with several other macrotensions: for instance, that between the mental and the material, or that between the centrifugal and the centripetal. Above these, hierarchically speaking, ecstasy functions as a sovereign structure, strategically placed at the apex of the conceptual configurations that determine the overall framework of the Powys world and Powys novel. My decision to view ecstasy as a master key to this large body of works is based therefore on the fact that ecstasy, as concept and structurational force, controls the interrelation between these other macrotensions. This situation cannot be reversed: you cannot, for instance, see animation (the inanimate/animate duality) as a topmost concept controlling everything else. There are too many factors in the Powys novel that are not directly related to this subsystem, and there are interrelationships between a number of other dualities that cannot be critically clarified *in terms of* that inanimate/animate polarity. By contrast, there is little that cannot be seen structurally subordinated to the overriding Powysian preoccupation with ecstasy-versus-nonecstasy.

If the Powys novel, then, is scattered throughout with moments of pure ecstasy, it is also scattered throughout with moments of pure animation, ecstasy being, as we have seen, something that will automatically tend to produce a dissolution of the subject/object duality. As the object enters the subject, so the subject enters the object. There is interpenetration. This interpenetration is "feminine." Penetration is "masculine." The Powys world gives way to the feeling of interpenetration, while at the same time resenting the diminuition of control created by this. Penetration and interpenetration begin to fight one another, and out of this anatagonism much of the beauty and subtlety in the writing is born.

Ecstasy creates geometry, but geometry does not create ecstasy. The typical geometry of the Powys world (the centrifugal/centripetal duality) is produced by the altered state of consciousness, the driving force behind the writer's creative powers. Since it is scientifically known that changes in mental arousal create a distinctive geometric-rhythmic ornamentalization of the visual field,[27] much of the aesthetic idiosyncrasy of the Powys novel can be traced back to the intensity of the altered state of consciousness. I shall unfold the structure of the Powys novel in terms of this pervasive centrifugal/centripetal polarity, but it must always be remembered that this visionary spatialization in Powys's writing is always effect, not cause. Ecstasy is cause, vision effect. When the writer describes his thought processes as the thought processes of the inanimate, we must not underestimate him, believing that he is on the level of some innocent savage, attributing to objects individual personality and consciousness. Rather he is trying to convey the difference between the common state of consciousness, in which we remain conceptually aloof and removed from the *being* of exterior reality, and the altered state of consciousness, in which this being is more fully taken in, *as being.* The seaside resort of his childhood becomes an integral part of his consciousness, rather than of his memory, because he is intellectually aware of the dangers of intellectual awareness. He is not the child who has never grown up, nor the child fearing the business of growing up. He is the adult, different from other adults in knowing the price of adulthood. This is why, in an extension of adulthood, the world of the child must come into vital interaction with the conceptually rigid outlook of the "mature." In those very early days

> every aspect of the Weymouth coast sunk into my mind with such a transubstantiating magic that it might be said that when I think now of certain things I think *with* St. John's spire and the Nothe, and the old Backwater, and the Harbour Bridge, and the stone groins, and the green pier-posts, and the dead seaweed and the windrow-flotsam and the stranded star-fish! Yes, it is through the medium of these things that I envisage all the experiences of my life; and so it will be to the end. (IV, 151)

Is this fantasy? supernaturalism? No: it is honesty, sensibility, largesse. Above all it is reality, because it is an accurate and spontaneous rendering of a real inner state of being. This only becomes unreal or strained for the one who is unfamiliar with the shift of existential strategy (from Ego to Self) underlying this special sense of spiritual expansion, this calm knowledge of the dense interbelonging of things.

The Powys world is visual and visionary. These are two different things, but they both accentuate the ocular faculties. Furthermore, as vision, ecstasy can be either translucid or opalescent. This variation is related to the two polar extremes in ecstasy that we will be dealing with in the investigation of the novels. The translucid variant is related to what we shall find Powys defining as the hard-little-crystal experience; the opalescent variant is related to the very different experience of quivering mirage or vibrant halo. This latter type of vision can cause the Powys hero to question the validity and reality of the dextral capacities. The greater complexity of multiple awareness forces a character like Richard Storm in *After My Fashion* to ask himself if this multimodal mentation is in fact an illusion, something misty and unreal. Perhaps there is no enhancement of consciousness in this special mental approach to the universe. Perhaps it all just amounts to a lazy immersion in some kind of thought soup, in which no act of the mind ever acquires any distinct outline: "Was he actually wanting in some normal human attribute; and did everything that occurred to him approach his consciousness through some vaporous veil like a thick sea mist" (XX, 262)? Yet this type of vision is never really out of focus. It is so only in the sense that we could say that William Turner's *Rain, Steam and Speed* is out of focus in comparison with a real life photograph of a locomotive speeding over a viaduct. The former is more precise, because it stays closer to the reality of the act of perception and to the shifting complexity of exterior reality. Or because, in Hegelian terms, it catches the Absolute as fluidity. In many fine scenes in the novels, the writer gives way to this pure and enlarged moment of visual receptivity in which the world, quivering in gossamer insubstantiality, is perceived as an iridescent, impressionistic pearliness.

Such superfine formalizations of the visual field also involve characteristically intense color ecstasies. These are miraculously retained from childhood in the memory bank of the adult writer and also, as in *Autobiography*, conveyed in full splendor to the reader:

> I had never seen this peculiar tinge of green covering the whole expanse of the Eastern sky, and it made a tremendous impression on me. . . . I have retained, ever since that day, a curious lust for that green colour in the sky, and a delight in it that has remained what I am inclined to call a purely aesthetic pleasure. Other effects of sunrise or sunset—for instance the more usual one of bars of massy gold, or of blood-red streaks against a watery-gold background—have often filled me with that vague spiritual nostalgia which seems one of our universal human feelings; but the feeling that a *green sky* gives me is quite different. (I, 30)

This differentiation finely illustrates the way in which ecstasy is not simply intense feeling. When you have an ecstasy you recognize its special and unique quality, and you do not confuse it with the sentimental, the more ordinary moment of repose ("vague spiritual nostalgia"). This is also why the poetic-descriptive, in Powys's writing, rarely acquires any tinge from stereotyped, petit bourgeois notions of the picturesque. In a rather remarkable way, the Wessex of the great Powys novels is removed from nearly all conventional concepts of the idyllic and pastoral; yet, ironically, it emerges, in its newness and otherness, as something even more idyllically pastoral, English. Again this ecstatic virescence reflects the way in which John Cowper Powys links ecstasy to the poetic as well as the nonpoetic—simply because he *acquires* ecstasy from both of these. An exceptional green sky may trigger the altered state of consciousness— but so may a totally unexceptional railroad engine. Far from being embarrassed by this, the writer sets out to take this experience with quite as much seriousness as the more traditionally poetic transport:

> The *colour* of the railway engines was one thing that transported me with excitement. That the Great Northern engines should be green, and the Great Western engines a different shade of green; that the Midland engines should be of a muddy purplish tint, so it seems to me now, while the Great Eastern engines were black—these things thrilled me through and through. And again with the railway stations! (I, 17)

Now this is not simply narrated within the context of traditional authorial reminiscence. The overall intention, here, is to suggest the manner in which these early color ecstasies come to link up with the chromatic raptures of adulthood. There is no nostalgia, because the writer still feels that he is in total touch with this dimension of perception and because he knows that the setting down of these memories is merely part of the will-to-power through which he acquires a position of central command vis-à-vis the whole realm of reverie. Thus color, and particularly green or bluish-green color, does not function symbolically in the Powys novel, within a specifically symbolic framework. It is instead to be conceived as the hue of ecstasy itself, related to the altered state of consciousness by pure laws of sensuality and psychophysics.[28] A certain green comes upon Powys as a shock (II, 64), and it is so intense that he will do anything to reactivate this particular stimulation. He does this, as a child, by rubbing his knuckles against his eyelids. Later, at Sherbourne, he produces such iridal effects through chemistry. He spends his chemistry lessons "in making celestrial greens and blues out of nothing, and causing golden rains to be precipitated in crystalline water" (IV, 136).

Color is "twenty times" more important to him than form (II, 72), and color itself gives him even as an adult a feeling of mysterious initiation into the unknowable (IV, 137). From the manner in which the color experience is related to the sense of the subject/object collapse, it is clear that the colorific is in itself a trigger device for the release of altered states of arousal in Powys:

> *Colour!* What a thing to have appeared at all under the sun! To anyone who like myself is . . . a confirmed sensualist, this phenomenon of colour is like a vast number of entrancingly delicious fragrances *grown visible.* No it is more than that. It is like a human body with which you are infatuated. It is at any rate something you touch, taste, feel, and embrace with your whole soul. It is something *you sink into* and enjoy like the revelation of an erotic Fourth Dimension. (II, 73)

This passage also reflects the overriding significance of the visual in Powys's perceptual repertoire. He tells Nicholas Ross that he judges everybody and everything by how they look (*LNR*, 130), and at the beginning of *Morwyn* the narrator tries to explain how the sense of sight alone can satisfy the three basic cravings that shape his maturity—those for nature, young women, and broadmouthed books:

> You will probably refuse to believe me when I say that I could satisfy all these three manias to the fullest extreme through one of my senses only, the sense of sight, but this is the exact truth. I could even enjoy the ecstasy of the climax of the Eleusinian Mysteries themselves without hearing or touching or tasting or smelling—purely by seeing! (I, 19)

Strangely, these color and sight ecstasies work simultaneously in two opposite directions. While breaking down the distance between subject and object that gives us our coldblooded perspective of the cubic solidity of things, ecstasy also magically preserves that solidity for us. Only through the ecstatic intensification of art can *we* come into contact with the concrete out-thereness of the stray objects that Powys retrieves from the past in *Autobiography* and elsewhere. Here is that tattered purplish volume of Euclid that once gave him a moment of intense satisfaction and transport (I, 37); here is that small, oval print of the Duke of Wellington, which "for some queer reason" had given him infinite excitement (II, 54); here also those tiny dark bottle-blue beads that he once strung together as a child (II, 73). Recalled through the magic of memory, possessed though the magic of ecstatic sight, they are somehow also magically preserved within the ecstasy of print itself. So the text, at its best, establishes what seems to be a one-to-one relationship between the extraneousness of the colored past, made unreal through ecstasy, and the inner coloration of imagination, made real through ecstasy.

In *Wolf Solent* (1929), the first really great Powys novel, the central theme is the eponymous protagonist's struggle to remain a Self, not to become an Ego. Wolf has an inner life, the magnetic center of which is the dextral faculty and which in the novel is referred to as his "mythology." This "mythology," broadly, is the stream of consciousness of the Self. Since I believe (with Powys, as we shall see), that the Self experiences a circle of consciousness rather than a stream of consciousness, the former term will be considered more adequate to express the nature of this "mythology." The novel's central theme does not only concern itself with the problem of whether it is possible to maintain a stable Self in life—the possibility of such a stability is outlined in *A Philosophy of Solitude;* the real problem is whether the supersensitivity of the Self can survive a violent or prolonged confrontation with the worldly. Can the Self mingle with the worldly, with all that represents Ego, and then retreat unscathed? Or will such an immersion cause a fragmentation of the Self so intense that there will result a feeling of personal dissolution and total spiritual disintegration?

> This killing of his "mythology" how could he survive it? His "mythology" had been his escape from life, his escape into a world where machinery could not reach him, his escape into a deep, green, lovely world where thoughts unfolded themselves like large, beautiful leaves growing out of fathoms of blue-green water! (XXIII, 544)

One notices, again, the importance of color, the blue-green ecstasy within the green reverie denoting a world totally hostile to the world of the Ego. The difference between the mental orgasm of the Ego and the mental orgasm of the Self is that the former has a severe aftereffect, while the latter has none at all. Why, Powys asks in *A Philosophy of Solitude,* do the champions of the Ego "prefer their orgies of riot, followed by reactions of infinite futility and disgust, to the experience of long ecstasies of happiness without any reaction at all" (IV, 105)? An effective "mythology" would kill boredom, destroy inertia, dispel lethargy, and overcome a general sense of weariness (IV, 107). The Ego is trapped in a destructive rhythm, "violent alternations of ennui and pleasure" (IV, 106). Yet as an alternative to this, the Self would not set up a "mythology" that would be a status quo. It would have its own movement, its own recklessness, its own will-to-power. Powys's temperament is partly that of a stoic, verging on quietism; but it is also that of a Jacobin influenced by Rousseau, "and with not a few anarchistic leanings" (A, X, 526). This temperamental bias entails a revolt removing the writer from the orthodoxy and dogmatism of established church, established learning, and established conduct; but it also entails a revolt that removes him from the orthodoxy and dogmatism of revolt itself. This revolt against revolt comes strongly over in Richard Storm's rejection of Karmakoff's impersonal logic in *After My Fashion.* Insofar as "historical materialism" implies a relentless determinism, beyond the scope of personality and individual will, it is for Powys something more to be feared than loved:

> Everything was reduced to a logical inevitable sequence of cause and effect, which could neither be hastened nor retarded, but which in its own predestined hour . . . would reveal a new order of society. Richard

felt, as he listened to him, as though he were present at some demonic unclothing of the hidden skeleton of the universe—a skeleton of cubes and circles and angles and squares, of inflexible geometric determination! . . . Nature was reduced to a chemistry. Human nature became mathematical necessity . . . *Art*, he thought to himself, is anyway safe from this man's logic. There, at least, will always be a refuge for the free creative spirit that lies behind all this cause and effect. (XIV, 195)

The impersonalism behind ideology is seen in vital relationship with the impersonalism behind certain brands of deterministic science. The Self's "mythology" comes in conflict with scientism, with the "long, cold clutch of scientific discovery, laid like metallic fingers, upon the human pulse" (*WoS*, XVIII, 376). Specifically, the form of science that Powys rejects is the reductionist science that culminated at the time when the writer was at the height of his own intellectual development. In *Mortal Strife* (1942), as in so many other works by Powys, the target is behaviorism, a theory of human behavior that denies the reality of will, spirit, and creative complexity in the individual mind: "It is easy to sum up what has happened in our time. Individual men and women in great numbers all over Europe have ceased to believe in the soul. This means the substitution of *behavioristic,* mechanistic, obedient Bully-Boys for men who stand on their own feet" (IX, 156). This statement introduces us to what must be considered a significant overall theme in the Powys world and in the Powys novel. This is the theme of spiritual decadence, of the twentieth century as a specifically evil century from the viewpoint of spirituality in general: "Our unfortunate human nature has never been subjected to conditions quite so anti-pathetic to all the most interesting stimuli to poetic human feeling since the beginning of the world" (*A*, X, 494–95). This view reflects Powys's belief that the Self is being annihilated by the tremendous forces released by modern science, modern technology, and modern economics. At the same time, this view does not express nostalgia for bygone days; the writer is quite conscious of the harsh reality confronting preindustrial man. Nor does this view reflect a kind of worldly innocence in John Cowper Powys. He was, to be sure, brought up in an atmosphere of rural retreat, in England; yet his intense transcontinental traveling in the United States can hardly support the idea of a man unfamiliar with the modern scene in all its vivid diversity.

The first shock comes with the Great War. At this time John Cowper was living in the United States; upon his return to England toward the end of the war, his contribution to the British campaign never became more than indirect and marginal. In *Confessions,* he looked upon the whole nationalist-military scene as a realm of rampant insanity, lamenting "the desperate, noble recklessness, with which our European youth is now throwing its life away, as a child's toy, at the command of its political leaders" (XI, 173). Yet after this war there comes another war. For Powys, the workaday world, as it has been formalized by industrialist-capitalist society, is nothing but "a kind of daily war" (*A*, XII, 631). With blood-and-iron industrialism, there is a general transformation of Self into Ego, as the rigid survival routines go on "forcing us out of our sensations into exhausting mass-production" (*MS*, IX, 151). It is particularly in *Wolf Solent* that we get this feeling of the hostility, vulgarity, coarseness, brutality, and inhumanity of the blind mechanical forces of our time. On all sides, even in the air, crisscrossed by airplanes, the protagonist is surrounded by a force that is stronger, colder, and more furiously demonic than himself. His belief in the reality of his Self depends on his ability to refuse to yield to the impact of the new machines (XXIV, 580). Yet as symbols of the Ego, even as actual physical externalizations of the Ego, these immense powers constitute a threat of considerable magnitude. They will come to destroy all that he values most. Against such forces, his mythology will ultimately be helpless and useless:

> They would dissect love, till it became "an itch of the blood and a permission of the will"; they would kill all calm, all peace, all solitude; they would profane the majesty of death till they vulgarized the very background of existence; they would flout the souls of the lonely upon the earth, until there was not one spot left by land or by water where a human being could escape from the brutality of mechanism, from the hard glitter of steel, from the gaudy insolence of electricity! (XXV, 624)

At this point it is time to consider various diagrams that clarify the structure of the complex psychological mechanisms underlying the process of literary creativity as it interacts with daydreaming and the altered state of consciousness. I have spoken, at the outset, of a fall line. As a slalom skier crosses the fall line of an alpine slope before every turn he completes, so the mind crosses a fall line as it turns from the dextral into the sinistral and then back again. In sleep, this is a quite regular movement, a kind of giant slalom with each turn taking about ninety minutes.[29] Dream sleep (REM sleep) is the "right" swerve, and nondream sleep (NREM sleep) is the "left" swerve.[30] The former is dextral because in this phase the right hemisphere is given a more disconnected, autonomous, and freewheeling status, similar to that which I believe it is given in the wakeful period of peak artistic creativity. Figure 1 presents a diagram that schematizes the crossing of the fall line in sleep.

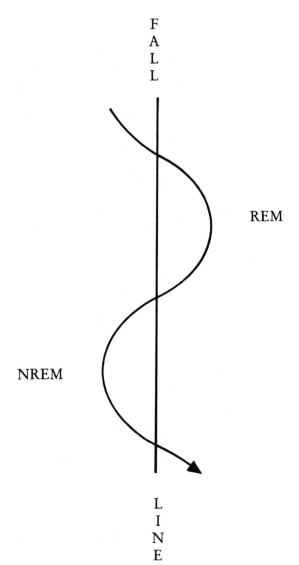

Figure 1. Crossing the fall line during sleep.

In *After My Fashion,* Richard Storm senses how the sinistral/dextral duality is two things—first, a rhythmic movement, or a movement seeking out a rhythm and an equilibrium; second, a destructive tension, denying us unity, coherence, self-completeness. The contemporary fragmentation of survival routines creates a glittering surface texture in life, suggesting that our daily existence is a single selfsameness containing infinite diversification. Yet below the level of quotidian appearances, the fundamental polarity is still at work. The "more complicated pattern of our modern days had not liberated us from the old accursed duality. Will the balance, the rhythm, the lovely poise of things, *never* be obtained by luckless humanity, torn and divided between the two natures" (I, 24)? Throughout the novel, the protagonist is conscious of the necessity to maneuver with the fall line always in view, sensed as a real presence. The division created by it can be worked out as the human/inhuman duality, or as the animate/inanimate polarity, or simply as the tension between the refined and the brutal:

> Had he, in this eternal division between the sensitive and the insensitive, slipped over to the wrong side? Had he ranged himself with the glaring advertisements and brutal sounds, with the lights and the iron and the paint and the roar, against the deeper voices that alone gave life any beauty or meaning? (XVII, 223)

This, essentially, is a dilemma corresponding to that worked out with far greater sophistication in *Wolf Solent,* the fear of destroying the Self's "mythology" through the intensity of the will.

Now if the downhill schuss of the mental night skier traces a flowing S-shaped line of travel with gentle serpentine windings between dream and nondream, the corresponding undulation in our waking state is far more complex and unpredictable. Indeed, the daytime alternations between Ego and Self are so subtle, despite their magnitude, that it is not likely that they can be described in meaningful detail within purely referential scientific discourse. Generally speaking, however, the contemporary psychologist will suggest that the duality of night is carried over into the duality of day:

> Like nocturnal dreaming (i.e. rapid-eye-movement) periods, daydreaming periods tend to recur in an approximately 90-minute cycle in adult humans. This cyclic variation in consciousness apparently involves changes in present-centredness as well as duration experience. Recent work on daydreaming has begun to clarify the nature of these changes. For present purposes, "daydreaming" is defined as any conscious activity that is not related to immediate external information-

processing demands. This definition emphasizes that daydreaming is stimulus-independent or task-irrelevant mentation. Daydreaming draws attention away from processing incoming information, so that consciousness shifts toward reconstructing the past or anticipating the future, often in ways involving considerable fantasy.[31]

The transition from night to day roughly corresponds to the transition from the line of giant slalom to the line of ordinary slalom. This latter alternative implies a more rapid and irregular sequence of turnings, more dramatic, exciting, and risky crossings of the fall line. The Powys novel knows both these rhythms. The S-shaped line becomes a more violent zigzag, as the skier, now with a closed ski stance, adapts his traverse to a more rapidly changing terrain: jostled by the random events of our work-aday world, we can hardly expect that daydream will alternate with non-daydream as smoothly as dream alternates with nondream. Awake, we are in a refined form of tight rhythmic parallel turning, the radius of our windings and bends having dramatically decreased. Our line of travel is shown in figure 2.

Despite the increased intensity and violence of the psychological change overs—corresponding to what the skier knows as edge checking, angulation, prerotation, sideslipping, and so on—this daytime line of travel is so close to the fall line that the unselfconscious observer will be deceived by his untrained eye, getting, in fact, the impression of a straight lineal descent, without turning, effort, or inversions. Powys's major contribution to the psychological novel is the application of an intensified self-observation revealing the discontinuity between awarenesses, or the illusoriness of psychic coherence.[32] His intellectual understanding of mutually exclusive cerebral repertoires enables him to give way to a somewhat ironic playfulness. Knowing that each of the two primary mental systems is merely a switchback from its opposite, he delights, sometimes with semisadistic intensity, in teasing the mysticist with pragmatism, the pragmatist with mysticism. This tendency is best observed in *Confessions* (VII, 94). While this alternation strikes the superficial observer as being some kind of self-contradiction or affectation, it is for the novelist himself the most natural, the most necessary, thing in the world. He is two beings, and the knowledge of this gives him a heightened self-presence—through the reality of duality rather than through the illusion of monality. The constant awareness of the absent hemisphere gives the mind the rounded sphericity that is denied to the one who will never acknowledge anything beyond what is at hand.

The model of consciousness I have described is the only one that will permit us to understand not only the reasons for Powy's intensely hostile attitude toward psychoanalysis but also the extreme caution that the

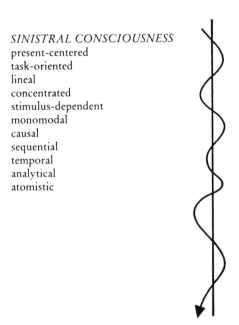

SINISTRAL CONSCIOUSNESS
present-centered
task-oriented
lineal
concentrated
stimulus-dependent
monomodal
causal
sequential
temporal
analytical
atomistic

DEXTRAL CONSCIOUSNESS
nonpresent-centered
nontask-oriented
supralineal
hyperconcentrated
stimulus-independent
multimodal
supracausal
holographic
multitemporal
synthetical
holistic

Figure 2. Crossing the fall line during wakefulness.

scholar must apply to any modes of critical investigation aligning the extrafictional John Cowper Powys with the intrafictional John Cowper Powys. As I shall presently show, the man in the novels, and the psychology of the man in the novels, only exists *in* the novels. The thinking that goes on in the novel (or which *is* the novel) is not the same thing as the thinking of the novelist that goes on outside the novel—for instance in a philosophical work of his. This is true of all novelists, for the simple reason that great novels are removed from other types of writing by the fall line. Since the altered state of consciousness plays a central role in shaping the final creative-productive strategies of the dextral center, and since the writer can make quasi-literary and metacritical statements about his own works *when totally removed from the dextral center,* the fall line becomes a watershed for criticism itself—and particularly for criticism involved with ecstatic texts.

Since only the writing of fiction (for the novelist) fully activates the dextral center, *Autobiography, Confessions of Two Brothers,* and innumerable statements made by the writer outside and beyond the context of his novels can never be considered magic keys to an understanding of the structure of the imaginative Powys world itself. They may, of course, be helpful in confirming certain tentative hunches suggested by specific patterns in the novels. But because of the fall line, they are eternally removed from the world of the novels, and particularly from its psychology. Indeed, in the case of most major writers of fiction, the writer (in his nonfictional capacity as he exists to the left of the fall line) is *less* capable of saying anything profoundly significant about his creative persona (existing to the right of the fall line) than the neutral observer. Most novelists, from Dickens to the average entertainer, have never been able to give any crucial clue to the real nature of their work. If they could do this, they would probably be unable to write, since they would no longer be motivated to shift from the sinistral to the dextral in order to understand themselves. If that understanding were a function of quotidian ruminations, there would be no desire for the ecstatic illuminations of the creative trance. The really great writer is only intelligent in the act of writing. Therefore the critic is only intelligent, and only comes into vital contact with the writer's intelligence, when defining the rationale of his critique in terms of that special (dextral) creativity rather than in terms of the writer's intellectual statements or commonsensical remarks.

In fact, the fall line is involved in numerous phenomena of crucial significance for an understanding of the Powys world. Why did Powys dislike reading his own works? Because of *delayed impersonality.*[33] When the creative act is over, the artist crosses the fall line from right to left, *leaving his work on the other side.* Creative people achieve their full potential outside and beyond the mundane world of everyday routine, outside and beyond the world of the Ego. And because the creative experience is so very different from that of the person's everyday experience, numbers of artists choose not to deal with this dextral world once the creative process is completed. They will frequently talk about it with a sense of remoteness and personal detachment, even cynicism.[34] Powys was no exception. In fact, he had an almost destructive relationship toward his own writing and creativity, and far from enhancing his literary achievement, he spent a considerable amount of time and energy in spreading downgrading statements that he knew would only harm his literary reputation.

The fall line also comes into operation in the novelist's attitude to his characters. Powys claimed that he left his plots to be worked out by his characters. This is a curious idea, but it is nevertheless almost universal among writers of fiction. What does it mean? Well, it certainly does not mean that the artist goes about his work casually, allowing it to unfold spontaneously in random patterns of diversification. What it means is that *after* the writer has crossed back over the fall line into the sinistral and prosaic, he will come to feel that his sinistral subpersonality is only to a slender extent (if to any extent at all) involved in the piloting of the events that structure the novel. If the sinistral system is totally out of touch with the dextral center piloting the creative project, the writer (as sinistral persona) will claim that the work comes together by chance and beyond the sphere of his active will. (*Within* the work, he is God, controlling the curlicues of each tiniest syllable, but that is another matter.) If, on the other hand, the sinistral center is still faintly aware of the lateral presence of the dextral pilot, a curious and special feeling will arise that may cause the writer to refer to his *characters* as control agents. He does this because the character, like the dextral pilot, is himself and not himself: is something removed from the control of the present subpersonality, yet somehow integral to the novelist's overall identity.

The cognitive psychologist's model of the mind has a peculiar relevance also with respect to the tension in the Powys world between presence and difference, universe and multiverse. I use the word *Cowperverse* precisely to signify this overarching conceptualization through which Powys achieves a compatibility between universe and multiverse within his creative vision and literary artifact. We may remember how Dr. Brush came to dismiss the idea of a Freudian subconscious in *Weymouth Sands*. This dark world was a kind of nether appendix to consciousness. The modern model, which is also Powys's, rejects this older model: first, because the whole of the mind is a rounded interconsciousness; second, because the *whole* mind is entirely unconscious. This phenomenon is obvious once we realize that the fall line always intervenes between the two principal awarenesses. There is always unconsciousness, because as soon as we cross the fall line, the relationship between the conscious and the unconscious is merely reversed: they merely change places. Thus, according to Roland Fischer, for instance, the fall line always comes to represent amnesia between normal awareness and altered awareness, so "that what is called the 'subconscious' is but another name for this amnesia."[35] In fact Powys's concept of a world that is somehow supremely a universe as well as supremely a multiverse fits in very well with the modern model of a consciousness that is holistic yet at the same time full of internally dislocated subsystems within a hierarchy of amnesias.[36] Novels such as *Weymouth Sands* and *A Glastonbury Romance* are constructed with this dual emphasis on difference and structure; the former novel allowing the dominance of difference, the latter that of overriding coherence. There is discontinuity within an overall continuity. Or, if you will, the process of discontinuities is never arrested, never prevented from coming full circle.

The Powys novel is a circle of discontinuities: not a discontinuity, and not a circle. To quote Roland Fischer again:

> Therefore, instead of postulating *one* subconscious, [we must] recognize as many layers of self-awareness as there are levels of arousal and corresponding symbolic interpretations in the individual's interpretive repertoire. The many layers of self-awareness, each with its characteristic "Self"-to-"I" ratio, remind one of the captain with girl friends in many ports, each girl unaware of the existence of the others, and each existing only from visit to visit (that is, from state to state). This is how multiple existences become possible: by living from one waking state to another waking state; from one dream to the next . . . from trance to trance; and from reverie to reverie.[37]

The fall line is the main amnesic barrier in the mind.[38] Normally, it is impossible to look across the fall line. Powys spent most of his life attempting to achieve such cross-modal awareness. In doing this he came to create a coherence of Ego and Self. This "double vision" required an ability to neutralize the phenomenon referred to by the modern psychologist as *state dependent retrieval.*[39] This erasure of the fall line means that the novelist is continuously making demands on the reader, testing whether he or she is prepared to abandon a flat, simplistic concept of reality. State dependent retrieval prevents *real* memory, prevents a transfer of sensibility, from a sinistral phase to the following dextral phase, and so forth. Instead, there is a transfer from one sinistral phase to the next sinistral phase. Since, as we have seen, the sinistral is task oriented and present centered, the left turnings in the S-shaped line of travel easily become linked up with one another. Yesterday, at three o'clock, I went shopping. Today, at half past five, I am also going shopping. These trivialities, contours in our survival routines, are strung together in a sequence of self-awareness that we call consciousness, or time. For us this lineal synthesis seems terribly simple and natural, but it is of course in reality a complex process that has required millions of years in order to come into being. It subsumes two operations that we take for granted. First, the act of self-consciousness: "I am shopping at half past five." Second, the act of recall: "I went shopping yesterday afternoon too."

Now the crucial point here is that it is altogether different with the *right* turnings in the mind's S-shaped line of travel. Because of the complexity of these turns, they are not normally linked up in the mind of the average adult. There are islands, or pockets, of dextrality (see figure 3). Because of the amnesic barrier, created by the fall line, the dextral moment of ecstatic awareness cannot be carried over into the "left," into our

Figure 3. Monadic dextrality in pre-Self awareness.

normal routine world of consciousness. If this transfer had been possible, the enislement of the dextral would immediately be broken, since, as we have seen, the sinistral has both self-awareness and memory. As it is, the dextral falls into complete oblivion. It is downgraded or dismissed. It is unreality.

Why is this so? Why can the moments of sinistrality interconnect so easily so as to form the Ego, while the moments of dextrality refuse such dynamic coherence? This was a major problem for John Cowper Powys, one that he overcame in part by writing his novels, for they reflect interconnected moments of dextrality. In fact, you could take the diagram above, turn it around so that the fall line became a horizontal line pointing to the right, and extending the whole thing you would have the basic pattern of the great Powys novel. You would only have to pinpoint the ecstasies and give brief accounts of the intervening strips, or nonecstatic intervals. By giving such enisled moments of ecstasy a co-habitation within the time-frozen framework of the artifact, Powys accomplished that ecstatic concrescence which alone affords the sense of sustained fulfillment.

But back to the question. Why do the dextral moments fail to link up? Well, we have seen that the dextral moment is neither task oriented nor present centered. This lack of lineality immediately complicates things. Self-awareness to the "left" grows rapidly out of the simplicity of that lineal being. An hour ago, I was task oriented. I was concentrating on one activity, on one line of thinking: that of getting my shopping done as efficiently as possible. But with the multimodal, multitemporal moment of daydreaming, there is little foothold for such linking up of one simplified mental process with the other. Daydreams are complex, so intricate that we are only now beginning to comprehend their significance. Far from being atemporal and connected to a primitive form of awareness lacking temporal structure, they are multitemporal: in other words, composed of manifold interlacing temporalities that fluctuate.

We can better understand the intellectual aspirations of nonfictional works like *A Philosophy of Solitude* and the artistic aspirations of novels like *A Glastonbury Romance*, if we come to see the emergence of the Self (whether in author, reader, or character) as the crucial moment of psychological inversion in the Powys world. This emergence seems to require two evolutionary phases. These will apply to the individual as well as to the species. The first phase is the phase of dextral self-awareness. Roughly: "This is an ecstasy." Or: "I am now having an ecstatic daydream." Here there is an attendant process of self-observation and analysis: "What is special about the thoughts I am now having?" "What are the distinctive features of this mood?" Through such introspection, there is a

Figure 4. Intervallic dextral consolidation in pre-Self awareness.

hardening or consolidation of the dextral moment. It takes a photograph of itself, or at least it tries to. The Self is now half-formed. (see figure 4).

The Powys novel is scattered throughout with descriptions of these special moments in which the individual begins to appreciate the quality of the dextral moment. This phase is to be distinguished from the subsequent stage in which the actual Self is formed. That happens when the remembered dextral moments are suddenly perceived within the unified structure of a single interior landscape, or "mythology." There is now a persona, the Self, monitoring the moments of peak awareness. There is also a concrescence of such awarenesses within a newly established network of memories and retrievals. A hierarchy of ecstasies has been formed.

1.3 Smoke Screens

With this model of a fall line, it is now possible to review some of the internal disruptions and contradictions in the thought of John Cowper Powys. Care must be taken here, for these dislocations do not form a homogeneous group of ruptures, all derived from a single geological fault in the Powysian mindscape. Sometimes this line of fracture is coextensive with the fall line itself, so that a tension is formed between the sinistral and the dextral. A more subtle tension, however, is formed in Powys world by a tension between this meridional position and the purely dextral, which, in turn, gives rise to a new center of gravity between center and right. It would be tempting to see the sinistral/dextral polarity as a tension between the Blakean Tyger and Lamb. But the demon in John Cowper Powys cannot be equated with the Tyger. The demon, instead, is in itself poised in daring equilibrium between two extremes. The demon becomes demonic in Powys by inhabiting the middle. It sleeps on the fall line. This means that apart from the left/right, or "masculine"/"feminine" tension between pure Ego and pure Self, there is also in the Powys world a more subtle antinomy between the demonic center and the tensionless dextral extreme: if you like, between the androgynous and the feminine. I shall return to this presently.

Certain caution must also be applied to a further group of polarities. Powys's self-analytical statements tend to quiver with an extraordinary degree of ambivalence, and while it is tempting to bunch all these statements within a single operative category for critical review, I think it is better to make a crucial discrimination between two clusters of such ambivalences. I shall discuss these clusters one at a time. The first involves a deliberate hide-and-seek that Powys plays with people in general, indeed, with the entire universe. The reader is deliberately misled. Ostensibly peeling layers off himself, like an onion revealing a receding infinity of interiorities, he is really putting out so many smoke screens. In the end, as with the onion, there is nothing left at the center at all, and in this invisibility the writer thrives.

Let us look at the smoke screen cluster first. A book like *Confessions of Two Brothers* (1920) is of extremely limited usefulness as a key to the intellectual substance of the major fictional works for a number of reasons. First this is so because of the amnesic barrier between the intelligence within the act of literary creativity and the intelligence outside that creative act. Second, this is so because *Confessions* is a book written at a period of great intellectual instability within the overall maturation of Powys's thought. The third reason for its limitations is its extensive use of pseudostatements. By this I refer to propositions that are profoundly insincere. They can be so either because the writer is trying to throw his weight around in general, impressing his audience with the metaphysically blasphemous or the psychologically unexpected. More specifically, these pseudostatements function as self-tormenting or self-annihilating propostions. They deny the metaphysical position that the author clung to with passionate intensity the year before, the month before, the week before. The writer always has this overriding desire to pounce. To startle. The end justifies the means. In a sense a certain portion of Powys's writing is lacking in what we normally come to think of as integrity. Even in the novels, or perhaps particularly in the novels, there is this motivational primacy of the functional, the strategically convenient. While *Autobiography* (1934) would seem to be a movement toward an unprecedented sincerity, differing radically from *Confessions* in this respect of authenticity, it is not difficult to argue that this book merely comes to perfect this whole art of dissimulation. With time, Powys was to develop this gamesmanship into something quite sophisticated, leaving much of his work embedded in a kind of slyly oriental mystique. But in *Confessions*, as we can see from the following selection of pseudostatements, this technique fails to transcend the crudely dishonest:

I [have] no ideas of my own. (III, 27)
I cannot bear to recall my childhood. (III, 34)
I am all for the bare, bold, merciless determinism of drastic conformity with fact.
   (III, 38)
I have no Philosophy. (IV, 43)
I know no human being less of a mystic than I am. (IV, 60)
The "something far more deeply interfused" of the Wordsworthian ecstasy leaves
   me contemptuously frigid. (IV, 61)
I have no passion for life. (VII, 90)
I am superficial. (VIII, 105)

When writing *Confessions*, Powys (following a Nietzschean paradigm) is clearly aware of the way in which he is teasing his reader by giving a unilateral (sinistral) version of what is really a bilateral (sinistral/dextral) complexity: "In reading what follows the reader must be on the lookout for indirect betrayals and unmaskings. He must follow me suspiciously, guardedly, furtively" (I, 11). Generally speaking, *Confessions* is the most misleading of all Powys's works. Unlike all the rest of the books, it is written in a kind of rebound phase. It is, so to speak, the only book that Powys wrote to the left of the fall line. Conceptually, metaphysically, psychologically, it is an antibook in relation to the rest of his nonfictional works. The author senses that he is betraying himself, and occasionally he gives the reader hints to maintain sufficient caution in the act of interpretation: "Nothing is more interesting than to lay one's finger on the false hypocritical gestures into which at times nearly all of us are betrayed. I do not profess to be able to unmask myself at every point" (VI, 83).

What has happened with Powys here in *Confessions*—and there are traces of this in *The Complex Vision*, too—is that after having lived through an initial rapturous communion with the dextral, he then goes through a reactive, antithetical phase. This spans only a short period of time and literary creativity, and as soon as it is over, Powys continues where he left off—once more embracing the champions of the dextral angrily disqualified in *Confessions*: "I once fancied that I shared with Bergson and James—those plausible sophists!—a predilection for the 'instinctive,' over the 'logical'" (IV, 53). In this rebound phase, he also leaves behind him the adherence to the Jamesian concept of a multiverse which he was to return to with such intensity in *Mortal Strife*. There, the multiverse stands in triumphant contrast to Hitler's Block-Universe. Here, in *Confessions*, more than two decades earlier, it is temporarily dismissed from the framework of the writer's conceptualizations (IV, 47–48). Significantly, and because he has crossed the fall line, the writer is unable to comprehend how he could ever have become involved with such a pluralistic theory. He feels that it is totally alien to his temperamental disposition, and therefore it is now to be seen as a "treachery to my own disposition." The dextral center that he calls the "better self" in *After My Fashion*, "conscience" in *Morwyn* (IV, 230), and various other things elsewhere ("will," "imagination," "personality," "individuality," "higher I," "deeper I"), is in *Confessions* held to be an illusion. Since it is related to multimodal awareness and multiple thinking, the dextral easily becomes the multiverse when conceptualized cosmically. Conversely, the sinistral becomes the universe in cosmic projection, because its mode of awareness is unilineal and unicausal. Lodged now to the left of the fall line, in *Confessions*, Powys not only looks upon the dextral as treachery; he also looks upon its multilayered complexity as anarchy and chaos:

> I must have been betrayed into this treachery to my own disposition by some species of proud and mischievous spleen, and by an unconscious following of literary fashions. As a matter of fact these "chaotic" forms and shapes, these sudden groupings and miraculous chances of contact, though they seem to have about them all the arbitrary magic of the unknown depths, and to be quite independent of the uniform procession of cause and effect, are really as much a determined part of the whole inexorable stream of things as the most mechanical sequences. (IV, 51)

This position is entirely reversed in *Mortal Strife*. Here Hitler is a monist, the potential governor of a Block-Universe (XI, 192). World War II is essentially a conflict of the One against the Many, "the logical Block-Universe against the real, living, mysterious, anarchical Multiverse" (X, 178). Put simply, the sinistral is monism, the dextral pluralism. *Mortal Strife* denies the validity of the proposition quoted above from *Confessions*: "I say 'multiverse' rather than 'universe'; for although the unfathomable levels of Being and Not-Being, into the midst of which we have been flung, are too much of-one-piece to be called chaotic they are far too disconnected to be calmly treated as one simple *continuum*" (*MS*, III, 41). This is the mature Powysian position, recognizing multiplicity and difference within an overall structure that may or may not be real. It is this latter view, poised strategically a fraction to the right of the fall line, that gives the great Powys novel *(A Glastonbury Romance, Owen Glendower)* that overall impression of autonomous and disconnected subworlds so characteristic of Dickens's majestic volumes. The subworlds do not know of one another, *cannot* know of one another—are in fact incompatible. Only the author's vision manages, just barely, to hold the thing together, to make knowledges knowledge. This is practical pluralism, viewed from the metacritical heights of a vague monism. On a purely pragmatic level, whether in terms of events or ideas, the novel "takes place" just to the right of the fall line. Yet through the unifying force of the medium, the act of writing which unifies all dislocations within the framing borders of page and cover, the final vision nevertheless becomes centrally poised on the fall line itself. Thus the artist achieves through art that cancellation of the divorce between "conscience" (dextrality) and "intellect" (sinistrality) that is envisioned in *Morwyn* as the psychological ur-harmony of the Golden Age (IV, 230).

The "treachery to [one's] own disposition," mentioned above in *Confessions,* is of course a permanent and integral state of affairs, if one accepts the modern theory of mental dissociation. We can view *Confessions* as pure sinistrality, *Mortal Strife* as pure dextrality. This would allow us to see these works as deliberately polemical—as propagandistic simplifications involving the reduction from duality to monality in the writer's psyche. In the novels, however, the writer is able to work out this civil war of the mind within the space of a single work. Thus in *A Glastonbury Romance*, John Crow—indeed the Crows in general—comes to represent the sinistral, the matter-of-fact; while Geard, Evans, and others come to represent dextrality. This polarization is undermined by a contrapuntal movement in which John is suffused by the dextral, while Geard is given some strong sinistral-materialist streaks of personality that ostensibly fail to be concomitant with his main inclination.

Always, in this body of writing, there is a hidden observer: a cold-blooded, sinistral persona overlooking dextral intensity with smooth and calculating aloofness. This is the metallic, steely side of John Cowper Powys. It is always there, in the background, and the only really strange thing about *Confessions* is that here, for once, the writer has given primacy to this harder and colder side of himself. Here he claims that his "general bent is toward what is roughly called materialism" (IV, 43-44). He returns tentatively to this position in *Autobiography*, discussing a "vein of ferocious realism" in himself (XII, 649). One also senses the strong presence of this colder, harsher persona, virtually absent from the last works, in the early romances. As Richard Storm delights in the raw ferocity of New York in *After My Fashion*, so the harder, denser, more "masculine" side of John Cowper Powys must have experienced the primal aspects of the New World as things previously denied him. "Many people in England," he writes in *Confessions*, "wonder at my love for America. Fools! How shall I ever pay back the debt I owe to this dear, mad, chaotic, scandalous country . . . No one with a tendency to love the great driving fatalistic rush of simplified elements, can help loving America" (VIII, 112). Richard Storm's experience echoes this mood:

> He exulted in the rawness of the iron frameworks, in the great torn-out gaps, like bleeding flesh, that were being laid bare in the sides of the old Dutch houses, in the subterranean thunder and the whirling puffs of air and dust that came up through the subway's gratings. He exulted in the huge grotesqueness of the gigantic advertisements, in the yells of the truck drivers, in the flapping clothes lines, in the piled-up garbage, in the hideous tenements and vociferous children. (*AMF,* XIV, 185).

Now it is very clear that this expansive persona, requiring space, and striding gigantically like a Miltonic demon through megastructures of steel and glass, is a very different "I" from the comfortably English or comfortably Welsh fireside persona of the later works.

This difference, to be sure, is related psychologically to the process of ageing. By this I do not refer to the phenomenon of diminishing vitality—mocked by the accelerating pace of Powys's creative career. I refer, rather, to the quaint psychological inversion that takes place as an individual or a culture or a planet comes to sense a reduced future-centeredness with progressive ageing. Maturity involves the wider recognition of life's complexity. That in itself works for pluralism and against monism. But with the approach of death (which is a cancellation of structure), there is also a different psychological mechanism at work. A negative one. This is a kind of escapism, sublimated as metaphysics.

Life is unity, coherence, structure. Death is the dissolution of these. Death is antistructure, nonunity, difference. Accordingly, by a subtle trick of the mind involving no small degree of self-deceit, we can abolish death (as a tangibly unpleasant concept or presence) by conceiving life itself as structureless—as a thing essentially lacking presence, unity, meaning. Death is the end of structure; but if there is no structure there in the first place, there is really no death. To die in a total world, in a Block-Universe, is something terrible. It is a total annihilation. But in an infinitely receding pluralism of worlds within worlds, death is merely a displacement, a skidding phase within a series of disruptions initiated by birth.

I am stressing this point for two reasons. One is that I think it enables us to clarify some of the fractures within the Powys world—both diachronic (between antithetical periods of creativity) and synchronic (between antithetical levels of meaning in the text). The second reason is that the issue of structure versus nonstructure may suggest the need, for future criticism, to deal with the Powys novel from the poststructuralist viewpoint. Insofar as poststructuralist criticism defies structuralism and structure, for instance within deconstructive criticism, it is significantly related to the mechanisms that progressively removed Powys from a metaphysical monism. I submit, here, that such deconstruction at heart always mirrors a situation of exhaustion. In a situation of cosmic weariness, the planet seeks a meaning in the crevices formed by its old age. It conceives wrinkles as text. It conceives crumpling as philosophy. It looks at the cracked skin with an eye that will uphold fissure, rift, cleft, ravine, canyon, fracture, *difference,* as the only alphabet. To glorify difference, to celebrate otherness, is somehow to make metaphysical profit out of physical loss. It will be seen that this analysis is significantly related to the tension in Powys between the physical and the metaphysical, as well as to the tension between the metaphysical and the antimetaphysical. By the latter I refer to the writer's combination of extreme metaphysical playfulness with extreme metaphysical skepticism (skepticism toward the metaphysical). Even in *Confessions,* this Pyrrhonism denies the validity of any theory. We are probably as far from a real clue to the structure of the universe today as in the times of Heraclitus (IV, 46–47).

This relationship between the thought of John Cowper Powys and the thinking of poststructuralist criticism also has a crucial bearing on the novelist's treatment of time and temporality. The final pages of *A Glastonbury Romance* are conceptually suspended in a tension between time and the timeless. At the same time, this conflict is vitally related to the tension between structure and nonstructure. This is mainly so because structure seems to give way to nonstructure as the great flood dissolves the social, communal, biological, industrial, religious, and mythological structures that have been displayed in unfolding complexity throughout the novel. Yet in characteristic style, the narrator refuses to acknowledge any one-way solution here. Is not this flood in itself an overriding structure? If so, is it not more intimately affiliated with certain structures (humans, ideas) in the story than with others? And did not, in fact, one of these dissolved structures (anarchism) in itself contain the idea of non-structure?

In *A Glastonbury Romance,* the dextral and feminine is affirmed with triumphant occult overtones. It is linked to the idea of the goddess Cybele: "Out of the Timeless she came down into time" (XXX, 1120). The novel ends in duality, the sinistral being the antiworld of the dextral, and vice versa. The sacred cause of the dextral is said to be the cause of the weak and the invisible, the cause of that which is weak *because* it is invisible. The distance from *Confessions* is immense. The cause of Cybele is "the cause of the unseen against the seen, of the weak against the strong, of that which is not, and yet is, against that which is, and yet is not." An affinity between poststructuralism and Powysian thought emerges in the delight taken in constructing a metaphysical system that denies the validity of metaphysics. In this grand new scheme, no structure has meaning in itself (as presence); it has meaning only within a play of differences (a multiverse of absences, relativistically interdefined). This notion is implicit and central in *A Glastonbury Romance,* and in this respect, the novel is profoundly modern.

For quite some time, it has been fashionable in criticism to align the structuralist desire for presence and center with the idea of the Platonic Timeless, and to align the acceptance of difference with the idea of temporality: the latter alternative giving an existentially authentic stance, it is claimed, recognizing the relativity and ephemerality of life. This view is so widespread and doctrinal by now that it functions as a tacit component of critical respectability in general. The model of dextrality and sinistrality should have made it clear, however, that there is really an opposition between the multitemporal and the unitemporal rather than between the timeless and the temporal. Moreover—and this is why it is significant to trace Powys's development from *Confessions* to *Mortal Strife*—the idea of an infinite play of differences is in a sense far more Platonic, far more "timeless," than the theory of centrality, unity, and structure. A self-present structure dies, in time. But an infinitely receding play of differences goes on forever. It is a kind of reincarnation theory: Time is infinitely different from itself in every flowing second, and through this it ceases to exist. There is difference, infinite difference—infinity.

In tracing Powys's overall development from the monism of *Con-*

fessions to the pluralism of the later works, we should perhaps understand this gradual shift of emphasis precisely in the context of a changing strategy vis-à-vis time and death. It is easier to die in a multiverse. It is easier to think in a universe.

Synchronically, we cannot avoid being struck by the Jekyll-and-Hyde doublesidedness in John Cowper Powys. Diachronically, however, we sooner or later must find an answer to the question of the internal relationship between the "soft" and the "hard" Powys: which of these comes first? The answer, as we have seen, is obscured by the constant use of smoke screens. How are we to determine which side represents the exaggerated, which side the normal? "I exaggerate my eccentricities; I parade my adversities; I expose all my most secret and scandalous thoughts. I love nothing better than to be the butt of my friends' ethical and intellectual indignation" (*C*, VIII, 111). A revealing statement. But then, on the other hand, perhaps it is only a further smoke screen. Where is there foothold in this slippery terrain? Here in *Confessions,* there is much of the demonic side of Powys: the hard-core skeptic, driven from within by a kind of Machiavellian arrogance. Yet how does this fit in with his professed goal in life? His ideal, he claims, is that of "some happy iridescent jelly-fish," a harmless sunlit organism placidly lingering in the aqueous eternity of an insignificant rock pool (V, 66). The central question then is this: which comes first, demon or jellyfish? Is John Cowper Powys at bottom a demonic individual, softened by this jellyfish ideal? Or is he primordially the jellyfish, artificially demonized?

While both of these alternatives are grotesque simplifications, I do not hesitate to favor the first alternative. I favor this interpretation not primarily because I attach much critical significance to the various accounts in *Autobiography* of Powys's alleged sexual demonism: his obsession with pornographic material, his delight in cerebral forms of erotic sadism—projected into the character of Mr. Evans in *A Glastonbury Romance.* All of this is a bit too *recherché,* as are the various accounts he gives of neurotic obsessions of different kinds. Who is free from these things? Powys gains most of his dramatic effects by his intense manner of self-exposure. He exposes man's normal fear of war; he exposes man's normally intricate erotic daydreamings; he exposes those quaint daily aberrations that we would hate anyone to know of, that we do not really know of ourselves. Posing and exposing, *Autobiography* perhaps does differ from most autobiographies in its ruthless, clinical dissection of various lower aspects of personality. But does this make it a work of superior honesty? Not a bit! In fact, the author manages to ramble on for some 650 pages without giving me the least clue to what I really want to know about him: his real-life intimacy with women. Innumerable details are given on the subject of erotic thought, but they are nowhere near the real center at all, nowhere near the love and the passion out of which so much in the novels must have sprung. Here too the writer knows what he is up to: "in this book I have made myself out at once more of a sinner and more of a fool than I really am" (XI, 599).

Having dismissed various specific aberrations as fairly innocent, we still acquire an overall picture of an extremely intense and passionate nature. There is indeed cause to believe that Powys only prevented himself from burning himself out at an early stage by transforming his demonic willpower into a nondemonic willpower. Somewhere along the line, he managed to complete a kind of psychic eversion, a kind of total transformation of internal affairs. The intellectual clarification of various psychic strategies in *The Complex Vision, A Philosophy of Solitude, The Art of Happiness,* and *In Defense of Sensuality* can be seen, partly, as spin-off phenomena resulting from an intricate self-therapy. (Yet again, this was not therapy for a fundamentally sick person, but for a person with excessively high aspirations for spiritual well-being.) Likewise, it is hard to believe that the great mass and volume of the literary output in general is unrelated to the need for getting rid of surplus electricity. (*AFU,* 16). Far from believing that Powys actually succeeded in cooling off into any real peacefulness, I think it is more likely that he remained quite restless and "demonic" all along—as the following statement from *Confessions* seems to suggest.

> I talk of this art of lingering delicately by the way, tasting everything as it passes in its sweet confusion, and committing oneself to nothing, as though it were an art I myself followed in my own life, and wherein I were a master and adept. As a matter of fact I am the very opposite of all this. . . . I plunge madly about, from hunting ground to hunting ground. I sink desperately into this obsession, into that vice. I let the most gracious moments go by utterly unremarked as I plan and plot the satisfaction of some absorbing desire, some ill-balanced greedy wish. . . .
>
> It is curious how one can be inconsistent with oneself, and yet profoundly consistent. Even in love-affairs it has been my experience to find myself combining this tendency to treat things as if they were alcohol or drugs, with this other tendency to be indirect, evasive, sentimental. (VI, 84–85)

As far as I can understand, the psychic eversion achieved by Powys in midlife, giving "jellyfish" ascendency over "demon," involved the sudden acquisition of control over the mental systems triggering the altered state of consciousness. This control meant that ecstasy came to override emotion, even intense emotion. It meant an end to those fevered quests in which the writer would hunt down a certain object or person that alone could trigger the desired heightening of awareness. More precisely: the discovery of this mechanism was sudden, but its application to behavioral patterns was something gradually refined so as to be completed toward the end of the period in which he lived in the United States. The turning point had come during the academic years, when Cambridgeshire, rather than Cambridge (*A*, V, 201), provided Powys with the necessary background for a psychic switch over:

> But the real discovery that I made while I was at Corpus was so important to me as to be alone quite sufficient to explain the vanishing of sadism, and the vanishing with it of so many dreads. For it was while I was there, that I consciously came to realize that mysterious thing, the thing which, after that became the secret within the secret, the essence within the essence, of my whole life. (V, 193)

Far from resulting in a kind of annihilation of sexuality, the new command over altered awareness led to an erotization of the act of perception itself (*AFU*, 16), which is why John Cowper Powys, in his great fiction, is the most erotic of novelists. Between this demonic sexuality, tamed to vision through ecstatic dissemination,[40] and the sexualized world of a Lawrence or a Hemingway, there is interposed an infinitude of sensibility. Being, as I have argued that he is, quintessentially "demonic," Powys never has to resort to playing up the "manly" and wolfish, an embarrassing pose in a soft and "feminine" artist. Masculinity, in the Powys world, whether in Sam Dekker's desire for Nell Zoyland in *A Glastonbury Romance* or in Jobber Skald's desire for Perdita Wane in *Weymouth Sands*, comes over as a primal thrust, not as a swooning emotion to be intellectualized or disintellectualized. This does not mean that there is not a full spectrum of masculinities tapering down to the more or less androgynous. It means that when the demonic is fully released by this writer, it is unmistakably authentic.

Insofar, then, as the writer is nondemonic, he is postdemonic, never predemonic. If he is different from the structure of himself, if he himself chooses difference as a modus operandi for the business of living, this is so because self-difference is conceived as an existential clue. He speaks in *Autobiography* about the art of becoming a *Cowperist*, letting his American readers know the correct pronunciation: "Cooperist" (XII, 626). This is the act of becoming a Self, abolishing the Ego. It is a postdemonic act.

Insofar as this mental gesture involves paradox and self-contradiction,[41] it is in alignment with the vaster scheme of things:

> [My] mania for acting the zany, together with the "sacred malice" from which it springs, contains, just as does my contradictory blending of sanctity and satyrishness, a quite definite philosophy of life, and a philosophy, moreover, that combines reaction with revolution in a way in harmony with Nature's own devious and yet magical method of going to work. . . . My writings—novels and all—are simply so much propaganda, as effective as I can make it, for my philosophy of life. It is the prophecy and poetry of an organism that feels itself in possession of certain magical secrets that it enjoys communicating. And, by the way, I certainly feel conscious of conveying much more of the cubic solidity of my vision of things in fiction than it is possible to do in any sort of non-fiction. (XII, 641–42)

The release of the ecstatic capacities of the dormant Self is accompanied by the most exalted feelings of self-presence and self-completeness. Out of this grows self-confidence. Having discussed the extremely slow mental development of each member of the Powys family (I, 24), he declares, well into his sixties, that he has no thoughts of retiring from the public scene until he has written "a shelf-ful of first-rate romances" (XII, 624). Looking back at the publication of his first collection of poems (1896), he describes, here in *Autobiography,* the strange anticipatory undercurrent that seems to have swept through his innermost being from the very beginning:

> I knew then, just as I knew twenty years later, when I had not pub-lished anything else, that I *was,* in some way impossible to prove, a great and . . . terrifyingly formidable genius! . . . I had the power of tapping some deep reservoir of magnetism that could be used—when I was driven to the wall—to blow the wall up . . . I regard myself as a voice crying in the wilderness, an individual with a devilish shrewd inkling as to the hidden tricks of the creative and destructive forces of the cosmos. (VI, 225–26)

2
THE INTERIOR DISTANCE

2.1 Behind the Looking Glass

We now come to the novels and to the theme, in them, of introspection. For Powys, introspection uncovers no simple center, for Ego and Self come to divide the center. At the heart of the World-Mind, we experience this feeling of double interiority in *Mowyn*. Arrived down through a crack in the planet's surface at its central core, the narrator feels that he and Morwyn belong to an innermost infinity: "Down there in the heart of the cosmos . . . we were two pips in the centre of an infinite orange" (V, 254). This is what Ego and Self are for us: two innermost pips.

John Cowper Powys differed from John Cowper Powys, as we have seen. He speaks in *Autobiography* about his contradictory interiority, a blending of sanctity and satyrishness, reaction and revolution (XII, 641). It is in *Owen Glendower* that this internal rift is worked out most clearly. The inner dislocation is actual for Owen himself, the Welsh Prince; but it is also actual for his secretary Rhisiart, the real hero of the story. What, asks the protagonist, is his life? It is "Rhisiart's feeling about Rhisiart." Life in itself is self-consciousness. Consciousness is self-consciousness. This is a profound insight, masquerading as truism: "Rhisiart is Rhisiart—*that is, I am I*" (X, 319). Yet once the individual has discovered that the I that is reflecting may be displaced from the I that is reflected, he suddenly acquires an advantage over his fellow beings. He can now consider his Ego from the viewpoint of Self, his Self from the viewpoint of Ego. He can play out one against the other, within himself. But in addition, he can send either of these two out into battle with the world. This is an advantage, first, because of the strategic superiority of two over one; second, because of the element of uncertainty created by such bifurcation (the enemy wondering *which* subpersonality he is really dealing with);

and third, because one of the two is always consciously left behind—intact, unconquerable, aloof, supreme.

In the Powys world, there is a dramatic polarization between characters who dislike introspection and characters who favor self-analysis. Several important figures look with constitutional and instinctive contempt on such modes of awareness. We are told that Rhisiart never analyzes his feelings (XX, 859–60). He has "all the average Norman's dislike of introspective analysis" (XVIII, 707). Similarly, in the *Brazen Head*, Lady Ulanda is described as being intensely suspicious of all mental analysis (XII, 171). Owen Glendower, by contrast, is the most introspective of all Powys's characters. Accordingly, he acquires an intense psychological proximity to the author himself. Yet throughout this great historical novel, Owen's faithful servant, the giantlike Broch-o'-Meifod, looms as a psychic counterweight. He views his master's introspection as an essentially futile operation of the mind. It is a centripetal negativism, a false psychology:

> There was rarely anything in the motion of his feelings, in the drift of his intentions, that Owen missed in himself. "You're a mirror-man—*drych dyn*," old Iolo had often told him; and Broch himself had once said, and he remembered the very spot where he said it, that his was the only soul he knew that actually and without pretence obeyed the oracle "Know thyself." "But all you do," Broch had added, "is to push the unknown *further in;* and *that* only makes it darker than it was before. In fact"—Broch had gone on—"your lantern of self-knowledge only creates more darkness. 'Light the candle, and you'll see how dark it is,' as the old Powys proverb says." (XIII, 453)

John Cowper's consciousness, like Owen's, played "juggler's tricks within the circle of itself" (XVIII, 695). If there is self-scrutiny in these mental tricks, there is also self-escape. During his first major intestinal operation in a London nursing home, Powys deliberately used self-distancing mental acts similar to the elaborate self-regulations of Owen Glendower. These are suggested in *Autobiography* (IV, 138). It is also clear that the writer considered the concept of introspection an integral aspect of his practical propaganda for an enhanced life-style:

> There is a very widely spread view, current in educational circles, that what we call "introspection" is a dangerous and immoral thing, a thing from which our youths and maidens ought to be protected. . . . Introspection and analysis are supposed to be a prerogative of degenerate natures, of natures that spend their time in useless brooding because they are inefficient in action. . . .

It is indeed by reason of this deplorable prejudice in favor of "reserve," and this ridiculous view that unreserved people are conceited and degenerate, that so little progress is made towards an intelligent understanding by man of his relations to himself. . . . The fear of self-analysis is a cowardly fear. (C, II, 18–19)

When Catharine, Owen's youngest daughter, runs with Rhisiart through the forests of Tywyn, she thinks about her dead nurse and her future husband—a Frenchman she does not love. As Rhisiart, her real love, runs beside her, he begins to see that it was only to "put the figure on the balcony, *between herself and her life,* that she kept up this ridiculous running" (XVI, 590). For Catharine, there is a difference between *"herself"* and *"her life."* What difference is this? It is the difference between Ego and Self. Catharine, in fact, has decided to abandon her Self forever. She has made up her mind to live the rest of her life with a man who will always be making love to her Ego but never, like Rhisiart, to her Self. It is as if each nucleus has its own stream of consciousness. Now that Rhisiart has failed to make erotic contact with her Self, her hectic running serves to pilot the relentless onward impetus of the Ego. The physical onward thrust of her accelerated stride accentuates linearity and this reinforces the Ego. Closer to the body than the Self, the Ego also establishes a hold on Catharine's whole person through the very physicality of bodily motion. Owen himself, by contrast, is so immersed in Self that the body belonging to his Ego is like a ship without captain. He is not *in* his body. His Self is so strong and his Ego so weak that his whole physical being seems to behave in an entirely mechanical and impersonal fashion. It is a machine controlled by an autopilot (Ego), the real pilot (Self) being somewhere else, projected into some romantic or utterly trivial corner of the cosmos. Having flung his soul out of his castle window, he fails even to notice how he grazes his ear while jerking his head back out of the stone aperture. Absently he feels the wound, registers the blood, unconcerned (XIX, 718–19).

In *The Brazen Head,* Albertus Magnus of Cologne is a quite different figure. His mind is centrifugal and anti-introspectionist: "Albertus had by nature an outward-working mind . . . [It was] extremely repulsive and even loathsome to him to indulge in any sort of introspection. It was pain and grief to him to analyse his own thoughts, feelings, impressions, and reactions" (XVIII, 268). Yet if introspection is a trick to escape, so is also, it would seem, the avoidance of introspection: " 'All my life,' thought Albertus Magnus, 'I've been escaping from myself. What I've been always secretly afraid of is neither God nor the devil, neither man nor beast: it is simply and solely myself' " (XVIII, 269).

The Powys hero is typically caught in a tremendous struggle between Ego and Self. Such is the case with Wolf Solent and Owen Glendower, but also with Sam Dekker in *A Glastonbury Romance.* Escape, here, is the desire of the Ego; and to prevent this escape, the Self has to put a *leash* on its companion. Sam's Ego wants to possess a married woman, Nell Zoyland. Intrinsically, the Ego is possessive. But Sam's Self wants to live the nonpossessive life of a saint. *This act of nonpossession is the Self's egoism,* and, as it turns out, it is stronger than the Ego's egoism. In St. Patrick's chapel in Glastonbury, Sam's Self grabs hold of Sam's Ego through a tremendous act of will. With its own diffused eroticism, the Self conquers the violent sex drive of the Ego:

> Yes, the soul itself, in this grotesque swaying body with clenched fists, exulted in what it was doing! Sam's soul seemed to be able to gather to itself a peculiar consciousness quite apart from the rest of Sam's sensibility. His soul seemed to be holding his body and his will in a tight leash, as a man might hold a wild-eyed bull, by a ring through its nose. (XVIII, 551).

The image is appropriate, for man's Self is superior in strength to man's Ego precisely in the way that a human being is stronger than a bull. The leash metaphor is repeated in *Maiden Castle* (1937), where Dud No-Man realizes that he cannot achieve the absolute self-transcendence shown by Claudius, the philanthropical communist. Dud feels, however, that he *could* live for the spirit, in the manner of his mother's old lover Uryen, if he were only allowed to retain his cerebral eroticism. In the sharp Mai-Dun wind, the invisible hostility between Ego and Self rages recklessly at the center of his being:

> But what this wind was doing was dividing him like a sharp sword. Half of him was crying with savage finality: "I! I! I! I! I!" while the other half was threatening to put a leash around the neck of this "I" and turn it into an obedient servant of Evolution, or Communism, or the Will of God! (VI, 258)

Under pressure from an expansive Self, the Ego is likely to fall into nonexistence. Then the Ego is no longer felt to be part of the mental world. This, now, is inhabited only by the Self. At this point, the Ego becomes associated with that which is not mental—with the body. This rejected Ego-as-body takes on various strange forms. It can, for instance, be viewed as a detached automaton severed from the conscious life. In *A Glastonbury Romance,* this perspective comes to dominate Nell Zoyland just before the erotic climax of her life, the illicit lovemaking with Sam

Dekker. The chapter "Consummation" holds what is perhaps one of the most magnificent renderings in fiction of a full sexual encounter between man and woman. Some time before this moment, Nell strips herself with eager fingers of every piece of clothing and begins to sponge her soft naked skin from head to foot. "She felt, as she did this, as if her flesh and blood were something entirely apart from the deep consciousness where-with she loved her lover" (XI, 304). This body/soul alienation, as projec-tion of the Self's ousting of the Ego, also haunts Wolf Solent. He frequently has the sensation "that his body was a lump of contemptible putrescence, on the top of which his consciousness floated" (XXIV, 574). This feeling culminates in a very strange description of an eerie self-absence in Wolf when he nears Lenty Pond in order to drown himself. As in those painfully unforgettable dream windows in *Wuthering Heights,* where the Self and the Ego fail to reach each other across the visible/ invisible translucence of glass, a membrane separates the estranged and polarized aspects of Wolf's personality. At first the alienation seems to involve a disconnection of the mind and body. Then things become more complicated:

> Was his mind going to issue the final mandate now, at this very moment? What was his body doing that it revolted like this? . . . His consciousness, hauled up, as if by a string, from the bottom of the pond, began beating now against the dark wall that separated him from the portion of his being which was unrolling that map! . . . There was no "I am I" to worry about; no Wolf Solent, with a mystical philoso-phy, to look like a cowardly fool! But whose hand was it that was unrolling the map? His own hand? . . . He felt as if his consciousness were already ensconced, like Banquo's ghost, at the Otters' table, while some quite alien force was dragging across the field a numb, inert, apathetic human body, that raised one leaden foot after the other. (XXIII, 560–62)

This obliteration of the Ego, or of the Self, may be something that just happens, something that makes the Powys hero feel uneasy, half dead. At other times, however, it is clear that Powys believes in reinforcing the individual's ability to consciously achieve such a condition through sheer willpower. He talks about this phenomenon as a trick he used to perform on himself during his lectures. "I succeeded eventually in *hollowing my-self out*" (A, X, 449). Owen Glendower, in similar fashion, makes "use of every mental art he possessed to reduce himself to non-existence" (XVIII, 693–94), and in *A Glastonbury Romance,* John Crow feels "that he pos-sessed the power of becoming so nearly nothing at all—a speck, an atom, a drifting seed, a sand-grain, a tiny feather, a wisp of thin smoke—that he

was completely liberated from the burden of competing with anyone"
(III, 101–2).

The individual, of course, lives under the illusion of mental unity.[1] In
some cases, however, the Ego and Self profit from the acquisition of a
double name: one name stands for Ego, one for Self. In *Owen Glendower*, Catharine discovers on her wedding night that she enjoys hearing
her husband pronounce her name in the French manner. Her Self feels no
love for this foreigner, only for Rhisiart. But through this distortion of
her name, she can identify her Ego, in isolation from her Self, and give *its*
love to her husband without guilt, without unfaithfulness: "Once more
the French pronunciation of her name gave her a curious relief. She began
to feel as if the Catharine who loved Rhisiart needn't be so stern with this
other Catharine whose name sounded so different" (XVI, 614).

One of the most beautiful moments in the novel comes toward the end,
when this name fission becomes a true fusion. Again it is the name
"Catharine" that is involved. This time her name does not split into two.
Instead, it merges with "Tegolin," the name of Rhisiart's other great love.
As Rhisiart and Talbot symbolically duel with daggers after Rhisiart's
burning of the seal pardoning Owen, he cries out "Catholin" in the most
intense moment of physical assault. The fusion of identities marks not
only the dissolution of individuality in love, but also the common Welsh
origin of the girls. That which is shared by the race neutralizes the individual traits of the rival Egos. Considerable psychological insight is
shown here: when close to death in extreme danger, the individual tends
to experience a curious form of self-alienation. In *Owen Glendower*,
there is also the parallel event in which Prince Henry accidentally injures
his wrist while playing with Rhisiart's dagger. At this point, David Gam
tries to hug Rhisiart to death with the immense brutal force of his hairy
arms: "And in his breathless pain he was surprised to find himself becoming two Rhisiarts. One Rhisiart was savagely biting the bare shoulder of
the ruffian who was hugging him. The other Rhisiart, quite cool and
collected, was looking on as if he were totally uninvolved" (XI, 357).[2]
Then, suddenly, there is a change. We see in what follows not only the
problem of name and the otherness of an alter ego, but also the confusion
sensed by the Self in the vicinity of the Ego made physically insistent:

> And then he thought, "Am I going mad?" For the pain had begun to
> take a palpable form; and the form it took was the form of a corpse,
> which was himself, and yet not himself!
>
> With this corpse he was wrestling; and as he wrestled he kept crying
> out, "I know your name! I know your name!" And sometimes the
> corpse had an evil stench, and sometimes it had a lovely heavenly smell
> like lilies of the valley.

And he kept crying out to it, "I know your name!" though how it could *have* a name when it was only himself remained one of those problems that often confront a mind under some cracking tension. (XI, 358)

Carried to its extreme, self-alienation becomes a doppelgänger phenomenon. Owen himself looks upon his Ego "as if it were somebody else thinking a tiresome thought" (XVIII, 710), and in *After My Fashion*, Richard Storm wakes up one morning after exceptionally deep sleep with a strange sense of a coexistent and synchronous counterpart. An invisible identical twin seems to inhabit the same room: "He had the queerest feeling as he washed and dressed as though it were necessary to move very quickly, very stealthily and solemnly, about the room. Was some shadowy dead self, some phantom corpse of everything he had been before, actually lying on the bed he had quitted" (VII, 98)? Here the mental self-division is internally experienced. With Mary Crow's vision of *two* Miss Drews in *A Glastonbury Romance* it is different. Here it is an outsider, her employee, who sees the internal rift. Mary Crow tells Euphemia Drew that she intends to leave, and the spinster begins to speak like an automaton: "Her words seemed to come, not from her own mouth, but from some other Miss Drew—a towering image of devastated frustration—that hung and wavered in the air between them" (XX, 639).

Mary shares with Owen Glendower a preoccupation with the inner duality as it is projected in mirrors:

> It was indeed a fierce mania of Mary's to stare into her own eyes at the looking-glass. She did it as a rule more angrily than with any other feeling; and, when she did it, she always thought of the self that looked back at her there as something quite different from the self she was conscious of really being. Her real self didn't seem to have eyes at all; didn't, in some mysterious way, seem to need eyes or nose, or mouth! Her real self seemed compounded out of pure ether and totally independent of bodily form. (XX, 631)

In *Mortal Strife*, John Cowper Powys claims that those who understand the secret of Jesus are "born again into a Looking-glass Land where everything is *the other way round*" (IV, 52). Ego and Self are reversals of one another. Mary Crow's feeling that the Self *ought to have a body* reflects the enormous disparity between the body-Ego and the body-Self relationships. This difference probably underlies some of our feelings about posthumous life. The body is so intimately "attached" to the Ego that the Self gets the impression that it has no relation to the body at all.

The real mirror man is Owen Glendower. Not only is he obsessed, like

Mary, with the idea of another part of him having eyes. Also, this mental dichotomy is visible from without, from the viewpoint of a detached spectator who will hardly fail to notice the "*interior* distance" (V, 120) in Owen's green-gray eyes.

If the mind is a duality, as Powys insists, then it is a Self/Ego duality; if it is a multiverse, as Powys also insists, then it is a tetralateral multiverse. This is a configuration of four basic relationships: Ego/Ego, Ego/Self, Self/Ego, and Self/Self. Mary's weird experience in the looking glass suggests the third of these alternatives. The interplay of all four can for instance be studied in the description of how Catharine and Rhisiart both *want* to reach each other in the forests of Tywyn, yet fail to do so because there are two Catharines and two Rhisiarts. This we have already seen in Powys's bisection of their names. There is a crucial moment when Catharine is actually ready for Rhisiart. Yet his Norman equilibrium, the solidity of his Ego, refuses to act in perfect synchronization with Catharine's far more dramatic Celtic switch into physical abandon, into an expansive etherealization of the bodily. Rhisiart never really leaves his Ego, and when he finally does make his move, Catherine is already in transit from the periphery of Self to the centricity of Ego, her blood "reverting inwards, ebbing inwards" (XVI, 588). The Self knows All or Nothing. It resents the idea of copulation as something less than this All-or-Nothing. The Self would prefer, as we see with Catharine, to let its companion-Ego have an affair with another Ego on a quite different level. That, at least, would not be treachery.

That other edition of the individual that is found in the mirror serves as something capable of holding the contents of a twin identity. But if the mirror can do this, so can the shadow. Rhisiart's sexual relationship to Luned, a lady in waiting, is far more casual than his affairs with Catharine or Tegolin. Only his Ego is involved, and it is a question of pure lust generated by the lavish dimensions of Luned's figure. There is a memorable scene, however, when the two lovers come to form an Ego—Self—Ego—Self foursome in conjunction with their two shadows as these are projected onto the castle wall by the candlelight. Rhisiart is for no special reason thinking about Luned at five in the morning. Then, suddenly, she actually materializes, coming down the corridor with a candle. Luned informs him that she is pregnant, and at this point their shadows "seemed, as he stared at them, to have taken the whole situation into their hands" (XVIII, 680). This, no doubt, is because the Ego/Ego quality of his relationship with Luned suddenly changes to a Self/Self quality from the depth of feeling created by the urgent and vertiginous question of parenthood. Later, Rhisiart is immensely relieved to find that he and Luned slip back to their normal, casual personalities. Luned, he feels, has "taken the control of the situation out of the hands of their shadows" (XVIII, 682), and he can now relax to the sound of her cheerful gossip.

Owen Glendower's inner cleavage is suggested not only by the interior distance in his eyes but also by the bifurcated shape of his beard. He is extremely fussy about his appearance and keeps trimming his beard in front of the mirror. On the day of his coronation, he begins a profound dialogue with himself. He feels as if only half of his personality is involved in all the pageantry. Only his Ego participates. Facing, as Self, this Ego, externalized in the mirror, he initiates a process of ruthless self-examination and self-annihilation:

> "But *is* there anything to confess? Owen confessing to Owen!" And then he drew a deep and bitter sigh. And as if fishing for his own self-treachery in his fluctuating eyes he spiked with his spirit a terribly glittering fish, and as he caught it he thought, "That's my reward for knowing you so well, old cloven-beard. I can detach myself from you till my soul *isn't in you at all*, till my soul is there, or there, or *there*"— and he made motions with his head—"till my soul's so independent of you that it can make you do anything—*perhaps even live after you're dead!*" (XII, 392–93)

A configuration of two Egos and two Selves then creates a psychic quadrature in the mirror scene that takes place after the grazing of Owen's head in the stone aperture of the castle window. First, there is a kind of confidential intimacy between Owen and his mirror partner, as he recollects his habit of mentally undressing Tegolin in front of this particular looking glass. But this simple mirror duplication becomes a quadruplication at the precise moment when Owen begins to indulge in his special mental trick of simultaneously bifocusing Ego and Self:

> The moment their features had relaxed, however, a quite different and still more complicated phenomenon occupied that portion of the magician's chamber. For if the power possessed by the body of Owen of seeing itself in a mirror created one "mysterious double," the power possessed by the mind of Owen of analysing its own thoughts created a second mysterious "double"; so that the Prince of Wales at that moment became a four-fold being, became, in fact, what might be called a *Quaternity*. (XIX, 720–21)

Put simply, the Ego is possessive, the Self nonpossessive. More precisely, the "possessions" cherished by the Self are of a nature that does not make sense to the Ego. Put simply, also, the chief enemy of the Ego is boredom, while the chief enemy of the Self is pain. Schopenhauer saw man torn between this polarization of negativities. There is no way of escaping both of these at once. With pain and possession, we move into the world of *A Glastonbury Romance*. Here, for Sam Dekker, the switch from Ego to Self means giving up possession, giving up Nell Zoyland's lavish breasts: " 'I could bear it,' he thought, 'if she'd never leant against me with her breasts. Who could bear that and not want to "possess"; and not *have* to "possess"?' " (VII, 208). Love is a central force in the Powys novel primarily because it intensifies the conflict between Ego and Self. In the refined love relationship, the Ego is at first entirely out of sight. The exhilaration of the erotic encounter is largely derived from the sense of release from the Ego, encapsulated as it is within the mundane world of everyday routine. With time, however, the Ego shows up even in the most finely attuned rapport. In the Powys novel, this first glimpse of the Ego in the individual supremely representative of Self is shocking. Wolf Solent seems quite overwhelmed by the fact that Gerda is a rather ordinary girl:

> Why did all girls introduce into life an element of the conventional—into that life of which they themselves were the most mysterious expression? He became suddenly aware of the existence, in the beautiful head opposite him, of a whole region of interests and values that had nothing to do with love-making and nothing to do with romance. Was love itself, then, and all its mysteries, only a kind of magic gate leading into a land full of alien growths and unfamiliar soils? (*WoS,* X, 229)

Here John Cowper Powys becomes involved in a problem that he keeps returning to in his fiction: the negative aspects of empathy and extreme altruism (*AFU,* 13). Wolf Solent at one point meets a begging tramp, and he is tormented by the idea that giving this man a half crown is the only right thing to do, though it will at the same time prevent his own purchase of a railroad ticket to take him home (XXII, 531). In *A Glastonbury Romance*, Sam Dekker encounters this problem on a much wider scale. He witnesses the cancer suffering of old Mrs. Bagge and comes to realize that absolute identification with suffering would mean death. He fixes his gaze on a large bug on the sooty wall and contemplates the necessity of hardening the heart and ceasing to think of the pain of others. Sympathy with infernal suffering would kill all happiness. There comes a point when survival means forgetting, drawing back from the hell we glimpse close to us (XXVIII, 931–32). The motif returns in *Maiden Castle*. At the beginning of the novel, we find Dud No-Man in a churchyard on All Souls' Day. He contemplates the difference between the two women who have shaped much of his past: his mother and his wife. Both are now dead. Survival of death, he reflects, may not be universal. It may be an art, dependent on the discovery of some cosmic clue. But which clue? If survival of death depended on sinking into our individual life with a maximum of intensity, then it would be his mother who would be likely to dodge annihilation; if, on the other hand, such survival depends on our ability to sink our individuality into the life of others, then his dead Mona would have a far better chance (I, 21).

Usually, however, such antagonism between egotism and altruism is not worked out as such a simple polarization. *Mortal Strife* was written during World War II to encourage the people of Britain. The author views the Briton as essentially an individualist, a pirate-anarchist (X, 174), but this individualist acquires his strength and resilience from the Self, not the Ego. This is the central thrust of the whole argument in *Mortal Strife*, and it is based on sophisticated interpretations of cultural-psychological difference. Put simply, the Battle of Britain, for Powys, features squadrons of Selves defeating squadrons of Egos. When the writer discusses "our young men's recklessly individual supremacy in the air" (X, 172), he is suggesting the altruistic benefits to be derived from the "selfishness" of the Self.

The divisibility of human identity into centripetal and centrifugal extremes is also given a social projection (history) in the novels. This is so in *A Glastonbury Romance*, where the Glastonbury commune is defied by Philip Crow's capitalist egoism and by John Crow's pagan egotism. With greater subtlety in *Owen Glendower*, history is seen as a conflict between William the Conqueror's feudal system, with its vast collective hierarchies, and "this mad splitting-up of estates" (III, 64) endorsed by Owen and others. Owen can only destroy. Through military operations and political intrigue, the Welsh prince makes history out of his own personal and internal disruptions.

The erotic aggressiveness of the Ego saturates many memorable passages in the fiction of John Cowper Powys. The Ego is "the vulture on the wing, and the hyena on the prowl" (R, XV, 204). Frequently, the phallic presence of this Ego is suggested by various symbols: Hamish Traherne's white rat Ricoletto in *Rodmoor;* Jobber Skald's seashore pebble in *Weymouth Sands;* Petrus Peregrinus's lodestone in *The Brazen Head.* All these things are pocketed, pressed, and clandestinely squeezed. There are also female counterparts. In *Rodmoor* (1916), Linda slips a fir cone into her dress. Brand has twined it in her hair during their lovemaking, and now she keeps it from day to day between her breasts. Its symbolic pregnancy is diffuse, however, when in her jealousy Nance plucks the treasured object from Linda's dress, flinging it "into the centre-current of the inflowing tide. 'So much for Love!' she cried fiercely" (XVIII, 262). The emphasis on the centripetal/centrifugal forces of flinging out and flowing in makes this scene a precursor of that vivid one in *Wolf Solent*, where the protagonist throws away his fetish, the rain god Mukalog, to the panting of his own indrawn breath (XXII, 533).

This in-sinking often characterizes the emotion of the Self *as motion*. Hamish Traherne speaks of the self-encapsulating warmth of "love," meaning the centripetal gravitation of the Self: "When the passing hour's cruel to it, it sinks away within, below the passing of every possible hour, beyond the hurt of every conceivable stroke. . . . It does not ask to be recognized. It is its own return, its own recognition" (R, IX, 121). There is a self-sufficiency in the Self, then, that is not the self-sufficiency of the Ego, discussed earlier.

In the reality of practical love and sexual encounter, the Ego/Self polarity tends to entangle lovers, as travel in inner space from Ego to Self and Self to Ego is troubled by an appalling lack of timing and synchronicity. In the seventeenth chapter of *Rodmoor*, Brand's masculine Ego first sweeps Linda's feminine Self off its feet; then, as Linda herself moves into Ego, Brand recedes into the gentler understanding mood of the loving Self (XVII, 231). The faultiness of this inner timing is accentuated when Adrian Sorio passionately embraces Nance in chapter 6. For his Ego, her Self lacks the fire and blood of real love: "I can't always make love to you as if we were two children, can I—two babes in the wood?" (VI, 82). But Nance, failing, like Adrian, to perceive the divisibility of personality, interprets his physical intensity, not as the language of the Ego, but as the ferocity of mere animal passion (VI, 81). Sexuality, here, is interpreted by the characters as being either present or absent. There is no understanding of that complicated mechanism through which the eroticism of the Self only communicates with the eroticism of another Self, the sensuality of the Ego only with the sensuality of some other Ego. It is perhaps also this erotic asymmetry which explains some of the strange hatred that the Powys hero will direct at woman. This, in Powys, reflects the quaint admiration that the Self always feels for the freewheeling Ego.[3] As Selves, Magnus Muir, Wolf Solent, and Dud No-Man are so infatuated with their paramours that these females become pure mental torment when they switch between Ego and Self. This switch over is wistfully fascinating as well as obsessively destructive. Most painful of all is the vision of Ego from the perspective of Self, the manipulative and autonomous seen from the vantage point of the receptive and communicative. The Powys hero, being male, sees this Ego in the female, and therefore females in general tend to be given a number of negative attributes that belong, essentially, to the Ego of both sexes. The proximity of Ego and body gives the Powys hero the impression that women are more "physiological." They are part of matter, matter itself. Men are not matter, not nature. The male is that which destroys matter, from without (R, XIV, 178–80). There is a greater body/spirit duality in man that in woman for the Powys hero. Man is outside the body, as spirit; man is inside the body as body. For woman this is not so. A "girl's body passes into everything round her, whereas the body of a man stays inside his clothes" (MC, IX, 486). It is perhaps in *Maiden Castle* that John Cowper Powys best captures this feeling of a saturating erotic diffusion emanating from the radiant nucleus of the feminine mystery and creating the haunting aura of an all-enclosing semi-occult magic. Wolf is obsessed by Gerda's Ego; Magnus Muir is obsessed by Curly's Ego: but neither of these two obsessions is quite as extreme as Dud No-Man's narcotic attraction to the ever-receding Ego of Wizzie Ravelstone:

> He had never believed that a girl's body could diffuse itself as Wiz-zie's did—quite apart from her mind—through the fabric of chairs, through the stuff of tablecloths, through the polish of door-handles, through the angles of looking-glasses, through the reflections on glass bottles, through the flickerings on coal-scuttles, and through all those meaningless scrolls and scrawls that the elfish artistry of time leaves upon walls and ceilings. (IX, 486)

Man, by contrast, is less diffuse and expansive. He does not share his secret feelings or radiate his eerie semicorporeal presence into the inanimate. In *Weymouth Sands*, Dog Cattistock has the sexist conviction that a man who does not live alone, even when living with a woman, is not a real man—only half a man (XII, 442).

It is, however, in the physical act of love itself, and in the mental convolutions accompanying sexual intercourse, that the difference in inner stances is at its clearest. After their lovemaking, in *The Brazen Head*, Peleg notices that Ghosta falls asleep before him, because in her, body, soul, and spirit are more intimately connected, while in him a certain dimension of mental awareness is always left intact, unaffected, detached (X, 147). The same erotic polarity is to be found in *A Glastonbury Romance*. At the height of erotic intensity, Nell Zoyland remains conscious of Sam Dekker as a human being, as Sam Dekker. She abandons herself to him, not to his body. For Sam, Nell is at this moment absolutely impersonal, "a woman's flesh in empty space;" for Nell on the other hand, Sam is still "the *actual, personal, conscious man she loved*" (XI, 310). While it is clear that some of the early prototypes for the

Powys hero, like Adrian Sorio in *Rodmoor* and Richard Storm in *After My Fashion*, have a rather primitive and callously conventional Byronic sexism at the heart of their stylized neo-Gothic psychology, it is also evident from much of Powys's writing that the novelist has a deep understanding of women and of the way in which woman may surpass man in her capacity for emotional depth and sincerity during the heat of passion. The fever of masculine devotion is archetypally quixotic and escapist, whereas even in its infinity, the female surrender never becomes a surrender of reality or humanity:

> There are levels of feminine emotion in the state of love entirely and forever unknown to men. Man's imaginative recognition of feminine charm, man's greedy lust, man's pride in possession, man's tremulous sense of the pathos of femininity, man's awe in the presence of an abysmal mystery—all these feelings exist in a curious detachment in his consciousness. They are all separate from the blind subcurrent that sweeps the two together. But with women, when they are really giving themselves up without reserve, a deep underflow of abandonment is reached, where such detachment from Nature ceases completely. (*G*, XI, 298)

In Powys's fiction there is a greater integration in the feminine than in the masculine. The male-female dichotomy comes to stand for the Ego/Self duality. In *After My Fashion*, the painter Robert Canyot tries to point out the difference between Ego and Self to Nelly. She, however, refuses to acknowledge any such divisibility. Nelly sees herself as belonging either to the world of art (Robert's painting) or to the world of erotic possession. Robert, on the other hand, sees Nelly's Self as independent of Nelly's Ego. Her Self he refers to as her "soul;" her Ego he calls "the *Nelly* part of you." If he were to possess Nelly in the personal world of sex, her Ego would drift out of his painting into the possessive embrace of his Ego; but Nelly's Self would remain, unpossessed and unpossessable, in his painting. We get a lucid picture, here, not only of the Ego/Self antinomy and of its projections into the erotic but also of how the Self overlaps the confines of sex, indeed of humanity itself. This, essentially, does not suggest an occult permeation of the nonhuman. It suggests the feeling of transcendence in the Self. This is a transcendence of Ego, and therefore also of that body to which Ego is felt to be so intimately glued:

> "I mean," said Robert . . . that my painting draws its life from every single thing which destiny takes away from me."
> The girl looked at him in whimsical gravity. "Then if you *had* had me," she said, "I shouldn't be in your paint box any more?"

"The *Nelly* part of you wouldn't, he answered solemnly, "but your soul would—because I should never have got hold of that!"

"But the *Nelly* part of me *is* my soul," she protested; "that's what I am really and truly."

He looked at her grimly and sardonically.

"No! No! my dear," he said. "*This* is Nelly," and he touched her shoulder. "And *this* is Nelly," and he touched her knee. "But the thing in you which says 'I am I' isn't Nelly at all. It isn't even a girl. It isn't even a human being." (X, 139–40)

Sex, in the fiction of John Cowper Powys, is rarely confined to the individual living organism. In the outspread expanses of its interstellar enormity, the cosmos can make love to itself by virtue of an internal fissure. In *Rodmoor*, Philippa Renshaw detests feminine sluggishness: "I'm like that myself—or half of me is. I betray myself to myself and lacerate myself for being myself" (VIII, 115). But this (in a Hegelian image) is also the fate of the universe as a whole, because "it Itself is divided against Itself in those ultimate regions of primal causation" (G, II, 77). Powys's fiction always comes full circle in the sense that the "cosmic" is eventually equated with the psychic. The cosmic dimension always denotes travel in *inner* space. The comprehension of the significance of all the cosmic imagery in the novels does not therefore require detailed knowledge of theosophical balderdash and occult myth. Instead, it is essential to grasp certain structural asymmetries in the human mind. We encounter a tension between a cosmic Ego and a cosmic Self, and this tension is merely the "cosmification" of that inner duality which has obsessed all great writers.

2.2 The Cosmic and the Collective

In *A Glastonbury Romance* we can see how the erotic Self gradually transforms itself into the cosmic Self in that haunting eleventh chapter. The planetary presence of the Sedgemoor moon comes to suggest the cosmic significance of Sam Dekker's feelings for a human being with two beautifully developed breasts. The moon is the controlling center of that creative-destructive Atlantic which eventually deals such a fatal blow to the vain human endeavors of Glastonbury. Yet the moon is also a symbolic circle of magic that controls those far more elusive tides involved in the inner drama of each principal character:

From that fragment of white mystery there slid across land and water into the soul of Sam Dekker a thin, long-rippling confederate stream of sweet disturbance. . . . He became a wave in the Bristol Channel, a bracken-frond in the Quantock hills, a crystal in a Mendip stone wall, a black-striped perch in the Brue under Pomparles Bridge. Sam and that old bent pollard, whose youthful sprouts he was clutching with such blind intensity, gave themselves up together so completely to the power of that obscured moon that an identical magnetism poured through the man's flesh and blood and shivered through the vegetable fibres of the tree. (XI, 307)

The moon represents the Self in *A Glastonbury Romance.* Its enemy, the sun, represents the Ego. This opposition is suggested by the overall structure of the novel. It begins with the individualistic John Crow walking under the bifurcated power of solar divinity. It ends with that all-encompassing, all-obliterating flood destroying the human-collective force of the Glastonbury commune. The movement is a simple one, vastly cosmic in its conceptual expansiveness: from sun to moon, from Ego to Self. The elemental transfer is from fire to water. In addition, on a different symbolic plane, the moon acquires a latent sociopolitical pregnancy, standing for the collective Self against the collective Ego. The moon "has always been on the side of the weak and the sick against the strong and the well-constituted" (X, 280). This macropolarity sweeps the novel from the divine-diabolical ferocity of its first solar paragraph to the never/always open-endedness of its final lunar line.

The centripetal/centrifugal interaction is brought out in the interconnecting of the planetary and the individual, the cosmic and the psychic. From galactic periphery to terrestrial centerpoint, there is an immense inward-moving astral mentation. At the same time there is a centrifugal countermovement. Both currents are divided into parallel streams of antagonistic energy. As John and Mary pray together while out on a love trip in a rowing boat, the duality of their prayer encounters the duality of the First Cause:

They prayed to this unknown Ultimate, out of their hollow boat, above that gleaming current, so simultaneously and so intensely, that the magnetism of their prayer shot like a meteorite out of the earth's planetary atmosphere. Something about its double origin, and something about the swift and translucent water from which it started on its flight, drove it forward beyond the whole astronomical world, and beyond the darkness enclosing that world, till it reached the primal Cause of all life. . . . Down through the abyss of ether, away from the central nucleus of this dualistic Being, descend through the darkness that is beyond the world two parallel streams of magnetic force. (II, 77)

Here in *A Glastonbury Romance,* Mr. Evans claims that God is outside nature and that matter is entirely evil (IX, 260). Sam Dekker, by contrast, argues that something has come into nature from the outside. The incarnation is the becoming-inside of the great outside, the dissolution of the inside/outside duality. Is this really a difference in cosmological theory? Hardly!

Salvation is certainly connected with the discovery of Self, the process through which Self is emancipated from Ego, or, rather, from the monopoly of Ego. The religious mysticism of the Welsh antiquary sees the glory of Self; but Sam Dekker's religious mysticism also celebrates Selfness. There is no difference in devotional content. The apparent polarity is derived from contrasting perspectives. To see God outside nature, as Owen does, is to contemplate the Self from the viewpoint of the Ego. To see God as being part of nature, or as actually being nature, is to choose to forget the Ego and contemplate the cosmic Self from the viewpoint of the private Self.

Evans has an Ego/Ego cosmology (psychology). Sam has a Self/Self cosmology. Evans has no hope of ever being able to leave his Ego behind, to find permanent release, in this life, from the pressure of the quotidian world of time and matter. Sam, on the other hand, comes to the Grail-moment that turns his existence inside out, that turns his daily routines and his life in terrestrial squalor inside out. This is why he can give an old man an enema immediately after his Grail experience without any sense of inner conflict. (The enema in itself carries the doubleness of the centripetal/centrifugal polarity: insertion *as* extrusion; the centripetal *as* the centrifugal.) God is that anus too, God and anus are one in that imploded/exploded cosmology which makes Syl*vanus* Cobbold reiterate his "caput-anus" in *Weymouth Sands.*

The crucial discussion between Evans and Sam takes place under St. Michael's Tower in Glastonbury. John Crow is with them, and as the three of them sit there, Powys stresses the synchronicity and parallelism of their divided thought. They are three Egos, three separate individuals thinking erotic thoughts about three separate female individuals. In this Ego*ness,* they are apart from nature, outside the world-soul. Yet at the same time they are three Selves. Or better, they are a triple Self, expanding as a triadic halo. Their personal diffusion matches that other atmospheric diffusion which is converting the atomic distinctiveness of matter into the aerial opalescence of a planetary envelope:

Before them to the westward stretched the green water meadows . . . while to the southwest, beyond the fens, rose the blue-grey ridge of the low Polden hills. All these were softly suffused by the cloud-latticed vapour-filmed sun; a sun which, though riding at high noon, lacked the potency to dominate what it bathed with that glamorous and watery light. . . . And as they sat there they each thought of a particular girl. They thought of these three feminine identities so intently that by the automatic preoccupation of their feelings the souls of all three girls were drawn towards them; three wraithlike eidola! . . .

To the supernatural eyes of that veiled sun as he dreamed his indescribable planetary thoughts, vaguely hostile and vaguely menacing, one of these feminine forms came naked to the waist—that was Nell; one came naked from the thighs downward—that was Mary; and one came garmented like a nun, from head to foot in black—and that was Cordelia!

Together these three men represented—in Remorse, in Renunciation, in Roguery—everything that separates our race from nature. (IX, 259)

Again we see how John Cowper Powys tends to associate masculinity with divisibility. We also notice the tension between nucleus and aura, between the centripetal and the centrifugal. This is the antagonism between the inner Self and the outer Self, and it is elaborated further in *The Brazen Head* as the conflict between the cosmology of Roger Bacon and that of Pierre of Picardy. Bacon believes in a centripetal force holding the whole universe together, and he is frightened by Pierre of Picardy's sense of the cosmogonic centrifuge, the ultimate negativity that casts all creatures into the cosmic loneliness—what the Welsh call *Diddym*, "the ultimate Void" (XVI, 239).

As we have seen, *A Glastonbury Romance* is suspended between the extreme points of the first and last paragraphs as the tension between sun (the cosmic Ego) and moon (the cosmic Self). Spatially, this conflict is worked out into the imagery of the Grail containing a tench: the Self encapsulating the Ego. Temporally, the sun/moon antagonism is expressed through the polarization of solar time and lunar time, of time and "timelessness." By solar time, I mean sequential clock time as it is experienced in daily routine existence; by lunar time, I mean that which is not solar time—because it is a richer human experience of temporality than that afforded by serial clock time.[4] The fissure in the mind (suggested by our fall line) can be projected as the bisection of the protagonist's lifeline. After retreating from Lenty Pond, Wolf Solent feels as though he were a beginning a "*posthumous* life" (XXIII, 567). In *Owen Glendower*, the Welsh prince decides to be generous to Rhisiart in his heart and cold to him in public. This procedure gratifies some perverse quality in his nature. Owen decides to indulge in this perversity without further reflection at this point. All will be analyzed at a later stage. He pauses in front of a polished shield in which he glimpses the outline of his own face (XVII, 655): he knows that a time will soon come when his Self, so deeply attached to Rhisiart, will chastise his Ego for its treachery and superficiality.

John Cowper Powys is conscious not only of temporal fragmentation but also, above all, of the qualitative difference between one fragment of time and another: "There are moments in almost everyone's life when events occur in a special and curious manner that seems to separate that fragment of time from all other fragments" (*WeS*, II, 48). *Inside* this special fragment, time is no longer experienced as fragmented. In *Autobiography*, John Cowper Powys speaks of the Cambridgeshire walks of his university years as belonging to a kind of *"half-eternity*, made up of a fusion of past and present, with the future, and all its wants and wishes, totally annihilated" (V, 170). This centripetal temporality, this temporal oneness, expresses itself in *A Glastonbury Romance* as a holistic and feminine sense of time. The future is part of the present and the eternal is part of the ephemeral. From the platform of such a temporal synthesis, the Self makes its more daring departures into the "timeless:"

> It is women's fatal susceptibility to passionate touch that hypnotises them into by far the greater number of their disasters; for under this touch-hypnosis the present transforms itself into the eternal, and their grand sex-defence, their consciousness of continuity, their awareness of the future as an integral portion of the present, is shattered and broken up. The ideal love-affairs for women are when it is easy for them, after these momentary plunges into the eternal, to fall back again upon their realistic sense of continuity; whereas the ideal love-affairs for men are when their feeling for novelty and for adventure is perpetually being re-aroused by the bewildering variability of women's moods. (XI, 296)

Powys would seem to be suggesting that it is a high-frequency Ego/Self oscillation that arouses men, whereas the male frequency preferred by woman is that of a single sweep from Self to Ego and back to Self.

Clocks, in Powys's fiction, evoke the temporal as well as the transtemporal, the temporalities both of Ego and of Self. Dwarfed by the elephantine architecture of the New York railroad station in *After My Fashion*, Elise lifts her head so as to be able to read the time by the enormous clock hanging above her. She is too close beneath it, however, for the hands to be intelligible: "She felt as if she had indeed reached some fulcral or pivotal point in space where time issued its mandates but was itself obliterated by some formidable super-time" (XVIII, 243–44). The centripetal/centrifugal polarity affects temporality too. A passage in *The*

Brazen Head suggests that ordinary time denotes a centripetal movement from periphery to nucleus, while super-time marks a dissolution of quotidian temporality and an outward moving radiance into an ever-widening stellar infinity. Albert Magnus of Cologne suddenly feels his Self expand centrifugally into infinite space, until the thought of time saves him by a kind of weird centripetal countermovement: "And then suddenly he spoke to himself in a still small voice. 'Albert, old friend,' he said to himself, 'there's no need for you to be alone in Space like this. You have forgotten what all creatures ought never to forget. You have forgotten that there is also Time' " (XVIII, 270). Time, here, denotes the lineal time sense of the Ego. In its outward-bound yearning for something more complex, the Self seeks a transcendence of this commonplace temporality, and we see this at its best in Wolf Solent's confrontation with the ticking of the cosmos inside his parlor clock. There appears to be a timer not only in the Ego but also in the Self:

> The cheap wooden clock on the mantelpiece of his small parlour made itself audible to the ears of Wolf across the little passageway as he stood above his kitchen stove. Eight times the clock struck; and the old vivid consciousness of what time was and was not caught his mind and held it. It was not a consciousness of the passing of time as it affected his own life that arrested him. Of that kind of individual awareness he had scarcely any trace. To himself he always seemed neither young nor old. Indeed, of bodily self-consciousness. . . he had nothing at all. What he lived in was not any compact, continuous sense of personal identity, but rather *a series of disembodied sensations,* some physical, some mental, in which his identity was absolutely merged and lost. He was vividly aware of these momentary sensations in relation to other feelings of the same kind, some long past and some anticipated in his imagination; but he was accustomed to regard all these not from out of the skin, so to speak, of a living organism, but from a detachment so remote and far away as to seem almost outside both the flowing of time and the compactness of personality.
>
> Eight o'clock in the morning of the first day of June was what that timepiece said to him now; and his mind paused upon the recognition of the vast company of clocks and watches all the world over, ticking, ticking, ticking—sending up, in tiny metallic beats, vibrations of human computation into the depths of unthinkable space. (X, 224)

This passage gives us a detailed view of the Ego. The Ego is "individual awareness," "bodily self-consciousness," a "compact, continuous sense of personal identity," the "skin" of a "living organism," "the compactness of personality." The Self is transindividual, supratemporal, and supraphysical. The Self is a "detachment" that finds its impersonality in the

peace beyond the "flowing of time," in a realm where identity is lost . . .
and gained.

In *Autobiography*, John Cowper Powys claims that he is not a narcissist, that, in fact, he is the opposite of a narcissist. This is constantly
stressed with confessional pathos, and yet it is clear that both the writer
and his friends could detect in him an overwhelming self-preoccupation.
How is this to be explained? I think it is fair to say that Powys was
extremely antinarcissistic as far as his Ego was concerned. His Ego was
not in love with his Ego. Yet he was extremely narcissistic in regard to his
Self. His Self loved his Self. Not only that. His entire doctrine of life
came to be founded on the idea that this should be so. Hence the title *In
Defence of Sensuality.* The Self must arrive at a state of intimate self-
reflexive sensuality in which it gathers itself together at the expense of
everything else. As the title of *A Philosophy of Solitude* suggests, this is a
kind of mental hoarding, the psychic life becoming humped up as a
luxuriant centricity. Only the Ego/Self duality will allow us to understand how this psychic gesture goes hand-in-hand with the most intense
hatred of egoism, greed, acquisitiveness, and so on. The ideal life is a Self
trip, not an Ego trip. Between these two there is all the difference in the
world. As a mode of being-in-the-world, Selfness can equate itself with
disinterestedness, considerateness, compassion, generosity . . . even self-
immolation and martyrdom. The saint is totally absorbed in his Self. He
is freed, *through that Self-absorption,* from the centripetal worldliness
and personal vanity of the avaricious Ego. To be wrapped up in one's Self
is the very opposite of being wrapped up in one's Ego. The difference is
the difference between the saint and the timeserver, the mystic and the
opportunist.

The comprehension of the nature of the interaction between the collective Ego and the collective Self is related to this primal understanding of
the difference between the egoism of the Ego and the egoism of the Self.
Every psychic system will want to preserve its stability, and it is precisely
this act of preservation that we must not confuse with the ideology of that
system itself: its outward-bound capacity as existential statement.

It is clear that John Cowper Powys was strongly attracted to the begin-
nings of communism. It is equally clear that he was intensely hostile to
communism. His ambivalence raises the same question and the same
answer as the issue of narcissism. The whole problematics must be discussed in term of the Ego/Self dichotomy. Insofar as communism pro-
motes the Self by cancelling the power of the Ego, Powys is *for*
communism. Insofar as communism destroys the Self by promoting the
power of the Ego, Powys is *against* communism. In the former case, the

collective Self gives the individual Self more air to breathe in a claus-
trophobic Ego-society. In the latter case, the collective Ego of capitalism
only gives way to the collective Ego of the totalitarian state bureaucracy.
Concerned as he is with the central issue of personality and individual
autonomy, Powys never goes for the cheap political naïvism that equates
capitalism with individualism, communism with nonindividualism. Nor
does he wholeheartedly embrace a reversal of this notion. Rejecting political vulgarism, he comes to see the dual implications of both ideologies,
and it is only through the complex network of tensions created by this
refusal to simplify things that the novelist is able to work out the sustained sociopolitical framework of vastly conceived works like *A Glastonbury Romance*. Intrinsically, there is nothing in either system that
guarantees respect for "personality." All depends on what kind of real-life
articulations these doctrines are given, and upon what tacit meaning the
word "personality" is made to carry. Both Ego and Self aspire to this
ideal, this nomenclature.

We can see these crosscurrents during the great Glastonbury christening. In a fierce argument with Will Zoyland, who defends the capitalist
division of labor, Lady Rachel Zoyland, his half-sister, tries to point out
how the individual Ego profits more from a commune than from a free
enterprise society where the profit is never adequately shared: "The point
you entirely slur over, Will, . . . is whether these labourers would prefer
working for a single individual like Philip Crow, or *working for themselves*—that's to say for the community" (XXVI, 844). Young David
Spear, the fervent communist, looks upon the question with an additional
amount of cynicism and psychological subtlety. In his view, the small talk
of the christening reveals how entirely each individual is absorbed in his
own little world of private interest and selfish benefit. In this group
narcissism, there is this stunning preoccupation with the sensitivity of the
Ego, with the petty altruism of the Ego, while the global charity and
planetary compassion of the expanding Self are swallowed up by egotism
and narrow-mindedness:

> And this sort of thing is what they call a personal life! These people
> are thinking of nothing else but their own personal emotions; and they
> are proud of it. . . . I'll teach these good friends of mine how to be
> impersonal! These people think that their feelings are the only serious
> thing in the world. *Their feelings!* When, at this very moment in
> China, in India, in New York, in Berlin, in Vienna—Good God! . . .
> *their feelings!* When, at this moment, if all the pain in the world caused
> by this accursed individual life were to rise up in one terrific cry . . .
> (XXVI, 860)

The vulgar simplicity of the individualism-versus-collectivism polarity is also undermined by an understanding of the immense role played by the individual in the shaping of the history of the people. In the library at Mark's Court, Geard of Glastonbury experiences a moment of ecstasy under the influence of strong tea. He withdraws into the Self, and this gives him the strange feeling that some magnetic force is pouring out of the "piled-up mystery of printed matter" surrounding him (XV, 426). He rides on "one of the great ocean-wave crests of his conscious life," as the presence of all the various books acquires a peculiar grip on his saturated mind. At this moment he suddenly realizes the overwhelming part played by individual genius in history: every moment in history is created by books, and so it will always be. As he thinks of Plato, Rousseau, and Marx, he is struck by "the dramatic pliancy, suggestibility, malleability, of the masses of human beings."

This sense of the historical superman is carried over into the view of the esoteric. The supernatural presents itself only to the few, to a sensitive élite porous to the more subtle planetary influences, the really drastic shifts of inner gear. It is in "this singular Person" (XIII, 359) that the violent storms of intense feeling are allowed to rage freely. John Crow "sees" the Arthurian sword plunge into the Brue because he is equipped with a type of sensitivity that is not to be found in most humans.

In the cruder psychology of *Rodmoor*, the intellectual fury of the early, Byronic Powys hero works itself out as a kind of complicated morbidity. The morose, out-reaching intellection of the exceptional mind differentiates itself from the commonsensical mediocrity of the conventional personality incapable of enjoying vaster vistas of thought. In this rather immature romance, dedicated "to the Spirit of Emily Brontë," the Italianate Sorio is understood by the passionate Philippa but not by the tame-spirited Nance, and in her jealousy Philippa cannot refrain from lacerating her rival with a fierce analysis of her negative effect on the heightened consciousness of the creative mind: "It's women like you, without intelligence and without imagination, who are the ruin of men of genius" (XXIV, 388).

Adrian Sorio's individualism is a creative individualism. He is writing a book, and in this book he is setting down his discovery of some cosmic master clue. This, in the present terminology, is the discovery of the antagonism between Ego and Self, involving the necessity for the one to destroy the other: "It will explain my life, my whole life, that book. . . . I show in my book how . . . every living thing really aims . . . to escape from itself . . . by the destruction of itself" (XXI, 324).[5] This individualism in Sorio is something rather different from that free-enterprise creativity which David Spear sees in the capitalist Philip Crow. That creativity is the ruthless expansion of the greedy Ego. The individualism of the Self has to be radically different from the individualism of the Ego. The industrialist creativity of Philip's Ego in *A Glastonbury Romance* can hardly be equated with that literary and metaphysical creativity championed by Philippa in *Rodmoor*. Philip's "creativity" shows no concern for the slums and back alleys of Glastonbury. These, in the inclusive structure and scope of the novel, are carefully described by Powys (IX, 264–65), carefully neglected by the industrialist. The slums *are* this neglect of his. They are the product of a centripetal Ego-creativity serving the private ends of industry and the personal motives of Philip Crow. By contrast, the Self-creativity of Sorio in *Rodmoor* is expansive and centrifugal. It is directed impersonally and imaginatively to the astral limits of a metaphysically romanced cosmos, but also personally and practically into a concern for the tiniest suffering organism—a fish that can be saved from gasping death in the forgotten nets of an East Anglian fisherman; a moth gyrating helplessly in some forlorn weir by a derelict windmill on the fens. It is this ruthless domination of the expansive Self that drives John Cowper, the living writer, to distribute alms to beggars, to rescue leaves and sprays of vegetation from the New York gutters (*A*, X, 466).

Behind the ideological pathos in *A Glastonbury Romance*, behind those emotive passages where Powys seems to be carrying himself off his feet in the manner of his impassioned characters, it is possible to detect the Self's rejection of the Ego's claim to own and possess. The Ego desires that which is an inherent and integral part of the Self: its planetary heritage— earth, air, and water. In the world of Self, which downgrades the subject/ object dichotomy, there can be no dividing up, no possession or nonpossession. There can only be being. In the practical world of political reality—always the world of the Ego—the transfer of private property from Ego to Self becomes the transfer of private property from the private Ego (industrialists) to the collective Ego (state). By the time of *Mortal Strife* (1942), John Cowper Powys has come to realize the full negative implications of this. Here, capitalism is viewed as a kind of necessary evil, preferable to the more systematized reality of centralized state government. But such winnowed sagacity does not really rob the passionate anti-Ego rhetoric in *A Glastonbury Romance* of its sumptuous fury. David Spear sees capital from a Marxian point of view as the body of an indivisible Self. In the hands of the individual Ego, this capital becomes a threat to that Self-embodiment. It becomes the obliteration of the free Self: "Money—the engine of life—is an engine of death when it is in the hands of individuals. . . . It is a crime to be rich. It is a perversion, an obscenity, a monstrosity. It is an offence against nature, against intelligence, against good taste. To be rich is to be a moral leper. To be rich is to be on the side of Cancer" (IX, 268).

The ideopolitical discussions between Philip Crow and David Spear now come to fuse conceptually with the motif of incarnation-versus-nonincarnation (the topic debated by Sam and Mr. Evans). Does the cosmos possess itself or not? It is this self-possession, this oneness of Ego with Self, that Adrian Sorio yearns so desperately for in *Rodmoor:* to be "safe from everything—safe from love and hatred and madness and pity—safe from unspeakable imaginations—safe from himself" (XXVII, 458).

The Powys hero senses the possibility of escape, of an existential implosion that would remove all incompatibilities. John Cowper may have chosen this escape himself as a practical strategy in later life, but his protagonists are never let so easily off the hook. The soul of the Powys hero is perpetually reinfected by the same cosmic ur-virus: duality. Owen Glendower may possibly be the happy exception in that he manages to externalize his inner torment as social strife and national conflict. He manages to escape from himself and from his divisibility, but in doing so he destroys the inner life of a nation. By detaching himself from himself—the Ego from the Self, the Self from the Ego—he attaches his country to its own self-inconsistency. Owen's "habitual attitude to himself was of such detachment that it only needed an extension of this detachment, till it included all those connected with him, to create a temper essentially dangerous to human happiness" (XVI, 561).

Here in *Owen Glendower,* the Ego/Self duality is also given both a social and a cosmic expression—in military conflict and theological dispute. Master Philip Sparrow, champion of the peasantry, plays a simplistic political part, corresponding to that played in *A Glastonbury Romance* by Red Robinson, ex-foreman of Philip Crow's dye works. Powys transcends the shallow plebian/patrician antinomy of many a "sociological" novelist by differentiating the revolutionary Ego from the revolutionary Self. David Spear is, like Claudius Cask in *Maiden Castle*, a radical Self. Master Sparrow, by contrast, is just a radical Ego—an egoist like Owen himself. They both lack the "spirit of a revolutionary" (*O*, XII, 424).

Owen Glendower, however, clings to no rigid political orthodoxy; he has relinquished "that unquestioning acceptance of the existing class-system which makes every innovator a criminal." This, of course, does not mean that he comes anywhere near Walter Brut's extremist faith in the common people's future understanding of radical ideas, such as those of

Wycliffe in theology. Rhisiart looks sadly upon the Lollard's naïve egalitarianism and feels that all his Lollardry, in fact, is "a thing for the few" (XI, 342).

At this point, I am focusing three essential aspects of the sociopolitical dimension in Powys's writing: (1) his general inclination toward a noncompetitive life-style; (2) his conscious use of class structures and class conflicts; (3) his effort to differentiate the revolutionary Ego from the revolutionary Self. The social or sociopolitical dimension is never the primary structural level of integration in the Powys novel. On the other hand it is never entirely negligible. As an integral portion of the entire scheme, the sociopolitical can be seen operating at its best in *A Glastonbury Romance*. Here the Ego/Self antinomy is allowed to play itself out on the three basic planes of life—the private, the social, the cosmic. The private plane is that of the various love affairs: notably, those of John Crow and Mary Crow; Sam Dekker and Nell Zoyland. The social plane is that of Philip Crow and the Wookey Hole mines versus the anarchist-communist commune of Paul Trent and David Spear (XXIII, 717). The cosmic plane is that of Geard's struggle for the reestablishment of Glastonbury as a spiritual center for the Grail cult, and of Sam Dekker's quest for the Holy Grail itself. These three main dimensions are astutely interwoven so that the socio-ideological neither becomes superfluous nor pure sociology cancelling occult suggestion. The result is an immensely satisfying conceptual cross-saturation. This makes *A Glastonbury Romance* full because of its inclusive richness, rich because of a full interpenetration. Each episode is like a fragment of colored glass imprisoned within a large crystal ball. In the compressed limpidity of this sphere, the jumbled heterogeneity of tightly packed color planes never permits the exclusive viewing of one particular segment in isolation from the rest—yet at the same time, it is only the distinct individuality of that particular segment which makes the full interplay of diverse colorations possible.

The last chapter of *A Glastonbury Romance* marks the triumph of Self over Ego, moon over sun, mass over energy, difference over structure, force over intention. It is the defeat of individualism within the context of the story: the triumph of individualism in terms of personality's (John Cowper's, Geard's) achievement of vision. The ultimate collapse of this individualism qua egotism is the establishment of the Glastonbury Commune, but above all, on a symbolic level, the final collapse and fragmentation of Philip Crow's new steel bridge. This gives way under the vast elemental pressure of the flood. It may seem, this destruction, to be the victory of the inorganic over the organic; but it is essentially the victory of organic Nature over atomizing human materialism. This is the tacit suggestion of the final paragraph. The Commune dissolves, too, but we are really never told how to view this. The flood may have confirmed its idea, or destroyed even that.

If communism satisfies a human craving, at least in utopian theory, for a noncompetitive mode of being, it is nevertheless possible, indeed essential, to distinguish it as the noncompetitive-yearning-of-the-Self from the *Ego's* yearning for noncompetition. In its former shape, communism is the ideology of a passionate collective Self, seeking—with semireligious, semimystic fanaticism—for some way out of the labyrinthine repetitiousness of the quotidian Ego. As such it is to be equated with other doctrines (ostensibly antagonistic), like fascism. John Cowper Powys is perceptive in rejecting fascism while at the same time refusing to dismiss it as a mere hoax "turned on" from the top. In *Maiden Castle*, Claudius sees the fascist movement as more than merely last-ditch capitalism. It is evasive and indefinable, and it seems to spring from "youth." Fascism actually appears to satisfy some deep contemporary craving for something different from that which modern civilization has to offer man. Tyrannical popes do not account for the existence of the church—nor do the leaders who gain by totalitarianism account for the existence of fascism (IV, 177).

As the collective Self, as a conglomeration of spiritually starved Selves, the communist movement would appear to promise release from the narrow world of the industrial Ego. From this point of view, such an ideology seems for Powys to have an emotional content and a personal, human significance. Yet Powys never fully swallows this. For he detects at the core of the communist spirit an emphasis on the impersonally cerebral and logical. This is an emphasis on what I called "sinistral thinking" in chapter 1. Such rationalism suffuses the doctrine of communism with a cold, inhuman pallor. It robs the underlying humane benevolence of its blood and warmth of appeal. In combination with its emphasis on no-nonsense materialism (recall the covenant of Ego and body), this clear-cut impersonality and mechanical determinism chill the initial wave of Powysian enthusiasm for a planetary panacea promising so profound an alleviation of human suffering. Suddenly, in a switch to the abstract, communism seems to become the doctrine of that Ego which it was originally intended to overcome and destroy. In the stereotyped rhetoric of Claudius in *Maiden Castle*, of David Spear in *A Glastonbury Romance*, communism becomes, like Mr. Evans's God, something outside nature, something outside humanity. It becomes the eternal otherness, infiltrating through the back doors of personality into the breathing soul of the living individual (*MC*, IX, 407; *G*, VII, 200). The impersonality of historical materialism, with its promise of an inevitable *"next phase* of evolutionary, planetary life" (*G*, VII, 200), comes terribly close to the Powysian wish for a personal transcendence of the competitive Ego. This must always be kept in mind. For Powys, especially in the early works, there is always a risk of sliding from the anti-*Ego*tistical world of the personal Self into the anti-individual world of the collective Ego—the Ego robbed of its aggressiveness and masquerading as the nonaggressive Self.

What is the collective Ego? It is the confederation of suppressed Egos striving together for increased personal advantage, for human survival, for a minimum of existential integrity. And the collective Self? It is the oceanic feeling of oriental at-oneness *in a social situation* of collective misery, compassion, brotherhood. We see both phenomena at work in *The Brazen Head:* the collective cynicism of the Ego; the collective mysticism of the Self. Clearly, the rising of the serfs at the end of the story suggests class war—a conflict springing out of social oppression and not, like other conflict in this novel, out of a quarrel between the lord and lady of Lost Towers (XXII, 321). At this moment, "something less personal and much more far-reaching" begins to happen. Private dispute becomes civil war. The feeling on the part of the exploited is centripetal. Emotionally, there is a tightening, a defensive contraction, a blocking out of all of that which does not belong to the enlarged realm of an extended, multiplied Ego. It is the feeling that the working men of Glastonbury turn toward Sam Dekker when he tries to commence a new, saintly life by joining the proletarian masses in the heavy physical labor of clayhauling. Finally, his "heathen goodness" breaks the class barrier; but before that moment, he is granted no access to the collective Ego of an alien class. They refer to him, with detached merriment, as "Holy Sam" (XXVIII, 921–23).

In *The Brazen Head,* the serfs follow their revolutionary leader, Dod Pole (XXII, 323). They are inspired, no doubt, by egoism, Ego-ism. But in the pathos of Dod Pole's rhetoric, we recognize once more that idealistic transcendence of the Ego which is the hallmark of the expansive Self. Dod speaks enthusiastically about "a planet that should be owned in common by all mankind" (XXII, 324), and much earlier, pouring out his thoughts over the bailiff, Master Sygerius, he feels "in his soul as if over all the countries in the world millions of serfs and slaves like himself were uttering the same thoughts" (VIII, 106). This, it is clear, is not the rhetoric of a power-hungry Ego; it is, on the contrary, easily recognized as precisely that oceanic feeling which only the Self is capable of generating. In *Maiden Castle,* Dud No-Man (no-Ego) has exactly the same type of expansive feeling as he returns in old age from America to England, only to be disheartened by all the old men touching their caps to him. He feels infinite shame and considers the accumulated weight of centuries of oppression. He sits down to write, and in the ensuing half hour he enters one of those creative raptures in which the Self is freed from the Ego and therefore also from the Ego-dependent body. He feels as he writes—as the Self writes—the dissolution of the object/subject duality as well as the dissolution of sequential time. He is freed from body, from Ego, from sinistral temporality. His Self and each suffering Self in the expanses of the eternally present past become one agonized collective Self looking for a voice:

> As he wrote . . . he felt as though he really had become a "medium" for the expression, not only of one unavenged wrong, but of a thousand, all interpenetrating one another, all overlapping and per- forating one another, like separate magnetic currents within one great heaving sea of psychic tragedy!
> He wrote furiously for about half an hour, letting the feeling that obsessed him pass, as it seemed, from his receptive soul into the words formed by his pen, as if he had been a bodiless presence himself, rather than a bony, middle-aged man bending over a cluttered table. (V, 201)

2.3 On the Edge of Individuality

"Homo Sapiens," writes Powys, is "the creature who wants to be let alone" (*MS*, I, 9). Not only does man *want* to be alone: man *is* alone. This is the ultimate loneliness that confronts Wolf Solent: "Alone ! That was what he had learnt from the hard woman who had given him birth. That every soul was alone" (XXV, 634). These words come from the final page, and it is on this note that *Wolf Solent* ends. This essential human loneli- ness undermines all grand illusions about "love," and John Cowper him- self gradually moves toward that eccentric individualism which Pierre of Picardy looks upon in *The Brazen Head* as an inner compactness to be defended against sentimental humbug (XVI, 243). As long as we are considerate toward our fellow creatures, says Friar Bacon, we have got to live "to ourselves, for ourselves, in ourselves and by ourselves" (XXII, 341). There are, Powys will admit, love relationships of an extraordinary intensity. These awaken our somnambulist psyche to a heightened mode of consciousness. But in such extreme cases of human passion and inti- macy, the loved one, whether sexual partner or child, only reinforces solitude. We become "a crystal within a crystal, in the circle of our hard, integrated soul" (*DS*, IX, 285).

An ecstatic love experience annihilates the competitive aspects of life. In *A Glastonbury Romance*, John Crow decides never to compete: he uses his will to destroy his will. In *Autobiography*, it seems as if noncompetitiveness is not so much the result of an act of will but an emotional insufficiency, or psychic impotence (IV, 142). It is perhaps also from this perspective that we are to sympathize with Sorio's idealism in *Rodmoor.* He believes in the arrival of an era when sexual jealousy will disappear from the face of the earth (XXIV, 389). This will come from the destruction of the love/hate phenomenon rather than from any refinement of it. Here again, however, we must remember what was said in the preceding chapter about the *post*demonic nature of John Cowper's easy-going persona.

The most casual reader of the Powys novel will quickly perceive the central position occupied by the solitude-versus-love motif in this body of fiction. The Powys hero is centrifugal in his violent passion; he is centripetal in his equally intense quest for an ecstatic autonomy that provides the electricity of love without the emotional commitment of the love affair. Again, this tension between solitude and love can most easily be analyzed from the viewpoint of the Ego/Self polarity. We can see this in *Ducdame* (1925), the novel preceding *Wolf Solent*. Chapter 19 in *Ducdame* gives a curious account of a blackout in which the protagonist, Rook Ashover,[6] moves into a strange state of consciousness (307–10). This is written off as a kind of epileptic fit, featuring the upsurge of the "subconscious" (310). Yet the remarkable intensity and coloration of the whole experience suggest that we are dealing precisely with one of those crossings of the fall line described in the first chapter. This impression is reinforced by the writer's reference to amnesia (312). A few pages later (and the proximity is significant), there is a description of a nature ecstasy. The thrill of such a moment is seen in vital correspondence with the hallucination just described. They are both forms of what I have called dextral consciousness. Before the hallucination, we are informed that what Rook really required in life "was not an impassioned love with an equal mate, but certain faint, vague, elusive ecstasies that were entirely unspiritual, entirely unemotional, and entirely de-personalized" (XIX, 306). Women, to Rook, are not human individuals, integral personalities. They are "just vibrant quivering telegraph wires" stretching across the world and giving him the most delicious and mysterious raptures through their "magical hummings." This means that *woman is primarily an ecstasy-trigger in the Powys world.* Insofar as she triggers ecstasy, she enhances the Self-worshiping mind of the Powys hero; insofar as she

interposes her earthy humanity between him and his reverie, she is a
major threat to his unique happiness. Rook's marriage to Lady Ann is a
catastrophe,[7] because he feels deprived of his full access to the interior
Self. This foreshadows the way in which Wolf Solent feels that his
"mythology" is being threatened by real-life intercourse, by too social a
life stance. As Jeremy Hooker has pointed out, Wolf perhaps loses his
mythology by not going far enough in his introversion.[8] Here in *Ducdame*, the strange fit that removes Rook from an oppressively social state
of consciousness functions as a kind of safety device. For some reason
connected with "the tension in his brain" (XIX, 307), the entire visual
field turns from green to gray, and Rook is paralyzed by a sudden diz-
ziness. In the subsequent description of the nature ecstasy, Rook has
recovered. He has come to the edge of a little lake offering a magnificent
view of Comber's End manor house, on the farther side. In this serene,
undisturbed setting, Rook not only enters ecstasy. He also enters that
special Cowperesque mood in which there is consciousness of ecstasy.
This ecstatic self-consciousness produces *Self*-consciousness. As has been
suggested, this type of dextral awareness gives the individual access to
other ecstasies, experienced in the subjective past. The individual ecstasies
become part of an over-ecstasy. Such a linking up of dextral moments is
the mental act par excellence for Powys. It establishes the Self. The moment produces a transition from what I call sinistral time to dextral time.[9]
In fiction, and through fiction, this has often been represented as a transition from time to "timelessness." This fallacious notion of "timelessness"
has also infected science. What we have in fact—and Powys is very perceptive on this point—is two entirely different time nets, or temporal
networks: one to the left of the fall line (sinistral time, or *levotemporality*), one to the right of the fall line (dextral time, or *dextrotemporality*).
The former is experienced as "time" because it links up fairly simple
temporal experiences. The latter is a network of networks: each ecstasy
being a multitemporal event, the over-ecstasy being a further multitem-
porality (see figure 5). This is how Powys suggests the dextrotemporal
world of the Self in *Ducdame:*

> And such moments have another, a yet more subtle value; namely,
> their power of linking themselves up in some mysterious way with all
> the other past moments of a similar nature that we have passed through
> in the course of our life. Toward these other moments the present one
> seems to gravitate by a natural affinity, taking its place among them and
> establishing itself among them, in such a way as to draw them out more
> clearly, more definitely, from their hidden retreats, and to make us
> more vividly aware of them.

Figure 5. Formation of Self and dextrotemporality: individual ecstasies link-ing up into over-ecstasy.

It is then that we become conscious that in addition to the ordinary gregarious human life, led by us in contact with others and in the stress of our normal pursuits, there is another, a more intimate life, solitary and detached, that has its own days and months and years, such as are numbered by no measurings of common time, by no computation on any terrestrial almanac. . . .

They have nothing to do with the emotional or with the rational processes of our nature, these moments of vision. They are purely aesthetic. Yet they are not aesthetic in the sense of being entirely preoc-cupied with what is usually called beauty. The more definite and more suggestive word "magic" indicates better the quality to which they respond. (XIX, 314–15)

For Rook Ashover, the "life illusion" is outraged by marriage.[10] This anticipates the central dilemma in *Wolf Solent*. Rook cannot bear the thought that his life is no longer to be "a series of sweet solitary sensations" (*D*, XIX, 303). Moving from the psychic to the inanimate, from the human world to the exterior world of nature and objects, we find that this solipsism continues to orchestrate the quality of things. In the Powys world, objects greedily clutch their own personality and withhold it from the rest of the multiverse. In *A Glastonbury Romance*, the identity of the great Salisbury downland is "indrawn upon itself" (III, 96). Here, also, Mr. Evans is shocked to find a human being (John Crow) who can worship a stone simply because it is a stone (III, 98).[11] Stone as stone, as nothing more, is like Somerset moss: a perfect symbol of life, of something that returns upon itself in a "religious reticence" (XVII, 513). Even in the nonhuman world, the mystery of mysteries is personality, and Powys makes it clear that in this respect his cosmic outlook is the opposite of that favored by the Hindu philosophies with their dreams of the ultimate oneness of humanity (XXI, 665).

Between this human and this inanimate individuality there is the strange individuality that Powys gives to the most insignificant aspects of the animate world. As Sam Dekker tries to cope mentally with the sight of Mrs. Bagge's atrocious suffering in cancer, he has a tranced vision of a large bug on the sooty wall. The bug is there, all right. It is no fiction of the mind. But through the altered state of consciousness into which Sam slips, it acquires a strong occult personality. The bug becomes a nodal point in a world of psychic sorcery. Within this realm of filigreed telepathy, it seems to hold the ability to discriminate between various levels of ESP:

> This bug was a Glastonbury bug. Had it any message for him, a Glastonbury man? Can't *you* throw light on this? he thought, addressing the bug on the wall. But the bug was so extreme an individualist that it regarded the gibberish which reached it from the man's brain as the same sort of telepathic nonsense that it was accustomed to hear when in her heart Mrs. Bagge cried out:—"How long, O Lordy, O Lordy, how long, how long?" and it proceeded upon its tortuous way with less curiosity—not to speak of sympathy—than even ex-Mayor Wollop would have felt. (XXVIII, 931)

If we compare this Glastonbury bug with the seagull that drifts on the tide outside Harlech castle in *Owen Glendower*, we see that centripetal animal individuality ("the bug was so extreme an individualist") is counterbalanced by centrifugal animal supra-individuality. This seagull has "race-memories of sea-castles and sea-kings of thousands of years ago," and its thoughts mingle with Owen's (XVII, 646). Here the individual animal stands for the continuity of the species, for life itself, as opposed to the discrete autonomy of its own personality manifested in time; its "personality reproduced to the smallest particular that of its ancestors of two thousand years ago" (XVII, 645).

This introduces us to the treatment of the collective Self in *Owen Glendower*. Most obviously it comes over here as the idea of the ancient people of Wales. The Welsh form a collective whole that is aware of its own presence in time and space. This concrescence has a "neolithic self-control" (XIX, 760). Such a self-regulating capacity can only grow out of an inherent ability to stand outside the Self, and it is this potential, typified by Owen himself, that enables the entire race to slip back into its age-old psychic grooves when confronted by the overwhelming military superiority of the English enemy. In what seems like the conscious use of an atavistic reversion to the dormant psychic resources of the race, the Welsh retreat into a "secret passage" infinitely deeper than any hillside tunnel made by the ancient mound-dwellers (XXI, 906). This suggests "Difancoll:" the disappearance of the race into the earth, into the mountains. The Welsh identity of the collective Self is perhaps at its clearest in the shivering dawn that precedes the battle of Bryn Glas:

> And as they rested there it seemed as if the miracle of the dawn drew their general consciousness towards itself, so that their life-sense ceased to be an individual thing and became a common thing, a multiple entity, that had grown spell-bound by what was happening in the firmament. (XV, 547)

John Cowper Powys is here suggesting something psychic that transcends the herd instinct and the pack loyalty that he despised so much. When the Glastonbury Pageant is over, everyone becomes a separate individual again (XIX, 605), and, significantly, Powys connects the dissolution of the crowd hypnosis with the invocation of Christ, "the Redeemer of the Individual." Such dispersion of the collective Self into its constituent elements does not take place in *Owen Glendower*, for here, even on the very last page, there is a stress on the "impersonality" of race memories, of experiences that belong to something vaster and less palpable than the individual.

This race perspective is nevertheless challenged from a different quarter. As leader of the peasants, Master Sparrow views the whole Welsh/English conflict as an essentially "un-racial" business (XXI, 908). Beyond patriotism, beyond nationalism, and beyond the geophysical dimension, he sees the vast outlines of a commoners-versus-gentlemen conflict.

Here we have a simple dichotomy: plebeians and patricians. In *A Glastonbury Romance*, the stratification is more elaborate: the upper-middle-class world of Emma and Tilly Crow at the Elms is as different from the aristocratic and proletarian spheres as it is from the easy-going lower-middle-class atmosphere that envelops Mr. and Mrs. Geard (VII, 198). This novel, however, would not be the magnificent, spacious entity that it is, had not Powys outlined vaster and more subtle collective auras than those of class. To look upon human behavior from the viewpoint of class is certainly to be historical, to want to understand individuality as a function of historicity. But beyond that historicity, the mature mind perceives class conflict as a mere sideways thrust in a fuller historical perspective. The discontinuity of successive historical eras and epochs, the oligarchical diversification of power structures in the mosaic of historical time, is felt to be of secondary human-historical relevance compared with the continuity that binds man to man and woman to woman within the sex, person to person within the race, within humanity.

From such a cyclic and biological point of view, the "continuous stream of human awareness" (*WoS*, XIV, 305–6), absorbing the extended manifold of all lived organismic time, conveys the essence of "some deep race-memory in which these things are stored up" (XIV, 306). Patches of sky, trodden grass, clumps of weed, drizzle at noon, segments of derelict masonry—all these things have their own history: not that of their genealogy in an evolutionary time stream running parallel to that of mankind and leaving their exteriority unredeemed by the phenomenology of consciousness—but the history of their recycled sensory identity within the whole evolutionary organization of life itself. The inanimate is not out there, not out-thereness. The mineral and vegetative archetypes are carried intact from century to century, telescoped from the present into a receding past and nearing future. Powys returns to this view in *Mortal Strife*:

> But in mingling your soul—through your sensations—with these things you are really mingling it with the souls of your ancestors, you are calling up again, like bodies raised from the dead, all those surprises and shocks and raptures of inexplicable happiness that brought, in *their* day, such thrilling feelings, at such odd moments, to our grandparents! (IX, 142)

Despite his emphasis on personality, John Cowper Powys recognizes the enjoyment of life as a "race-sensation" (IX, 148), and it is the establishment of a tension between the continuous and the discontinuous, between eternal recurrence and evolutionary change, that permits the writer to evoke history as something more than a sequence of events. This tension allows him to see the historical moment as something more than a halted playback of the celluloid film strip. This is true not only of the "historical" romances but also of novels such as *A Glastonbury Romance,* where historical belonging is a convoluted multiplicity, an overlapping and interpenetration involving racial, religious, sexual, political, cultural, and professional interdependences, as well as psychic guilds, occult cooperatives, esoteric corporations, hidden freemasonries.

A Glastonbury Romance begins with John Crow, just arrived in England from Paris. As John makes his way toward the great funeral of his celebrated ancestor, Canon William Crow, the novelist does not stress John's class belonging so much as his belonging to Norfolk and East Anglia, his belonging to a quasi-Norman race, the blood of which is made throughout to remain hostile to that less commonsensical blood of the West Country. As a Crow, he belongs to a network of Crows—a network that is temporal, with its own particular genealogy, and spatial, with its own special regional dispersion: Thorpe, Yaxham, Thetford, East Dereham, Cringleford, Methwold (IV, 125). These Crows share certain idiosyncrasies, irrespective of class. They have been evolved through the hereditary siftings and winnowings of the slow centuries. The love shown by the Crows is nonideal, earthy, earthly—"muddy, weather-washed lust, like the love of water-rats in Alder Dyke or the love of badgers on Brandon Heath." This common heritage carries its drifting intimations of a shared past in the codification of a particular grimace. In John Crow there appears a curious pulse at the corner of the nostrils and a certain twitching round the cheekbones. This facial sign is a kind of racial coding trick. It has gone to the Norwich fair, to Cambridge book shops and silk merchants. It must have "appeared in the depths of old-fashioned looking-glasses, above mahogany chests of drawers, before the pushing open of innumerable ivy-shadowed front-bedroom windows to watch visitors come over the home-meadows" (II, 85). We see, here, that in this dwindling perspective of Crows hereditarily lodged within one another, consciousness appears as something too mellow and saturated for any individual claim. It is a multiple identity that is intercreated, each Crow and each moment of Crow-ness being but a grain of consciousness in the overall granulation of an awareness thinner and more diffuse than the tail of a comet. Each quantum of time is itself more than itself, realizing simultaneously the blood-infinities of all possessed pasts, all faintly dreamed nuances of race-futures. Scanning the expanse of this field of collective cognition, John Cowper Powys suggests the present moment of experience as a mere speck in the flow of mental events that have filled race-time since men rode in Elizabethan ruffles, cavalier ringlets, or eighteenth-century wigs, down the Norfolk lanes familiar to each individual Crow (V, 129).

In the middle of *A Glastonbury Romance*, the Crow cousins, Mary and John, share a moment of great spiritual intimacy with Tom Barter, another Norfolk character. Here Powys emphasizes individuality as well as racial belonging. First they form an inert consolidated trinity. Then they fall apart into individual personalities, each suffering from a physical disorder that does not affect the others—Tom Barter with his indigestion, Mary with her cold, John with his constipation. When conversation flags, a strong numbness seizes the group:

> It is an inertia made *cubic,* so to speak, by being shared. It was, at that second of time, as if the souls of these three East Anglians had suddenly clung together and plunged down the great backward slide of biological evolution. . . . All three were standing now in the centre of the room . . . [T]he sensation of oneness which their staring together into the fire had generated fell to pieces. . . . Any small group of human beings gathered close together acquires a certain warmth of protectiveness against the Outside, against all those unknown angers of which the outside world is full. A curious psychic entity—like a great, fluffy, feathery hen-breast—is evoked at such times, under which these separate beings crouch, into which they merge, beneath which they are fused. Every human creature is a terror to every other human creature. Human minds are like unknown planets, encountering and colliding. . . . Every pair of human eyes is a custom-house gate into a completely foreign port . . . Unable to shake off their selfish preoccupations, they all three went out into Northload Street in a fretful, troubled mood. (XIV, 394–96)

This tension between the collective Self and the individual Ego fascinates Powys in all his major fictional works. An extreme individualist and an extreme champion of individualism, he cannot help being attracted to all those collective atmospheres in which the individual is somehow freed from the tick-tock of his self-analysis. Personality, he keeps claiming, is the ultimate mystery. But in the novels where individuality *is* celebrated, there is also a celebration of the collective Self as a mysterious Individual, as an individual Mystery. Here, in *A Glastonbury Romance,* the long-dead medieval monks form such a mystical entity. To be a monk is in itself to renounce the preeminence ordinarily given to personality, and this supra-individuality is reinforced by the notion that the monks from all layers of the past gather in the abbey on Maundy Thursday. Here they form one huge, timeless collective throat existing in present matter (XIV, 376).

It is clear in these descriptions of the collective Self that Powys suggests not so much the existence of an actual physical aura round the group but, rather, the existence in our consciousness of the *feeling* of such an attendant halo. It is this feeling, and the intellectual abstraction underlying it

(Race, People, Mankind) that generates the sense of oneness and personality involved. Thus, in Glastonbury, the various enemies of the Grail legend *happen* to be going to sleep at the same time on the night of December the tenth, and they *happen* to be of the same sex. Yet these circumstances are sufficient to give birth to a conception of them as a confederate multiplicity with a tacit metaphysical or existential manifesto (XXIV, 746).

What is the real dividing line? This question is repeated throughout Powys's fiction. Is it the dividing line between race and race? or between class and class? or between sex and sex?

In *Owen Glendower,* there is a convergence of collective paradigms at the battle of Bryn Glas, which can be interpreted as the victory of the Welsh over the English, or else, as Master Sparrow would have it, as a victory of the people over their masters. This latter interpretation is based on the massive desertion of archers to the Welsh side (XV, 552–53). After the battle, however, Rhisiart comes to see the crucial universal conflict as neither of these. It is instead the conflict between all men and all women. He comes to this view when Lowri ferch Ffraid and the women of Pilleth strip and massacre the corpses of fallen English soldiers in an outrageously insane witch-dance under the moon (XV, 556). Ultimately, though, the collective Self is one that includes the whole of mankind, or even the cosmic life-aggregate itself. As Owen Evans hangs as Christ on the cross in the Glastonbury pageant, the temporal is the centripetal, the spatial the centrifugal. Life becomes a biological whole, divided, and turned (as whole) against itself. The passage, indeed, can be seen as a dramatization of the entire Ego/Self duality, the Ego being collectively all tormentors, the Self being collectively all the tormented:

> All the *eyes* that in the long history of this place had looked in vain into those of the killer—all these tormented *eyes* gathered now about Mr. Evans! And it was all connected with his deadly, his irremediable vice. The figures that flooded his brain were all torturers or victims, every one of them; and as the thing grew and grew upon him, as he hung there, all the victims flowed into one and became one, and all the torturers flowed into one and became one. Then it came about that between Mr. Evans as the torturer and this one victim, who yet was all victims, a dialogue arose; so that from their divided localities in space they addressed each other, and from their horrible association in time they answered each other. (XIX, 615–16)

One notices here that the planetary self-division that takes place around Evans as a cosmological drama is a projection of his personal sadomasochistic sex-perversion. Now within our binary model of Ego and Self, the individual is in a state of perpetual masochism. Man is either wounding his Self with his Ego, or wounding his Ego with his Self. In this light, the projection in question must be seen as one of psychological realism as well as one of allegorical suggestibility.

The sense of belonging is enhanced, even propelled, by the megastructures of time and space. In *Wolf Solent,* the macrotemporal is historic continuity: the eternal presence of human beings moving across the surface of the earth (XXI, 484). In *Weymouth Sands,* one of Powys's finest achievements, the macrospatial is the spire, the Hardy monument, the old deserted fort of the Nothe. Together with other inanimate objects and landmarks, these form a kind of magic circle of spatialized completeness. Within this circle, the various events and happenings are given a meaningful interconnectedness. The different buildings have been in sight of each other for so many years that they form an animated group with a peculiar and distinctive personality (X, 342). More intermittently, in some other novels, such an inanimate foil may be purely atmospheric—present, only, in the evanescent vapor of the passing hour. In *A Glastonbury Romance,* the unpleasantness of a particular early spring day is sensed by all animal nerves and all human nerves (VII, 184). In *Wolf Solent,* a portion of the protagonist's inner space is soaked in a lovely and irresistible bluish light, a crepuscular efflorescence that causes him to send his spirit into the consciousness of his fellow beings. The sense of belonging is to mankind, to humanity as a whole—not to class, to race, or to any other subpopulation:

> At how many hearths, that winter afternoon, were human beings watching this strange blueness, flung against their casements like the dreamy breath of the earth itself, caught ere it dissolved into space! That aerial transparency might easily be something that never again in all the days of his life would appear exactly as it did now! Oh, how he longed to scoop it up in great handfuls and pour it forth over every wounded spirit in the world! (XIX, 437–38)

The sense of human continuity is evoked visually here in *Wolf Solent* through the unbroken spatial presence of a winter twilight. In *Owen Glendower,* such continuity is suggested aurally when the protagonist faces the vast oneness of the sea in a corresponding serene contemplation of elemental sublimity. With Mad Huw and Master Brut, Rhisiart finds the volatile sounds of various animals and humans—a horse, a rook, a fisherman, a lamb—merged in a fragile, ethereal sound envelope: "Fused together, these isolated sounds evoked a sense of the continuity of life by sea and land, a continuity simple, tranquil, universal, detached from individual hunger or desire or pain or joy" (XVIII, 686).

Most striking of all, perhaps, is that unforgettable solitary tree in Water-ditch Field at the beginning of *A Glastonbury Romance*. In its smooth expansiveness, it sympathizes with the upward-clutching love embraces of John and Mary Crow: "It is extraordinary that we should ever have met!" says John to his cousin (II, 89). He happens to have uttered a sequence of words that, just like his facial tic, connects him physically with the lost presence of bygone humanity. Here the inanimate is a focal point for the human—a reversal of the mechanism just reviewed in *Wolf Solent* and *Owen Glendower*. The tree becomes an emblematic quincunx suggesting not only the deterministic and aleatory dimensions of human existence but also the centricity of the novel's centripetal structure and the centricity of the organismic cosmology at the heart of its conceptual geometry. In the vicinity of this arboreal reticence, John and Mary Crow partake of the events of inner race-experience that are normally removed from the individual by time, circumstance, and chance:

> Five times in its life of a hundred and thirty years had the ash tree of Water-ditch Field heard those words uttered by living organisms. An old horse had uttered them in its own fashion when it rubbed its nose against a young companion's polished flanks. An eccentric fisherman had uttered them addressing an exceptionally large chub which he had caught and killed. A mad clergyman had uttered them about a gipsy girl who did not know of his existence. An old maiden lady had uttered them to the spirit of her only lover, dead fifty years before; and finally, but twelve months ago, William Crow himself had uttered them; uttered them in the grateful, attentive and astonished ears of Mr. Geard of Glastonbury! (II, 89)

This tree is an individual tree but also something with a collective significance, housing within its single personality the vast concourse of the drifting generations. It has absorbed innumerable human thoughts—"absorbed," that is, in the sense of being symbolically weighted rather than paranormally saturated. In *A Glastonbury Romance*, we find that the inanimate in general (and tree life in particular) is torn, like humanity, between the individualistic and the collectivistic. From first page to last, the elemental confronts the individual. The tree is threatened by the forest, just as the raindrop is threatened by the flood. Much later than the passage above, individuality is once more stressed, now as the supremacy of atom over molecule, difference over coherence:

> In the summer when the wind stirs the trees, there is that rushing, swelling sound of masses of heavy foliage, a sound that drowns, in its full-blossomed, undulating, ocean-like murmur, the individual sor-

rows of trees. . . . *Floods* of rain destroy the quality and significance of rain. Drops they must be, many, many drops; an infinity of drops if you will; but still numberless separate drops, grey or brown or whitish-grey, in order that they may retain that rain-smell, rain-taste, rain-secret, which separates rain from ordinary water. (XXV, 786–87)

We see here that the element of water itself destroys individuality. This is negative, suggesting a loss of Self. The process is reversed in *Maiden Castle* as air, that other element, drowns the Ego ("the personal Wizzie") in sleeping Selfness ("impersonal sensations," "the depersonalized Wizzie"). When the southwest seawind dies at dawn, Dud No-man and his mistress Wizzie Ravelstone return to their separate Egos from the conjugate Selfness of night-consciousness:

This salt wind from Chesil Beach must have numbed and atrophied all those touchy centres of egotism in our friends, wherewith their personal minds spoilt their impersonal sensations; but when the interlude was over, and the depersonalized Wizzie with hot cheeks and glowing limbs, had become the personal Wizzie with tantalized nerves and unsatisfied feelings, the wind dropped, and a pallid light . . . drew the girl's wide-opened eyes towards it in impatient longing for the day. (IX, 420)

The inanimate, we observe, is torn between centripetal fusion and centrifugal dispersion. In addition, it is itself capable of fusion, of the act of fusing. In *Wolf Solent*, the paraphernalia of Wolf's entire life is gathered by a wishbone on Gerda's plate into "a heap on the kitchen table of Number Thirty-Seven Preston Lane" (XIX, 448). We have here a collapse of nonhuman individuality into collective indistinctness. Powys often describes a similar process of physiognomic dissolution in his characters. We see this as a subjective phenomenon in *Maiden Castle*, when Dud No-man looks at Uryen: "As he glanced at the vague dehumanized lineaments of the man beside him, every particular feature blurred" (IV, 172). The effect is heightened here, as in *Owen Glendower*, by an atmospheric dimness. When Simon the Hog struggles with Walter Brut during the monstrous postbattle massacre at Bryn Glas, the diversity of features in Simon's face is erased by the dominating insistence of a single feature: "Master Simon's face was convulsed with an emotion so great that its individual features in that pallid light seemed to merge into one another, seemed to become one single feature, a quivering, twitching, licking, straining *tongue*" (XV, 558).

The prevailing atmospheric conditions favor this kind of convergence of inanimate identities on a particularly filmy and vaporous day in Glastonbury. The outlines of every object are lost in the luminous suffusion that emanates from the veiled liquidity of the sun:

> All were equally blurred and softened. Thus it came about that a moon-like circle of pallid whiteness looked forth upon a world from which every harsh projection, whether of stone, or wood, or metal, or horn, or scale, or feather, or bone, or rock, had been obliterated; a world of flowing curves and sliding shadows, a world of fluctuating shapes and melting contours. (G, IX, 254)

As Perdita Wane moves through the narrow old streets of Melcombe Regis after her arrival to Weymouth by steamer from the Channel Isles, she experiences a similar sense of an inanimate confluence that robs objects of their individuality. Hulls, masts, and rigging are confused in the darkness; gables and lofts flow into each other, become lost in a "conglomerate mass" (WeS, II, 42). The same pattern is repeated in *Owen Glendower*. There is a merging of the identity of separate ships when a Bristol pirate captures a French vessel just off the Welsh coast. Watching the dramatic event, the constable of Dinas Bran, Denis Burnel, is struck by the violent mating of these two sea monsters, heading together for the horizon in surrealistic copulation (XIX, 782). The general sense of a loss of identity in the swallowing element of water is further emphasized by a curious metamorphosis. A drowning sailor is in fact discovered to be a large drowning chimpanzee. The dissolution-versus-individuation motif is then given one final twist at the end of the novel, when Lord Talbot of Goodrich uses the word "dead" in reference to Owen Glendower. At this point, each individual Welshman is instantly transformed "into one single multiple personality" (XXI, 906). Then, after a while, the race-spell is broken, and the collective Self becomes "four separate Welshmen again."

This cyclic variation also affects the sexually formed couple. A psychological tide brings the lovers together, giving them an all-pervasive sense of absolute certainty. Yet this mystical feeling of oneness is extremely fragile, shifting with the slightest change in level of arousal. In the mundane dimension of nonexalted awareness, the Ego of man faces the Ego of woman. Worse: the *Self* of man faces the Ego of woman, woman's *Self* the Ego of her man. We see this worked out in *Owen Glendower*. To save Rhisiart's life, his beloved Tegolin decides to sleep with Master Shore. This means a temporary sacrifice on her part, of Self to Ego. To retain life itself, Tegolin has to harden her Ego against her Self. In the process, something is lost, and facing each other, the two lovers become curiously estranged in binary divorce from the lost inner landscape of a deeper compatibility. They search each others' souls with their eyes but remain alienated from one another (XX, 836).

The origin of the independence/interdependence fluctuation resides in the child's independence/dependence relationship to the mother. The quest for an autonomous Self, freed from the Ego, retraces, therefore, on a higher turn of the spiral, the child's quest for an autonomous Ego. This process is perhaps at its clearest in *Wolf Solent,* where the protagonist becomes retrospectively nauseated by his loss of individuality during tea with his mother. The meal becomes "an obscure reversion to those forgotten diurnal nourishments which he must have shared with her long before his flesh was separated from hers" (XIV, 304). Having left his mother after this meal, Wolf becomes once more conscious of a stream of Selfness that feeds on the English countryside; he feels the reemergence of his Self confirmed. As Ego, he is attached personally to his parent; as Self, he reaches out impersonally to a vast humanity sensed as an expansive abstraction but also as a concrete collective Self:

> Roads and lanes! Lanes and roads! What a part these tracks for the feet of men and beasts, dusty in summer, muddy in winter, had played in his mental consciousness! The thrill that this *idea* of roadways gave him was a proof to him that his mind was returning to its independent orbit, after its plunge into that maternal hypnosis. His spirit felt indeed deliciously free just then, and expanded its wings to its heart's content, like a great flapping rook. Every object of the way took on an especial glamour; and never had he enjoyed so deeply one particular trick of his mind. This was a certain queer *sensuous* sympathy he could feel sometimes for completely unknown people's lives, as he passed by their dwellings. He enjoyed it now with especial satisfaction, thinking of the people in each cottage he came to, and *gathering their experiences together* as one might gather a bunch of ragwort or hemp-agrimony out of dusty hedges. (XIV, 305; emphasis mine)

The umbilical cord runs from Ego to Ego here, and its severance, or reseverance, suggests a release of the suffocated Self.

In *A Glastonbury Romance,* by contrast, the umbilical cord running between Nell Zoyland and her embryo child is a cosmic bond to be preserved as something biologically sacrosanct from the masculine abstractions of ideology. No political doctrine is going to be allowed to remove the child's autonomy by theorizing some utopian nonpossessive state (XVI, 460–61). The embryo has been conceived within Nell's and Sam's total love for one another. The invisible bond that holds together the race-group (Tom Barter and the Crow cousins) or the casual group

(John, Sam, and Evans) is intensified to an almost insane extreme in this love affair. Nell and Sam "plunged into it so desperately, so utterly, that in the mingling of their identities there seemed no portion of either of them—body, soul or spirit—*left over,* that was not merged and lost in the other" (XI, 311). Yet it is the more pagan eroticism in the lascivious lovemaking between John and Mary Crow that most beautifully brings out John Cowper Powys's sense of the tensions involved in all sensual attraction between man and woman:

> What was remarkable about their love-making was that during their embraces, in which the man held her and caressed her, first with her body front to front against his, and then with her face turned towards the river, their male and female sensuality—he "possessing" and she being "possessed"—was, in its earth-deep difference, of exactly the same magnetic quality. This was not due to his experience or to her inexperience; for, in these matters, Nature, the great mother of all loves, equalised them completely. It was due to some abysmal similarity in their nerves which, after making them fall in love, made them "make love" in exactly the same manner! (II, 70)

With this image of a duality turned *into* itself (breast to breast) and *from* itself (back to front), we are now prepared for a more penetrating investigation of the inner landscape as it projects itself spatially in the Powys novel.

3
CRYSTAL AND AURA

3.1 The Zones of Ecstasy

Is the innermost core of human awareness Self-centric or Ego-centric? To begin with, it is clear that it is the Self, and not the Ego, that is involved in the expansive, "oceanic" feeling—the sense of ecstatic circumference. It is the Self that gives consciousness its totalized spatiality, its spatialized totality. This sense of the outer rim of the World-Spirit comes over to us through recurrent references to a sense of spiritual projection "beyond the limits of the astronomical world."

But if the Self is circumference, is the Ego center? Is Ego the absolute centerpoint? Of course we are not asking this question from a neurophysiological point of view. We are not thinking in terms of expansions or contractions of wiring patterns within the actual neural networks of the brain. Instead, we are considering the mental world as an epiphenomenon. We are defining the way in which the individual typically *feels* consciousness to be extended in space, within or without the body, within or without the skull. The clearest answer to these questions is to be found in *In Defence of Sensuality* (1930), a nonfictional work written at the time of Powys's most acute and luxurious fictional creativity. But let us first take a look at Philip Crow in *A Glastonbury Romance.* He is the most obvious Ego in the novels, and an analysis of the spatial nature of his self-consciousness may give some clues to the present problem. As pure capitalist, as masculine Ego-beast asserting his wolfish individuality, Philip Crow feels like some Napoleonic tyrant of the business world when he is in the presence of his mines and machines (the spacings in this passage are Powys's own):

I . . . I . . . I . . . riding on electricity . . . I . . . I . . . I . . . grasping electricity . . . I . . . I . . . I . . . alone . . . all-powerful . . . under the

123

Mendips . . . letting loose my will upon Somerset . . . my factories
above . . . my electricity beneath . . . I . . . I . . . Philip Crow . . .
planting my will upon the future . . . moulding men . . . dominating
Nature. (I, 51)

Now it is absolutely clear that this passage suggests the centripetal limit
of Philip Crow's consciousness. It cannot go further inward. This *I* is his
inner limit. It is also the inner limit of the Ego. By this I mean to suggest
that this type of inwardness is totally different from the type of inwardness experienced by the ecstatic Self. Philip's inwardness is merely the
hardening of his personality. We shall see how different this sensation is
from the interiority described in *In Defence of Sensuality* and elsewhere. I
think indeed that it will be found that the interiority of Selfness goes way
inside the inwardness of the Ego: so that in fact the Self comes into its
ecstatic totality both as pip and periphery, both as experienced center
within the most contracted Ego and as experienced circumference outside
the most expanded Ego. In other words, I submit that in its contracted
form, the Self is an achievement of a center that is more intense than the
center of the Ego. *The center of the Self exists inside the center of the Ego.*
This more central centricity of the Self can only be achieved at the expense of the Ego. With the destruction of the Ego, its interior limit is
transcended, or imploded. *Its interiority becomes exteriority.*
    Ecstasy (the altered state of consciousness) changes our experience of
time and space. This fact is common knowledge. My thesis, however, is
that these changes come in two opposite forms: two opposite forms for
space and two opposite forms for time. In my study of the fiction of John
Fowles, I have shown how the ecstatic sense of time, which is usually
merely referred to as "timelessness," is in fact composed of two opposite
forms of temporal intensification.[1] In the first of these forms, time is
infinitely small. This gives the *eternal moment:* that fractional electric
moment when all is decided and when all is known. In the second form of
ecstatic time-intensification, the opposite happens. Time becomes enormous, infinite, oceanic. You become all Time . . . timeless: but now an
inverted timelessness. My thesis here is that exactly the same transformation occurs with space in ecstasy. Space either becomes infinitely
small—a state I shall refer to as *crystal;* or else space becomes infinitely
large—a state I shall refer to as *aura.* This aura corresponds to the temporal ecstasy we may call the *eternal now.* Just as John Fowles provides us
with a unique map of ecstasy through intricate explorations of inner time,
so John Cowper Powys provides us with a unique map of ecstasy through
intricate explorations of inner space.
    I have worked out the present model of ecstatic space (ecstatic being-

in-space) from the novels themselves, where it can be apprehended as a vaguely present structuration. It is not explicit, and only juxtapositions of a wide range of quotations will prove this to be a megastructure of the Powys world. Only after having formulated the theory, however, did I actually encounter it in explicit form: chiefly in *In Defence of Sensuality* and *A Philosophy of Solitude.* In quoting extensively from the former work, I do not therefore wish to initiate a movement away from the novels—I merely introduce extrafictional material to confirm beyond doubt what is suggested, rather than directly stated, in the novels.

In the model that I shall call *the circular triad,* we find the Self as crystal at the center. Outside this center is the operational field of the Ego. Farther out, we come to the Self as aura. I shall call these three areas *cognitive zones:* Self-as-crystal being the first cognitive zone, Ego the second, and Self-as-aura the third (see figure 6).

As we analyze *In Defence of Sensuality,* two points should be remembered. The first is that Powys uses the words "ego" and "self" at random. His "selfishness," "egoism," "selflove," "egotism," and so forth have no discriminatory value whatsoever in relation to the current Ego/Self duality or Self/Ego/Self triality. John Cowper uses these words because "there is no other vocabulary available" (*ISO,* VIII, 252). His random use of words does however not imply that he is theoretically muddled. The concentric triality is rigorously worked out and defined, as I shall show. The second point to be remembered is that this model of ours has nothing to do with the theory of focal consciousness and fringe consciousness. Aura, in our analysis, in no way signifies any dispersion or dissolution in the sense of evaporation, loss of focus.[2] The Self's "concentrated trance" (*DS,* IX, 283) may be just as "compact," just as intense, in aura as in crystal. Aura refers to the *spatial* quality of the experience. The outer circle is an expanded luminosity, the inner circle is a contained rotundity. As focused periphery, the third cognitive zone is Donne's "gold to airy thinness beat."[3]

In Defence of Sensuality defines the first cognitive zone as the "ichthyosaurus-beast," the second cognitive zone as the "humanity-ego," and the third cognitive zone as the "ichthyosaurus-god" (II, 68ff.). Notice that ichthyosaurus here corresponds to Self; notice also that it is opposed to Ego ("humanity-ego") and that it takes two opposite forms: as beast below man, as god above man. Beast/God is one polar extreme, the polar extreme of the Self. The other polar extreme is social Man ("ego," "humanity"). A crucial difference between the two polar extremes is that one is divided and the other is not. This is why Powys keeps mentioning a *double* polarity in the cosmos. It is the key paradigm to his thought and to his artistic vision of the world. Because the polarity is a double polar-

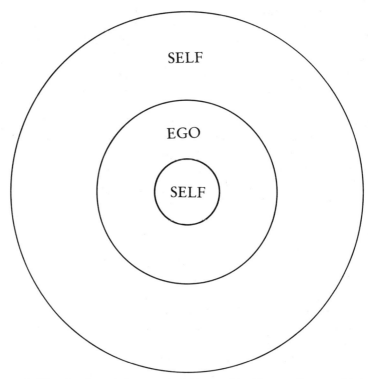

Figure 6. The circular triad: ecstatic Self sensed inside as well as outside Ego.

ity, our theoretical model for the Cowperverse must be based on a duality *and* a triality. The ciphers 2 and 3 interact. First, there is a macropolarity. (This gives the cipher 2.) It is the tension between Ego and Self. But then one of the polar extremes is divided. Now we have a subpolarity (crystal/ aura; or beast/god) *at one extreme end of the macropolarity* (see figure 7).

It is soon clear that Powys (as well as the critic) can analyze the structure of the world either from the viewpoint of the cipher 2, or from the viewpoint of the cipher 3. We face a triadic duality or a dichotomous trichotomy. Such a complex notion is central in *A Philosophy of Solitude* and *In Defence of Sensuality*. When the writer chooses to view this paradigm in terms of time (evolution) rather than space, we proceed from subman (beast) to man to superman (God) instead of from crystal to Ego to aura. In the following section from *In Defence of Sensuality*, this conceptualization is apparent; so, too, is the way in which the image of two millstones, squeezing out the intermediary zone between them, comes to reflect the figure of a circular triad outlined in figure 6:

> Here we reach the crux of the whole matter and the main theme of this book. Human nature—this gregarious thing of false idealism, savage cruelty, and mean, acquisitive greed—lies in every individual midway between the life of the plants and the life of the gods. In the ichthyosaurus-ego, in all of us, we revert to the life of the plants. In those faint feelings by which, in all of us, we approximate to the emotions of the saint, what we really have is a premonition of that future state of being when men shall have become as gods.
>
> And here I touch the question of the quality of happiness. It is my opinion that the most rapturous feelings of happiness we experience come rather from these two extremes of our nature—the ichthyosaurus extreme and the saintly extreme—than from *the hot, feverish, fussy, agitated, possessive, competitive middle-distance*, where the gregarious instincts of normal humanity predominate. . . .
>
> Now it is clear that all the ordinary ideals of humanity lie between these extreme points of sanctity and vegetation. That is why it is so necessary to keep them in their place; and, to speak grossly, to squeeze

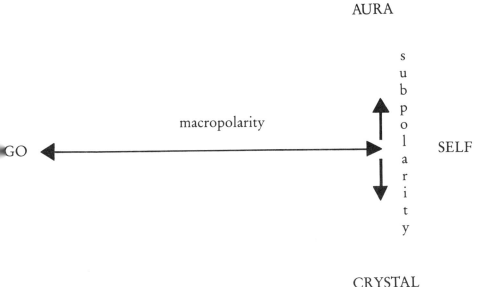

Figure 7. The double polarity.

them out between *the millstone of earth-dreaming* and *the millstone of godlike dreaming.* (II, 68–70; emphasis mine)

This passage is central because it so firmly places Ego ("the hot, feverish, fussy, agitated, possessive, competitive middle-distance") between the two extreme poles of the Self. One notices that Powys considers both these poles in the Self to be superior to the Ego. The Ego is a "gregarious thing of false idealism, savage cruelty, and mean, acquisitive greed," and as such it is "midway" between the two Self-states.

This section from *In Defence of Sensuality* can be seen in vital and significant relation to the corresponding section of central importance in *A Philosophy of Solitude.* Here, three years later (1933), the ichthyosaurus terminology has been dropped and replaced by the crystal/aura metaphor. Yet the theory is exactly the same. Below/middle/above has given way to center/middle/circumference: the middle term being negative in both cases, related, as it is, to the Ego. Crystal is only inferior to aura in the sense that the defensive is inferior to the expansive. These passages are crucially significant to the Powys scholar, since they articulate a formalization of inner space in the writer at a time when he was in the middle of his great novel-writing period: these nonfictional statements are from the early 1930s, and Powys's great creative phase runs from 1929 to 1941: *Wolf Solent* (1929), *A Glastonbury Romance* (1932), *Autobiography* (1934), *Weymouth Sands* (1934),[4] Maiden Castle (1936), and *Owen Glendower* (1940). Following is the key section from *A Philosophy of Solitude:*

In our deliberate, habitual creation of a lonely self two clear and separate evocations must be emphasized and held firm through all changes.

The first of these is a clear-cut, hard, resistant nucleus of consciousness.

This is the inmost "I am I" within us, felt and known, let us say, as a round, polished, inviolable crystal.

This hard, lonely pebble of the undefeated self is what we need to feel as our "soul" during periods of suffering. This . . . is what we need in wretched habitations, in squalid surroundings, in the workshops and offices of bitter labour, in the thoroughfares of relentless traffic, in destitution and want, and above all when invaded on all sides by the brutal clamour of the crowd-consciousness.

But the second of these—the second imaginary form which, in our habitual thinking, we can compel our consciousness of self to take—is, so to speak, a wide circumference of airy memories gathered about this inviolable crystal.

For round and about this undefeated, defiant, detached self there assembles, in the case of everyone, a fluctuating aura of precious memories. . . .

The most miserable and harassed among us carry about—wavering and flowing round the hard central self—these airy impressions . . .

Thus the self-creation of the soul is a two-fold achievement.

Like the projection of a spiritual body, within and around the material body, it creates at one and the same time this hard crystal of central resistance and this fluctuating, wavering nimbus of gathered memories.

With this hard indissoluble centre, with this flowing and undulating circumference, the lonely self is prepared to cope with the world. (II, 59–61)

The notion of a polarization within one polar extreme (within the Self) is by no means confined to these specific works or to this specific period in Powys's writing. Indeed, the very first pages of his first novel, *Wood and Stone* (1915), outline a conflict between mythologies that can be seen to illustrate this idea of a subpolarity at one extreme end of a macropolarity. In the village of Nevilton, an east-west line of tension polarizes the Holy Grail and the Holy Rood, both wrestling for mastery over the magnetic force that is to counter unbelief (I, 3). The pleasure there is in life, we are told in *Mortal Strife*, "is at once sub-rational and super-rational" (IX, 141). Some years later, in *The Art of Growing Old* (1944), we observe Powys using *within, beneath, above,* and *beyond* to describe the pivotal center of consciousness as something that is both outward and inward, both exploded and imploded, both internalized and exposed: "The circumambient etheric location of these thoughts, *which are himself,* which are essence within, beneath, above, beyond his corporeal frame, is a dark, limitless inward extension, without boundary or end, an inward extension which is fearfully and tragically *exposed*" (VI, 95).

Moving on to *The Inmates* (1952), we find there too this idea of a Self/Ego/Self triad. Just as the two "millstones" were to destroy the intermediary Ego in *In Defence of Sensuality*, reducing the triality to a duality with Ego eliminated, so here "we should reduce our lives to two dimensions, and cut out this damned personality once for all" (VI, 114). Powys tells us "to reduce the embodiments of our identity from three to two" (VI, 115).

As I have emphasized, ecstasy for Powys is not simply trance: it is the consciousness of trance, even the idea of the possibility of the consciousness of trance. Even further: self-consciousness *is* trance, can only be totalized as trance. Trance, also and conversely, is self-consciousness. Accordingly, Self is not just a state. Self is the feeling and awareness of a state. It is an awareness of an altered state and an awareness of an alteration. I shall refer to this psychic gesture as *selfsation*. By selfsation I mean the *sensation of the Self*, or ecstasy as Self-sensation, Self as sensation. Selfsation "must be something that attends the flicker of a fish's tail, the thrusting-forth of a snail's horn, the swish of an elephant's trunk, the stir of a wolf's penis" (*DS*, I, 18). This delicately altered state of consciousness is the ideal of John Cowper Powys and of the Powys hero.

Selfsation is the Self feeling the Self. But it is also the Self feeling the cosmos, feeling the entire mineral-vegetative-animal envelope. That envelope is now for the first time directly in touch with the Self through the thinning out of the Ego. The "inward extension" of inner space gives a feeling of accessibility to the outward extension of astral space. The Ego is now transparent or invisible, and the inner and outer space-thrusts intermingle so as to become coextensive. At one with itself, at last, the conscious organism now senses its self-completeness as a rhythm, a breathing. There are "only two cosmic gestures possible to man" (VII, 213). One is centripetal, the other centrifugal. In the sane human "there must be a centrifugal and centripetal rhythmic beat, a systole and diastole, an in-breathing and out-breathing, between one's soul and these images in the great Mirror" (IX, 279).

So far so good. But Powys was not a systematic thinker; better, he was a systematic thinker, but he never managed to express himself as a systematic thinker. Few great novelists have ever been able to achieve metaphysical clarity outside the element of their medium, and Powys is no exception. His own thoughts on this subject in the preface to *Wood and Stone* show that he was fully aware of how the medium of the novel permitted his thoughts to grow infinitely more complex and lucid there than outside fiction. The failure to sustain terminological differentiations creates no end of confusion in many of his theoretical digressions in the extrafictional works. In one work he will be attacking "personality"—as we have just observed him doing in *The Inmates* (VI, 114). Then, in a different work, such as *Mortal Strife*, this word "personality" will suddenly be used to denote the Self rather than the Ego. Now it is used as the most positive word in the English language. Accordingly, readers and critics may find "trends" and "developments" in the Powysian world view that simply are not there. A random quotation from the nonfictional writing will highlight this slack vocabulary. (The following passage is from *In Spite Of*.) With our model in mind, the underlying idea is nevertheless clear:

> Although you use your hidden "self" as your *post of observation* that does *not* mean that our philosophy encourages you *to make a lot of yourself* . . . They tell us we must have an "integrated self." They tell us

that we must "realize ourself," that we must strive to develop our originality, our personality, our uniqueness. . . .

In opposition to all this false prophesying . . . the chief thing to do is to be forever losing yourself in the enjoyment of embracing life. In place of "integrating" yourself the great thing is *to get yourself out of the way* as much as you can. (I, 17–18)

It seems difficult to imagine a true understanding of this passage outside the context of the Ego/Self duality or indeed outside the model of the circular triad. What, from a general, commonsensical point of view, can be made of this polarization of making a lot of oneself and losing oneself? of integrating the self and getting the self out of the way? Things fall into place only when we see that the "integration" of the self under attack is an integration of the Ego—an integration that has nothing whatsoever to do with the integration of the Self into crystal.

3.2 Kernel and Aureole

In *The Brazen Head*, the giant Peleg tells Lil-Umbra that everything in the world is a "Double Opposite" (I, 19). This is a reference to the psychological mechanism formalized in figure 7. We move on now to deal with the subpolarity between the inner Self and the outer Self rather than with the macropolarity between Ego and Self. In *Rodmoor*, we learn that the real truth of life lies in its "frozen chemistry" (XXIII, 367). This truth is crystal, the inner Self. It is contrasted with man's erotic-imaginative escapism, which is like a "blurring cloud." This is aura, the outer Self. The art of selfsation consists in striking a balance between the movement toward the inner Self and the movement toward the outer Self. We can see all three cognitive zones in operation in a scene in *Ducdame* during a tender moment between Rook and Nell. At this point, the trisection of Rook's identity comes to suggest not only our circular triad but also the theory of multiple personality and hidden observer, discussed in chapter 1. The rifts between Rook's three personae are so clear that we are informed that his words do not come from him but, initially, from "the second being in him," then from "the first being in him," and so on (VI, 82). These "beings"—really, of course, mental subsystems—are described consecutively from center to circumference. The first is the inner Self (crystal, beast, ichthyosaurus); the second is the fussy, social Ego; the third is the outer Self (aura, god):

Rook did not speak a word to her for several minutes. His soul seemed divided into three separate beings. One of these beings was obsessed with a simply concentrated desire to get hold of the inmost fluttering identity of this passive creature. To get hold of that—to take it for his own—to make it his unresisting, helpless, abandoned possession.

Another being in him was full of nervous considerations that were tremulous with a thousand fears, like the quivering antennae of moths, the agitated feelers of sea anemones, the twitching nostrils of horses; considerations that included Netta, Cousin Ann, his mother—Nell herself.

But the third being in him just looked on, with absolute detachment and indifference,[5] at the whole turbid stream of his life. It hovered over both their heads, this third being, and over the gravestone of Timothy Edward against which they leaned. It hovered over the ragged, mournful trunk of Lexie's elm tree. It voyaged out over the misty fens, over the gates and dams and poplars and ditches—over the rim of the horizon. And it was already out of its body, this third being, out of its malice-ridden, nerve-jangled body, drinking with deep, thirsty draughts the great calm under lake[s] of hateless, loveless oblivion! (VI, 81–82)

It seems to me that *The Complex Vision* (1920), *Ducdame* (1925), and *Wolf Solent* (1929) reflect formative aspects of a transitional phase prior to Powys's conceptual lucidity in the works of the 1930s. The passage above suggests some of the overall patterns in the Powysian design but there are still inconsistencies: for instance, in the possessiveness attributed to the inner center rather than to the middle. In this way, much of the strange, sometimes haunting, beauty of *Wolf Solent* arises from John Cowper's too intimate involvement with the mental conflicts of Wolf. One senses that there really *is* concern for the "mythology." It really *is* threatened: and not only for the protagonist but for the writer himself. The triadic paradigm has not been successfully worked out yet, and therefore the novel actually suggests the desperation of a man lacking any master clue at all—whereas the later novels, like *A Glastonbury Romance*, seem to spring out of a kind of appeasement, a kind of wisdom. These later novels describe the disappointments and riches of a quest, while in *Wolf Solent* the anguish of the quest seems to be an integral part of the work itself. Wolf, indeed, is no nearer the truth at the end than in the beginning. The question mark has not been removed, it has just grown much larger. By contrast, a novel like *A Glastonbury Romance* moves through a succession of stages all pointing in a similar direction and through a succession of perspectives all giving equally detached views of a central nucleus of problems. In *Weymouth Sands*, this detachment is even more evident: the author providing us with a spectrum of characters and visions, each replacing the other in a revolving pattern monitored by a central neutrality.

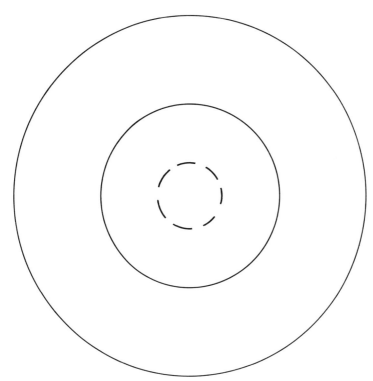

Figure 8. First and second cognitive zones merging into a single kernel of ambiguous status.

Unable to view the Self as both crystal and aura, Wolf Solent begins to see the quest for a deeper identity in an ethical perspective. The crystal (*WoS* XIII, 288, 289; XIX, 447; XXIII, 555) seems to be tied to interiority. This interiority locates good as Self (the first cognitive zone), evil as Ego (the second cognitive zone). Wolf cannot separate the center from the middle. He thinks they are one—a single kernel. This single kernel (zones one and two) comes to be polarized against aura, the aureole formed by the third cognitive zone (see figure 8).

This false perspective means that Wolf cannot see pure goodness at the psychic centerpoint. The kernel is now composed of a mixture of good and evil, and such a blurred and doubled center cannot be the pure home of his "mythology." Things rapidly become vertiginous for Wolf. The double kernel (inner Self *and* Ego) faces aureole: the pure aura. Wolf now comes to question the validity of his entire past life, for in the past, he felt that his "mythology" was firmly fixed within a centermost purity. Now that the Ego has been strengthened through erotic and obscurely vicious social entanglements, the center is a circle of inner confusion. Perhaps this crystal is an illusion? Perhaps he is right now losing his "mythology" with the destruction of this crystal? Then all that is left is aureole. Wolf moves out and away from himself. As his central identity disperses, he now makes the fatal mistake of seeing crystal *as* aura. He is becoming vapor with no internal solidity.

Wolf reaches an intensified and somewhat compensatory awareness of the Self as aura. But this movement from center to circumference is experienced as a dissolution (XXIII, 554; XIII, 289). He loses the sense of a "banked-up integral self" (XXIII, 543). No! he cries. His soul can never have been a round, hard crystal! What is it instead? It is aura, halo, aureole. It is a lake with drifting shadows (XIX, 448–49). Unable to see that the Self can take an inner as well as an outer form, Wolf Solent comes to deny the inner Self as he grows conscious of the reality of the outer Self. The danger of all this displacement lies in the instability of the outer Self. Suddenly it may be gone, this expansive feeling of ecstatic radiance. And what have you left then? All Wolf has left then is a blurred kernel in which the purity of crystal has been merged with the sordid worldliness of the Ego. Wolf has not learned the defensive trick of the Self described in such detail by Powys in *A Philosophy of Solitude,* a book published four years after *Wolf Solent:*

> In its fight for its identity against heavy odds, the soul has acquired one supreme device by which it can escape disintegration under the out-rush of another's personality.
> *This device is the self-obliteration of its own circumference!* . . .
> All the fluctuating images, all the essences, all the magical shapes and sounds and scents of this mysterious aura of its personality it deliberately destroys.
> What is the self now under this infliction?
> Nothing but a hard, impenetrable crystal, nothing but an adamantine pebble, nothing but a cold, smooth, recalcitrant stone. (II, 62–63; emphasis mine)

This passage, and especially the emphasized line, defines an act of the mind that is the very reverse of the mental dissolution in Wolf just described. Here aura is obliterated, producing crystal. In *Wolf Solent,* crystal is lost with the temporary achievement of aura.

Wolf's shadowed, ethereal "lake" is an image of the outer Self. It is a vaporous rotundity made fluid. Yet when this liquid aureole suddenly disappears and Wolf has to move inward from circumference to center, he does not come to the first cognitive zone, the centermost field of crystal. He only gets as far as the middle zone, which belongs to the Ego—or to what I shall call Kernel, a blurred centrality composed of the interpenetration of these two: "He had lost his whole inner whole; and the outer world—what was it but rows of puzzled, protruding ears, into which, for an eternity, he had to pump tedious, questionable information" (XXIII, 546)? In this situation, Wolf has lost contact with the outer Self (temporarily) as well as with the inner Self (permanently).

Powys's great aim in life as a child was to become a magician, one who controls the psyche. This is a central theme in *Autobiography*. And when he eventually did become a magician, he did so by learning how to preserve the Self by moving from center to circumference and back. Only by understanding the existence of *two* states of Selfness, did Powys learn the art of achieving stability and permanance for the Self. I believe he came to this understanding (semiconsciously) near the time of writing *Wolf Solent,* perhaps just after. This accounts not only for the peculiarly tremulous qualities of this novel but also for the coherence that characterizes the nonfictional works of the 1930s. The message in these works is always the same, and in this they differ from the earlier works that are not only in disagreement with one another and with later works, but also violently dislocated from themselves through a series of internal rifts and inconsistencies.

Once the understanding of the twin nature of the Self has been completed, the magician has eliminated the main obstacle removing him from a permanent sense of Selfness. This obstacle is the element of change and mutability. No state lasts forever, and this is particularly true of semi-ecstatic moods. By shifting from the extreme of center to the extreme of periphery, the magician achieves the impossible: change within permanency, permanency within change. Ecstasy can be eternalized and totalized through an act of ecstatic self-consciousness. It is now possible to view ecstasy from the viewpoint of ecstasy. Not only is this something entirely new; it is also something entirely liberating, intellectually as well as ecstatically. Intelligence and trance are beginning to work with one another instead of to the exclusion of one another. *In Defence of Sensuality* outlines this ecstatic interplay that Wolf never really grasps:

Every soul . . . has the power of changing its shape, its consistency, its field of operation, its location. It can retreat, if it pleases, into a little, hard crystal at the center of the creature's being. It can resolve itself into a hovering cloud that can float round the passive body of a person's life, so as to be immune to insults, attacks, degradations, humiliations, hostility, contempt. . . . It can turn itself . . . into an entity resembling an ancient moss-grown stone. So it can rest, indrawn into an aboriginal earth-life older than vegetation, while all the waves of circumstance roll over it. (VII, 220)

When Owen Glendower has a violent disagreement with his wife, this makes him feel that his spirit is "so light, so integral, so compact and free" (XIX, 769). This is Self-as-crystal. It is what *Mortal Strife* defines as the "solitary 'ego' at the centre of every-man's life" (VIII, 128). But this state of contraction eventually gives way to the feeling of radiance toward aura. And whereas crystal is smaller than the body (and creates a feeling of a self-presence less voluminous than the outline of the body), aura is larger than the body. These proportions lead to a feeling that crystal is lodged within the body, as part of it. By contrast, aura, because it is felt to be so large, is sensed as something outside the body, only loosely connected to it, if at all:

Our personality, even as we are aware of it, is so much more widely extended than our physical body, that the scope of the *antennae*, so to speak, of our identity is by no means confined to the space our body fills. It extends, this grasp, this touch, this reach, like a living and conscious *aura* projected from some point in time and space that feels to our own consciousness as if it were independent of the body. (VIII, 129)

A considerable amount of the psychological driving force in *Wolf Solent* derives from the protagonist's failure to see that the destruction of the interior Self does not incur the destruction of the Self. Alone at last with Christie in her room, and just about to seduce her, Wolf is "saved" at the very last moment by the sudden appearance to his inward eye of the face that has haunted him for so long. This face belongs to the destitute tramp he happened to see crouching on the steps of Waterloo Station before he went out to the West Country. There is a wonderful green lamp in Christie's room, and Wolf sees it reflected in a mirror. (This perspective in itself opens up the circular triad.) As he moves toward a swooning intensification of consciousness in which the mental cleavage is brought to a crisis, the greenness of the Powys ecstasy combines with the magic of his mirror fascination to form a dwindling perspective of ecstatic color. In its receding depths, the globular greenness comes to look like the "swollen green bud of a luminous water-lily" (XX, 458). In the phosphorescence of its green halo, his crisis shoots down a tunnel to the most secret recesses of his inner being. The passage contains all the megastructures of ecstasy:

rise versus fall, ebb versus flow, contraction versus expansion, crystal versus aura. Aura, here, is "mist" and "vapour." Within the overall development of the energy patterns in the novel, this section maximizes the thrust from crystal to aura. Wolf giving up Christie is Wolf giving up crystal. It is the act of a man who has only half-understood the laws of mind and ecstasy. He sacrifices half of ecstasy in order to retain ecstasy. But he only does this through ignorance of the doubleness of ecstasy. The scene is one of ecstatic suicide and, as such, intricately related to the scene at Lenty Pond where ecstasy saves Wolf from physical suicide:

> He reeled awkwardly to one side, and, snatching his hands away from her, sank down against her pillow. For a second or two the struggle within him gave him a sensation as if the very core of his consciousness—that "hard little *crystal*" within the nucleus of his soul—were *breaking into two halves!* Then he felt as if his whole being were flowing away in water, whirling away, like a mist of rain, out upon the night, over the roofs, over the darkened hills! There came a moment's sinking into nothingness, into a grey gulf of non-existence; and then it was as if a will within him, that was beyond thought, gathered itself together in that frozen chaos and rose upwards—rose upwards like a shining-scaled fish, electric, vibrant, taut, and leapt into the greenish-coloured vapour that filled the room! (XX, 460; emphasis mine)

Crystal here breaks into two halves: the inner Self and the outer Self. This difference between Self as crystal and Self as crystalline dust is perhaps at its clearest at the moment when Wolf is left alone with Mr. Malakite's body: "He recognized in that second that something had happened in his own heart that was like a wall falling outwards . . . outwards . . . into an unknown dimension" (XXIV, 592–93).

The ensuing sections of the novel are quite remarkable. First there is contraction. The intense reality of the ugly, lifeless figure beneath the bedclothes "narrowed the reality of his own life, with its gathered memories, into something as concrete, tangible, compact as the bony knuckles of his own gaunt hands" (XXIV, 593). Wolf now feels like a middle-aged gorilla watching the inanimate features of an older gorilla (XXIV, 594). Within "the abiding continuity of his days" (XXIV, 593), he senses the interiority of his inner Self. This inner Self corresponds in its animalicity and terrestrial grotesqueness to the ichthyosaurus-Self that we have seen described in *In Defence of Sensuality*. The inner Self is activated from within the marrow of Wolf's bones: from within his skull, his spine, his legs, "his clutching anthropoid-ape arms." The inner Self is a "vegetable-animal identity, isolated, solitary." The concrescence of this gravitational Self is so intensely inward-weighted that its awareness seems to lack the radiant abstractness normally associated with human thought. Moving inward toward the center of the body, rather than outward into air, this thinking ceases to be experienced as thinking. It becomes identified with the physicality of other interior processes. It is now an ingoing counterradiance reduced to pure physical being:

> Thought? It was "thought," of course! But not thought in the abstract. It was the thought of a tree, of a snake, of an ox, of a man, a man begotten, a man conceived, a man like enough to die tomorrow! With what within him had he felt that shrewd thrust just now about his true-love Chris? Not with any "glassy essence." Simply with his vegetable-animal integrity, *with his life*, as a tree would feel the loss of its companion . . . as a beast the loss of its mate! (XXIV, 593)

But Wolf is confused. He still does not grasp the interdependence of aura ("glassy essence") and crystal. When he tries to work out the mental connections between himself and Christie, he moves once more from center to circumference, without even noticing what he does. Suddenly Christie is again crystalline mist. Wolf now comes up with a new theory. He begins to differentiate will from mind, postulating will as nucleus, mind as a projection radiated from this nucleus:

> "And I know that my 'I am I' is no 'hard, small crystal' inside me, but a cloud, a vapour, a mist, a smoke, hovering round my skull, hovering round my spine, my arms, my legs! *That's what I am*—a 'vegetable-animal' wrapped in a mental cloud, and with the will-power to project this cloud into the consciousness of others!"
> As he articulated this thought he gave himself up to a vivid awareness of his body, *particularly of his hands and knees,* and, with this, to a vivid awareness of his mind as a cloudy projection, unimpeded by material obstacles, driven forth in pursuit of Christie. . . .
> "But if I send my mind after her, where is the will that sends it? In my hands and my knees? (XXIV, 594)

In *A Glastonbury Romance*, this antagonism between the inner Self and the outer Self is played out as the polarity between John Crow and Sam Dekker. Confronting John, Sam finds his mental aureole becoming so diffuse that he has to bring himself into some kind of artificial focus:

> "It's like this, Crow," he began; but he felt so much as if that tramp-ish figure at the window, even as he addressed it, might decompose, dissolve, disintegrate, that he couldn't go on. . . .

When he began saying—"It's like this, Crow," Sam could feel his own lanky, lumbering frame gather itself together, to express his new-grown purpose. (VII, 207)

Indeed, John Crow has exactly the same small-hard-crystal type of consciousness found in Wolf Solent:

> In the depths of John's consciousness something very lonely and very cold began to congeal itself into a little, hard, round stone. "I am myself," he thought, "I am myself alone. . . . What I really am is a hard, round stone defying the whole universe. And I *can* defy it, and get what I want out of it too! It's a lovely feeling to feel absolutely alone, watching everything from outside, uncommitted to anything. Why should I accept the common view that you have to 'love' other people? Mary belongs to me; but sometimes I wonder whether I 'love' even Mary. I certainly don't 'love' myself! I'm a hard, round glass ball, that is a mirror of everything, but that has a secret landscape of its own in the centre of it." (XIII, 370–71)

In the later nonfictional works, such as *The Art of Happiness* (1935), *The Art of Growing Old* (1944), and *In Spite Of* (1953), Powys attempts to bring the Ego/Self and inner Self/outer Self polarities into alignment with more rigorously defined ethical principles. I have discussed the sensation of the Self feeling the Self as *selfsation*. In *In Spite Of* Powys calls this *"selfness"* (VII, 222) or *"the feeling of selfness"* (VIII, 252). Now since the movement from the morally negative Ego to the morally positive Self can be a movement inward (to crystal) as well as a movement outward (to aura), there is an undermining of the normal clarity in the altruistic/egotistic polarity and a total subversion of the normal introvert/extrovert duality. Powys speaks in *The Art of Growing Old* of selfsation as the "ultimate selfish-unselfish gesture" (III, 53). This is "a double-edged movement, and one that includes both the selfish and the unselfish impulse." In the context of Powysian psychology, whether in the novels or out of them, words like "selfishness and unselfishness" become meaningless (III, 51). This should be remembered as the Powys scholar tries to come to terms with the actions and thoughts of central Powys characters like John Crow, Magnus Muir, Owen Glendower, and Dud No-man. Conventional moral standards cannot be applied to this imaginative world, for in it, tensions and polarities interact within a complex network of sensualities and moralities entirely different from anything we are usually familiar with in the novel or reality. The act of selfsation, we are told in *In Spite Of,* "is as egoistic as it is altruistic" (I, 14). Indeed, even if we *do* want to see a fundamental selfishness in these characters, we must acknowledge that this is "selfishness of a special and peculiar kind" (III, 59).

In *The Art of Happiness*, Powys speaks of the movement to the center as "egoism." This is a "commendable instinct" (I, 22), to be distinguished from "selfishness," which is the cruel gesture of the Ego in the middle ground, or second cognitive zone. Although John Cowper's thinking is quite lucid here, his terminology is not systematized and changes from work to work. In this case, above (in *The Art of Happiness*), it is curious to see how the *ego-* of "egoism" comes to reflect an act in the Self, while the *self-* of "selfishness" reflects the gesture of the Ego. A reversal of our own terminology would have simplified matters here but confused them elsewhere. Nevertheless, and despite this terminological problem, Powys moves in *The Art of Happiness* toward a clarification of the laws of the psyche that is quite superior to the tentative formulations of *Wolf Solent*. This improvement is tangible even when "egoism" comes to stand for the inner Self, and "egotism" for the Ego:

> What is popularly known as "Egoism" is therefore a mental attitude, not only lawful, but inescapable and inevitable, if we are to be in harmony with the main pressure of the cosmic tide; whereas what is popularly known as "egotism," or in plainer speech "selfishness," is simply the abuse of egoism, or egoism exerting itself in an unintelligent, clumsy, and insensitive way. (I, 21–22)

3.3 The Eye and the Stream

For John Cowper Powys, the twentieth century marks the ascent of the Ego and the assassination of the Self. The second cognitive zone expands, so that the middle invades center and circumference. Powys would like to see this trend reversed. He wants crystal and aura to destroy the middle, the "visible, palpable, circumstantial worldly life" (*DS*, III, 113).

With its three circles, the human eye—its pupil, iris, and white—is in itself suggestive of the circular triad in our model of cognitive zones. In this context, the novelist's preoccupation with the eye as literary motif is significant. So is the fact that he had a "lifelong terror" of the eye, as he informs us in *Autobiography* (V, 192). It is the gaze of the Ego that disturbs him (IV, 142). This fascination with the eye can take the fairly innocent form of Owen Glendower's obsession with his mirror gaze. But in the novel there are also more haunting and tremulous confrontations with the eye, as for instance in the case of Owen Evans and the externalization of his wicked sadism in *A Glastonbury Romance*. The following passage is typical in its use of animal imagery. Various animals, and especially insects, are given personalities corresponding to different mental subsystems in the writer or his character. In this way, the novelist incorporates into his work a variety of complex interactions, including multiple personality and divided consciousness. As Evans fights certain subversive aspects of his mental hierarchy, his willpower and his hidden observer are formalized as personae with subhuman or supernatural qualities. Toward the end of the passage, we recognize an inner dispersion similar to that of Wolf Solent:

> "If I yield to it—if I yield to it—" he kept repeating; while the image that worked the madness in him slid again into the fibres of his being and nestled, nestled there, like a soft-winged bird. And his imagination, as they drew near St. Michael's Inn, settled itself like a dung-wasp upon the nature of his conscious life if he *did* yield to it. He saw his soul in the form of an unspeakable worm, writhing in pursuit of new, and ever new mental victims, drinking new, and ever new innocent blood. *And he saw the face of this worm.* And it happened to him now that he obtained what is given to few to obtain, an actual certain knowledge of what thoughts they were, if they could be called thoughts, that would come to stir in the darkness under the mask of that face that was no face!
>
> Absolutely alone except for its consciousness of a certain little, round, red eye—the eye of the Evil in the double-natured First Cause—fixed upon it with a bottomless enjoyment of its suffering, the worst of the thoughts of this creature would be the intolerable effort required of it if it were to struggle to escape its doom. It would know that it *could* escape if it struggled. But the effort would be worse than what it suffered. And it would know its doom. It would see Remorse slowly changing its nature and becoming Something Else in the process of self-torture. It would know that its doom was no crashing annihilation, but a death as slow as the disintegration of certain mineral deposits which under chemical pressure gradually lose their identity and are converted into amorphous dust. (IX, 252)

The gaze that John Cowper cannot stand is the gloating look of the Ego. This is vision reduced to voyeurism, espionage. It is the dirty look of the vulgar mob, "the base, malicious, partly inquisitive, partly resentful look of the average people you pass in the street" (*DS*, III, 96).

This introduces the idea of the evil city, the idea of the city as the home of the collective Ego. It is perhaps at its clearest in *In Defence of Sensuality*. Powys's general dislike of the urban scene is intensified here by the Depression of the 1930s. In the "hideous commercial-industrial slavery"

(IV, 147) and "meaningless drudgery" (VII, 221) of the city, the Self is profoundly disturbed by the Ego's wink, leer, ogle, squint, stare. In this temple of the Ego, men and women seem to have become "galvanised puppets." The morality of the city is hard to understand, especially in an economic world where breadlines and jewelry shops exist side by side (II, 80). While the Self always remains sensitive to the pain of the fellow individual, the Ego becomes hardened to suffering and human misery (II, 79). Powys looks into the eye of the man of the city and in it he finds nothing suggestive of that semi-ecstatic bliss, that tranquil reverie, which he considered to be the most authentic form of happiness: "What is the cause of this strained, dull look, . . . this look at once so apathetic and so strenuous, so devoid of all living happiness, so empty of all peace, which stamps the faces of the people we meet in our great Western cities" (VI, 173)? As a "galvanised ant-heap" (III, 120), the city gives the impression of a ghastly insect world. Its energy is a kind of mechanical insanity (III, 111). Here Powys feels that the word "humanity" comes to stand for something quite the opposite of everything really human. And when the city culture uses this word, or the word "personality," John Cowper sees in it only some hideous mockery of central human values:

> How well one knows the sort of person indicated when one hears a man described as "so very human!" One even knows the kind of hand-shake he will give you—a handshake that is warm, fleshy, perspiring, and given so vigorously that one's fingers tingle. The cult of "the warmly human" has, indeed, been carried to such a degree, and the crowd "aura" has become so predominant there and has come to possess such a rank zoological smell, that it is an unbelievable relief when one encounters a really proud and lonely spirit. (III, 131)

At this point we are faced with a major problem. This is the problem of *movement*. It corresponds in magnitude to the question of interiority that we came to terms with through the idea of an inner Self situated within the compact Ego. (We did not solve the question of interiority versus exteriority by stating that the Ego was interiority, the Self exteriority, or vice versa.) Now in view of Powys's description of the City as anthill, with the individual lost in "the excitement of pursuing his immediate purposes" (AGO, II, 37), it would be tempting to see the world of the City-Ego as the world of movement, antithetically related to the tranquil world of the daydreaming Self—a world, apparently, of no real movement at all. The Ego seems to live within the swift flux of time, in "the clock-tickings and heart-beatings of this competitive world" (I, 29), whereas the Self seems to live outside time, outside any brisk stream or flow, in the serenity of an artificially achieved immobility. The Self thus comes to dwell in a timeless and arrested world, corresponding to the idyllic pastoral environment in which John Cowper grew up in England—fenced off from the swift realities of commerce, automobiles, and airplanes.[6] This past seemingly explains the writer's fierce denouncement of the metropolitan "herd-instinct" (DS III, 94, 98–99). The notion that the writer is escaping from the intenser currents of modern life could account for his opinion that the world of mass media "is nothing less than the collective soul of a vulgar epoch rejoicing in the contemplation of itself" (DS, III, 96). This "collective soul" is what I have defined as the collective Ego. It dwells in that middle ring of awareness that I have called the second cognitive zone and which we have just seen Powys refer to as the "crowd aura." The writer hates it because its "crowd-morale commands love for humanity, but condones abominable cruelty" (III, 97). ("City," of course, means more than just town, metropolis.) If this interpretation were correct, the movement in figure 9 would be formalized.

There is something terribly wrong with this schematization, however. There is something terribly wrong with the idea that the Ego is dynamic and the Self static. *Indeed, this very idea is an idea coming from the Ego.* For the Self, by contrast, there is very little movement in the second cognitive zone. For the Self, this Ego-movement and this City-flux is merely a pseudomovement. Even when it interrupts itself, the Ego-movement reveals itself as pseudomovement. When the City stops to breathe, there is only a pseudo-arrest, "just an interim of *no-life*" (III, 121).

This is a crucial point in the understanding of the nature of John Cowper Powys's psychology and philosophy, and it is significantly related to our earlier discussion of the difference between the writer as "demon" and the writer as "jellyfish." "Demon" takes precedence over "jellyfish": both in time and intensity, both historically and psychologically.

It is a dreadful mistake to believe that Powys rejects the Ego because the Ego is dynamic and because he is a static "jellyfish." It is a dreadful mistake to think that the *primary* reason for Powys's rejection of the Ego is fear. The primary reason for his rejection of the Ego is contempt. The Ego is simply not vital enough for John Cowper Powys. It does not move enough, it does not excite enough. Its electricity is faint despite all the fuss and bustle. *Ecstasy is maximized movement,* and therefore Powys finds all movement outside ecstasy to be an inferior or false kind of movement—ultimately no form of movement at all but merely the imitation of it. And this is precisely why the writer spends so much energy

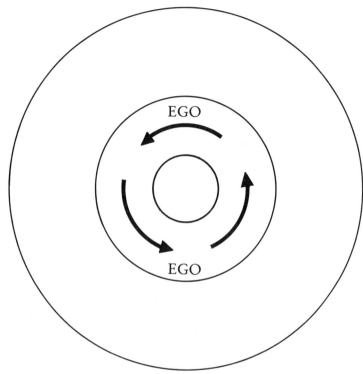

Figure 9. The movement of the Ego. This is a one-way stream in a middle zone of awareness, between the inner Self and the outer Self.

defining the countermovement, the opposite and real movement of the Self. This movement is the centripetal/centrifugal action of ecstasy: in-breathing and outbreathing, contraction and expansion (see figure 10). This is a larger movement, and one that intercepts the movement of the Ego at right angles, so to speak.

By considering for a moment this simple schematization of highly complex mental systems, we can achieve a tentative understanding of the difference between the ecstatic movement in the Self and the nonecstatic movement in the ·Ego. First (see figure 10), the movement of Ego is unidirectional. The Self, on the other hand, never ceases being dynamic. The Ego must stop in order to gain self-consciousness (a state in which, by momentarily being different from itself, it can know itself). In this arrest, it only senses a vague discomfort, the feeling that it is no longer pure movement, no longer blind, one-way energy. This is one of the reasons why the Ego resents self-consciousness. When the Ego steps outside itself it steps out into nothing. Nothingness. Then it swiftly returns to its blind onward-motion in order to shake off this unpleasant emptiness and sense of futility. But the Self cannot fear self-consciousness, since it is self-consciousness: for if it is the outer Self it can long for its polar extreme, the inner Self, and vice versa. This means that *knowledge for the Self is movement*. Self-knowledge. For the Ego, we perceive,

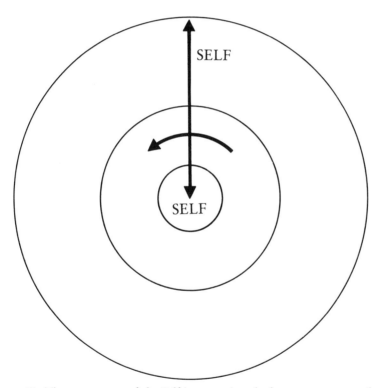

Figure 10. The movement of the Self intercepting the lesser movement of the Ego.

movement is the opposite of knowledge. For the Ego, *arrest* is knowledge. And since this arrest is nothingness, the Ego does not want this knowledge. Indeed, the Ego ultimately does not want knowledge as such; and this is one of the reasons why it has always taken so much trouble to build the most elaborate knowledge systems: hierarchies of subknowledges or pseudoknowledges that are self-explanatory and self-referential, yet wholly fenced off from the realities of insight, knowledge compatible with self-awareness.

This model of the difference between ecstatic and nonecstatic movement may help us to understand Powys's rejection of the popular concept of the stream of consciousness. But before looking at that problem, we shall consider how this awareness of two types of movement came to shape the writer's ambiguous attitude toward the thought of Henri Bergson.

Bergson seems to have had a profound influence on Powys's thought (*C, IV, 53*). Although Bergson, like nearly all philosophers in our Western post-Platonic tradition, works with stale dualities like time/space, essence/existence, ether/matter, interiority/exteriority, and so forth, he also works with the vital ur-duality: ecstasy versus nonecstasy, sinistral thinking versus dextral thinking. But in trying to make this ur-duality fit into the stock metaphysical polarity between time and space, he creates an intellectual confusion of which Powys was quite aware. At the same time, of course, Powys was attracted to this man of letters who so dramatically shared his own desire to foreground dextral awareness at the expense of sinistral intellection.

The main difference between Powys and Bergson is that Bergson saw space as stasis, whereas Powys saw it as movement. This is important: Powys actually saw being-in-space as movement. This is so because he connected the altered state of consciousness with optical awareness, so that the act of holding a field of vision, within which there is contraction/expansion, became something to be equated with the process of ecstasy itself. Bergson had an opposite temperament in that he connected space with nonecstasy rather than ecstasy. He saw a vital connection between pure time and ecstasy. Duration, for Bergson, meant dextral awareness. Sinistral awareness, the nonecstatic, therefore had to be the opposite of time. So, for Bergson, sinistral thinking (*la connaissance mathématique*) is a spatialization of duration.[7] In this philosophy, the nonecstatic freezes movement, transforms time into space. Bergson is unable to see what Powys sees: that there is movement in (experienced) space, too—that there is movement in (experienced) time and movement in (experienced) space, and that the movement in space is much vaster and more complex than the movement in time, Bergson's "pure duration." Of course, this phrase "movement in space" is somewhat nonsensical, not because it is impossible to "feel" space moving but, rather, because the whole Bergsonian idea of making the nonecstasy/ecstasy duality fit into the space/time polarity is absurd. This philosophizing currently takes the form of the equally absurd polarization between "logic" and "intuition." A large part of Powys's nonfictional writing was conceived with the specific intention of subverting this type of dichotomous thinking. He avoids the whole time/space fallacy by treating lineal time with marginal attention. The purpose, he states in *The Art of Growing Old*, is "to make Time our Pandar, to concentrate on the other" (III, 61). This stance enables him to survey consciousness in a way suggested in *The Art of Happiness:* "like a broken-winged Space-Bird, watching curiously this bubble of an earth-life" (I, 41).

We now see more clearly, perhaps, that when rejecting the whole stream-of-consciousness fad of his time in the arguments of *In Defence of Sensuality*, Powys is not throwing out another random thought in a medley of prejudices. Instead, his rejection of this concept is an integral and necessary part of a lucidly conceived model of the mechanisms of consciousness. This introduces what I shall call the eye-versus-stream motif in Powys. It is a central tension also in the novels and may help us to understand better not only the intellectual differences within the psychologies of various characters but also the very aesthetic structure of the Powys novel itself. This is always more of an Eye than a Stream, more a vision than a film: "The secret of life is the secret of consciousness; and the secret of consciousness is not 'a flowing stream,' but a creative-destructive Eye contemplating a creative-destructive Eye" (VI, 183).

This quotation from *In Defence of Sensuality* (published in 1930) and the longer one, below, may intensify our respect for the writer's ability to stick to his own intellectual convictions in a time of massive enthusiasm for ready-made pseudosolutions to the enigma of awareness. The fallacious "stream" theories have by now become part and parcel of our way of conceptualizing the inner life. This has been achieved through the impact of cinematographic techniques, spilling over into the post-Joycean novel.[8] Oscar Wilde said that the wonderful fogs and mists of the impressionists had actually been *created* by art: they were, so to speak, not there for the eye to see until the technique of the painter allowed them to come into existence. So, also, it may be assumed that the psychological mechanism through which we come to a state of awareness of awareness-as-stream is a mechanism in a sense "imposed" on us. This is a "natural" mode of self-awareness for us simply because it has been artificially maintained for so long by art, science, and technology. It is only quite recently, for instance, that psychology has moved toward the ironic treatment of the stream articulated by Powys in 1930. Following is a recent (1977) discussion of this problem by a professional psychologist anxious to replace Stream-psychology with Eye-psychology:

> Flow-chart diagrams of cognitive processes . . . show psychological functions (perception, memory, and so forth) as isolated points or boxes along a transmission line. In contrast with this approach are organismic metaphors taken from observations of biological structures and their development. . . . Immediate experience, for instance, seems to be controlled by a rapid integrative process (the scanner) . . . These rapid processes, in turn, appear to operate in an attentional field that provides a short delay in the flux of experience (the buffer), a delay in which impressions are held in simultaneous suspension, often called "multiple processing" or "parallel processing." . . .
> There is a broad and general principle . . . that describes the universe as being in continual flux . . . [C]onsciousness itself may be seen as the evolved capacity of living systems to cope with relentless flux and change. Imagine an organism for which there exists only immediate sensory events; such a creature would be forever at the mercy of the flux of its surroundings. . . . There could be no memory. Nor could behavior be organized under the direction of a unitary and enduring set, purpose, or control.[9]

Now consider that passage in relation to the following section from *In Defence of Sensuality*:

> The modern novelist tends to crowd a great deal too much into his "flowing waves" of consciousness; so also do many modern psychoanalysts.
> The truth seems to me to be that this whole image of "flowingness," this image of "the stream of," has been over-emphasised. I beg you to glance quickly now into your own consciousness, reader, as you reach this point and be honest with yourself. Does what you discover there in any kind of way resemble a flowing stream? Does it not much rather resemble a motionless Eye with a set of emotional retina-colours and retina-patterns held in reserve behind it, and behind *them* again a vibrant thought-goblin projecting waves of creative and destructive energy? (VI, 181)

John Cowper Powys could preach sensuality (as in the title of *In Defence of Sensuality*), yet at the same time he would totally downgrade sensuality as it is conceived by the City. The City's sensuality is entirely perverse and immoral. It is "self-indulglence" (*ISO*, III, 57), because it is the Ego enjoying itself, and Powys does not want the Ego to enjoy itself. It is not that he is begrudging humans any of the pleasures of the earth—the novels testify to a most liberal conception of the physically erotic, and so do many nonfictional statements.[10] It is simply that he fears that the pleasures of the Ego will prevent the individual from attaining the far more intense pleasures of the Self—whether erotic, nonerotic, or semierotic. To understand the difference between these two forms of enjoyment—the difference between selfsation and what the Ego refers to as "pleasure"—we need acute insight into the mechanisms of perception as these vary with alterations of environment and will. We cannot content ourselves with the idea of a supervening Eye, totally replacing Stream. For on closer inspection, the act of selfsation, so integral an element in the consciousness of the Powys hero, *is* a stream of sorts—though a stream that has very little indeed in common with the so-called stream of consciousness. Things do not simply flow through the Powys hero. He flows through them. He either allows himself to float into them, or else—if this does not work—he forces himself to float into them.

I believe this special state in which the Powys hero achieves an ecstatic communion with nature and objects is arrived at through internal dislocations, redistributions, or manipulations all somehow involving the shifting of the normal function of the "scanner," referred to, above, by the psychologist. A lot depends, here, on the level of input. In sensory overload the scanner will be working very hard, dismissing most of the incoming data. In sensory deprivation, on the other hand, the scanner will have little to do. Indeed, I think it reasonable to suppose that in a situation of extreme sensory deprivation, a totally different scanner will come into operation: one organizing our perceptions in an entirely different way. This is an important point for the simple reason that Powys consciously arranged his life to maximize situations of sensory deprivation and consciously turned his books into propaganda favoring situations of sensory deprivation (the title of *A Philosophy of Solitude* is in itself suggestive of this).[11] This is nothing new in literature. Only, with most writers, this type of awareness of the superior ecstatic potential of solitude tends to come in the very end phase of creativity—as for instance in Rousseau's *Rêveries*, or Maupassant's *Sur l'eau.*

If, then, you have a scanner and a flux, the "I am I" can either be centered on the scanner or on the flux. This involves monitoring operations usually referred to as "will." Usually, also, will reinforces the scanner at the expense of the flux: the flux is controlled, narrowed, thinned out, streamlined.

But with Powys, the will is used to reinforce flux rather than scanner, flow rather than filter. But how can this be? Did I not just state that

Powys was against Stream? against these flowing waves of the stream of consciousness? Yes! But remember that I am now discussing a situation of sensory deprivation totally outside the context of the City and its overwhelming masses of surplus stimulation. I am thinking of the situations in which we most often find the ecstatic Powys hero: the man alone with nature, alone with his woman, alone with his room, alone with his thoughts, alone with his daydream, alone with himself. Now if in *this* situation, the higher I, or mental control apex, shifts the focus of the attentional field from scanner to flux, there will be a sudden and dramatic heightening of the life colors; and in this special mood, magical doors swing open to that intensified world of ecstatic awareness which Powys has described with greater exactitude than any other novelist in the English language. The acute reader of this argument will already have come to the point I want to make at this juncture: that there in fact exist *two* streams, one within the other—and it is the inner one of these two that is the stream of the Self, hidden within the Eye of the Self, and removed by an infinite number of galleries and doorways from the hectic stream of the City-Ego.

This inner stream of awareness cannot be referred to as the stream of consciousness. I shall refer to it instead as the stream-of-ecstasy. It is not the movement from the inner Self to the outer Self, or the movement back to the inner Self. It is simply the awareness of very small shifts in the environment when the mind is in the state of outer or inner Self.

One of the prime reasons for critical concern with the nature of this movement is that it plays a significant role in shaping the rhythm of the Powys novel. Because of this stream-of-ecstasy, a number of other "streams" become superfluous as structural forces in the Powys novel. The novels acquire their forward momentum and propulsion from the dynamics of ecstatic awareness itself rather than from conventional build-ups of suspense. On the other hand, action is not internalized as in the psychological novel. Powys does not write psychological novels, he writes ecstatic novels.

Consider *A Glastonbury Romance,* John Cowper's best novel. The whole venture begins with an ecstasy; that is, it begins with a passage that can only be read as ecstasy, that can only be understood as ecstasy. If this passage is read as anything but ecstasy, it will be misread. And such a misreading (implying the superimposition of a nonecstatic grid on an ecstatic text) totally misses the movement and momentum that are so essential a feature of ecstasy and the ecstatic novel. If the reader is caught off guard, or deliberately refuses to cooperate with the ecstasy, assimilating it as nonecstasy, then everything is dead from the start, and the book can move nowhere. It merely becomes a whimsical, nonsensical jumble of disparate and overwritten trivialities, sprinkled with the occult and quasi-philosophical. The same is true for the beginning of Dickens's *Bleak House*. Read it as anything but ecstasy (fog-ecstasy, mud-ecstasy, eye-ecstasy, air-ecstasy) and what have you? The overwritten, the merely decorous. Above all, you have pages of fine writing *that move nowhere*. The whole thing is circuitous. Yet, read it as ecstasy, permit it to be ecstasy, and you have something entirely different—something that is overcharged with movement, that in fact implicitly contains all the movement of the rest of the book—held there, controlled, resisting explosion.

This ecstatic momentum is also a crucial factor in determining the failure of all Powys novels lacking ecstasy. In these novels, there is simply no movement whatsoever. The early novels with weakly developed ecstatic momentum rely on poorly exploited traditional tactics of creating suspense, while the late novels with weakly developed ecstatic momentum sink into a diffuse inertia. This, in my view, is why the much exalted *Porius* differs negatively from the golden works of Powys's fictional prime. Something has been lost, and this something is a thing with a central driving thrust, moving the reader from one ecstasy to another. At first, this lack of ecstatic momentum also seems to threaten *Owen Glendower*. Indeed, it is only after a few hundred pages that the novel somehow suddenly comes alive.

The transfer from the stream of consciousness (belonging to the City-Ego) to the stream-of-ecstasy (belonging to the Self) is described in *In Spite Of* as a shift in awareness from the Ego in the act of enjoyment to the act of enjoyment itself (I, 19). Also in *Mortal Strife* there is this emphasis on the "effort to enjoy" (VII, 115). In this process of pre-meditated Ego-transcendence, the individual can sometimes feel that the liberation from the monolinear sense of sequential time gives access to the vastness of the outer Self—but also, and at the same time, to the minuteness of the inner Self. Thus Porius can refer to a sensation that is at once microscopic and telescopic when he embraces Merlin, thereby entering dextral time: "The impressions of multiplicity for which he became a medium at this moment were as far-flung and telescopic as they were concentrated and microscopic" (*P,* III, 58).

This startling and original Cowperesque marriage of ecstasy and will means that the Self, in fact, is demonized in the Powys world. Far from becoming a kind of effeminate version of the Ego, the Self acquires a demonic Nietzschean willpower that gives it "the glow of victory" (*DS,* III, 90), "the feeling of a victory over an opposite" (III, 91). Sensing this superiority vis-à-vis its polar extreme, the Self is "felt to be *a triumphant opposite*" (III, 92).

Perhaps it is possible to take an even closer look at the psychological mechanisms at work when the Powys hero moves characteristically toward that moment in which—often at some erotic crisis—his consciousness seems to turn itself inside out.

As the City flings more and more stimuli toward the individual, his receptivity must restrict and narrow this influx. In this filtering and narrowing of his sensibility, he becomes more of a scanner and less of a pure recipient. If he fails to restrict his sensibility, he will become possessed by the City, merely drifting along with its streams of traffic and words. If he fails to become less receptive, he will become an anonymous part of the anthill—his will and his mobility will just be the will and the mobility of the collective Ego; his individuality will just be an individually parceled out share of something distributed in uniform quanta, impersonally. Now in the situation of sensory deprivation favored by the Powys hero, and by Powys himself, the individual's willpower no longer has to be tied to these fatiguing scanning operations. These become subject to what is known as *automatization*.[12] The Powys hero can transfer attention from scanning to flux. The flux is no longer a threat to the individual's stability and integrity. At the moment of tranced awareness, the Powys hero becomes pure flux, pure perception. This transformation can only happen when there is very little to perceive or, rather, very little to disturb pure perception. But, as I have suggested, this flux is the microflux of daydream, not the macroflux of City. It is the infinitesimal movement, the infinitesimal change of atmosphere, color, tone, that alone stimulates the stream-of-ecstasy. Anything cruder breaks the spell, brings back the scanner to deaden the receptive powers and protect them from overload. In a delicate mood near the very zero zone of influx, there is a magical sense of correspondence and harmony between the process of thinking and the process of perception. The tiniest exterior event will seem also to be an actual inner event, so that nothing at all seems to intervene between mind and world. Nothing that is "out there" fails to be taken in, and nothing within lacks a reverberating counterpart in outer reality. So the two spheres become one. Everything signifies. The world becomes text, and the reading of that text, ecstasy. The most insignificant thing is a signifier, inscribing trance: the movement of a raindrop across the minutest fraction of an inch on a windowpane, the morning toilet of the most inconspicuous insect, the random flutterings of some bit of refuse awaiting oblivion. This mood is as fragile as the faintest frostmark, and yet Powys turns it into a platform on which rest all his great moments of fiction. It is from within the poetry of this special mood that he makes us see the English countryside as it has never before been seen and yet has always been seen. It is from within the poetry of this special mood that he sees the killing nuances of erotic fascination in the idealized woman—

woman lifted out of the real into ecstasy, but also woman only real in ecstasy, only woman there, because she wishes this.

The important love affairs in the Powys novel are all ecstatic, even obsessively ecstatic: the love of Wolf Solent for Gerda, of Magnus Muir for Curly, of Sam Dekker for Nell, of Dud No-man for Wizzie. It is curious to note John Cowper's penetrating ruthlessness in revealing the exact quality of his fascination with the female. The intensity of detail—both of action and of desire—are immediately sensed as true to life in all possible senses. It is equally curious to see how the amnesic barrier operates in the writer's extrafictional modality. Significantly, in his nonfiction, he denies all knowledge of ravaging intimacies, the very birth of his son seeming to be an unlikelihood,[13] something that exists *on the other side,* in a world that is impossible. The same mechanisms underlie his inability to read what he has himself written.[14] Both of these self-obliterations suggest the ecstatic qualities of his life whether in love or in writing. The postecstatic simply cannot cope with the ecstatic, preferring to pretend for a while that it is unreality.

In a curious manner, ecstasy intensifies the sense of belonging and interpenetration as well as the sense of separation and autonomy within the love affair. In the passion of their lovemaking, Wolf and Gerda are like two poplars, their branches married by the fury of an electric storm. Yet once this storm is over, and still in ecstasy, they are again entirely autonomous, "completely themselves" (VII, 163). So also with Sam Dekker and Nell Zoyland. In their walks together, the overlapping of their shadows suggests a merging of identities that is essentially an illusion (*G,* XVII, 533–34). This tendency always to return to personality and individuality causes even ecstasy to be part of an atomizing force in the Powys world. Love, at last, is always weaker than identity. The Powys hero remains intensely concerned with the inner Self, "this dark void, which surrounds *on its inward side* the thinking identity of each of us" (*AGO,* VI, 96). This void is a centripetal infinity, an "inwardly recessive Boundless" (VI, 95). Even the mother, loving as she is, retains first of all this tendency to reinforce the solidity of a personal core. Her affection for her child may seem to deny this, but in the "insucking maternal eye" the writer traces in *The Inmates* a motion of the mind that is essentially centripetal rather than centrifugal (XII, 200). The female gaze that in all times has inspired the male and given him an intuitive sense of a thrilling beyond is also the eye of a creature desiring to swallow its offspring back into the womb. Where does the maternal Self end and the maternal Ego begin?

We see this double erotic effect of ecstasy on the lover in the seventh chapter of *Wolf Solent,* "Yellow Bracken." This chapter corresponds to the eleventh chapter in *A Glastonbury Romance,* "Consummation." The tranced intensity of the sexual encounter removes Wolf from the semi-impersonal detachment with which he has previously looked upon attractive females:

> Wolf had hitherto, in his attitude to the girls he had approached, been dominated by an impersonal lust; but what he now felt stealing over him like a sweet, insidious essence, was the actual, inmost identity of this young human animal. And the strange thing was that this conscious presence, this deep-breathing Gerda, moving silently beside him under her cloak, under her olive-green frock, under everything she wore, was not just a girl, not just a white, flexible body, with lovely breasts, slender hips, and a gallant, swinging stride, but a living, conscious soul, different in its entire being from his own identity. (VII, 156)

Ecstasy here intensifies the erotic desire for identity while at the same time heightening the acute awareness of erotic difference. In all such moments of erotic electricity in the Powys novel, a very complex network of psychophysical reactions and counterreactions is activated. Here there is not only a tensional heightening of the polarity between inner and outer Selves, but also a deepening of the conflict between Ego and Self. With the Ego, the erotic attraction to the body of the loved one is fairly straightforward. But as we see in Wolf's fascinated view of Gerda as enveloped body, the whole process of sexual attraction is far more complicated once the Self is brought into the matter. Things do not become less erotic, they become doubly erotic. Wolf sees in Gerda body, nobody, and nonbody. A gap opens between Gerda as clothed container and contained nakedness. In the following passage, we can see how ecstasy suddenly orchestrates a new reality for Wolf as he continues his walk with Gerda. We see how Wolf's transformation into Self causes him to apprehend a corresponding metamorphosis in Gerda. We then see how the commencement of the stream-of-ecstasy is pinpointed. Exterior reality becomes ecstatic reality. This is an expansive phase, Wolf flowing out into the landscape, retrieving its inherent magic. The mood is quintessentially romantic, gently undercut by the ironic naturalism of the animal droppings. Then in an additional development, the expansion changes to contraction, the ecstatic couple forming a kind of privileged center with exterior reality now hostile and ready to move in upon them with centripetal insistence:

> What he felt at that moment was that, hovering in some way around this tangible form, was another form, impalpable and delicate, thrilling him with a kind of mystical awe. It changed everything around him,

this new mysterious being at his side, whose physical loveliness was only its outward sheath! It added something to every tiniest detail of that enchanted walk which they took together now over one green field after another. The little earth-thrown mole-hills were different. The reddish leaves of the newly-sprung sorrel were different. The droppings of the cattle, the clumps of dark-green meadow-rushes, all were different! And something in the cold, low-hung clouds themselves seemed to conspire, like a great stretched-out grey wing, to separate Gerda and himself from the peering intrusion of the outer world. (VII, 156)

4
EBB AND FLOW

4.1 Ebb

It is now time to examine more closely what I have defined as the megastructures of the Powys world: ecstatic contraction and ecstatic expansion. In addition, I shall move toward a tentative definition of this ebb and this flow as the megastructures of ecstasy itself. I shall begin with the centripetal phase, the inward movement from circumference to center. In the subsection following that, the opposite, centrifugal phase will be reviewed. Finally, a subsection will be devoted to a chronological survey of the important Powys works, so that an idea can be formed of the pervasive nature of this ecstatic patterning.

We have seen Wolf Solent in search of an inner Self that looks like a hard little crystal. The loss of his integrality has been traumatic for him, and he continues to long for "an indrawn reality into which at any moment he might wake—wake despoiled and released" (XXV, 623). *In Defence of Sensuality* emphasizes this centripetal movement as a contraction to the inmost cognitive zone: his "ichthyosaurus-nature would like to gather all this [world] together, in one hard, compact, tight lump of dark-glittering life-quartz" (I, 27). "Quartz" and "crystal" are one and the same, obviously.

For the enthusiastic populace, grand social festivities mark a departure from the trivial world of quotidian monotony. But for the Powys hero, as we have seen, such wordly "pleasure" indicates no real intensification of consciousness at all. On the contrary: the more clamorous the worldly scene becomes, the more necessary he finds it to escape into a Self-enclosed mental sphere. At his coronation on 16 September, in the year 1400, Owen Glendower is anxious to withdraw from the interminable ceremony that has "driven his soul inwards" to the point of pure indifference to the entire pageant (XII, 413). Throughout the novel, also, castle walls stand for a symbolic barrier defining a psychological "in here" and a psychological "out there." In *Owen Glendower*, the in/out duality is significantly related to the down/up polarity. (We shall find this correlation important later, as we define our general theory of ecstasy.) This up/down tension gives added thematic and structural significance to the movement down toward water traced by the drowning chimpanzee, down into earth by Catharine in the "down-sinking vapour" of the forests of Tywyn (XIX, 781; XVI, 590–91). We see this down/up motif in *Owen Glendower* also in Rhisiart's desire to sink into the earth when ignored by Father Sulien and Broch-o'-Meifod (XXI, 878). There is a downward pull that affects individuals in the novel (XVIII, 703; XXI, 915). In this scene it becomes a nonindividualized phenomenon involving the entire Welsh nation. Like the Jews, the Welsh are said to win by losing, to expand by retreating, to attack by escaping. Owen feels that he can increase his power by sinking into the land of Edeyrnion; and why, then, should not the entire Welsh race "increase its power by sinking inwards?" (XXI, 914).

In *Mortal Strife*, close to *Owen Glendower* in time, this racial centripetalism is said to be a general British trait that contrasts with the psychology of the German fighter. The latter has a centrifugal psychology. The German is taught to live in order to fight, while his British enemy fights in order to live. Despite the simplifications of this war propaganda, it is fascinating to follow Powys's seemingly absurd but thought-provoking analysis of variations in the cultural psyche. Put simply, the German psyche inhabits the second cognitive zone, so that it has to fight a two-front war against the British psyche. Archetypally, according to John Cowper, the British fighter can keep a certain portion of his mind detached and in reserve. From this detachment he generates a superior self-reliance and a superior ability to act on his own (X, 177). Perhaps this ability derives from the duality of the Self: the interior Self being in reserve should the outer Self fail, and vice versa. Or perhaps it has to do with the fact that all wars are fought in the second cognitive zone, or *with* the second cognitive zone. If this is so, then the typical British fighter comes to this field as an outsider, as a Self forced to play the game of the Ego. At first this logic seems to imply that the British fighter will be at a disadvantage, fighting a battle on alien territory, on ground that he does not know. But in the long run, the fact that the home territory (Self) is left behind, intact, intensifies the war-psyche. For the Continental fighter, by contrast, war is really nothing new, nothing different. It is a realm that can never be visited, since it is home. The Ego, at war, can never be a raider. He is an indweller. Through a set of brilliant metaphors, Powys brings out the character of the British as something supremely reckless, individualistic—integrated, yet double; elusive, yet firm. Opposed to the massive, monolithic block of the Continent, Britain is considered first and foremost a sea nation fighting a land nation. This does not mean naval forces dominating foreign armies but, rather, that in the very idea of the sea, in the very feeling of being an island surrounded by sea, there is a power of extraordinary significance in times of war. Indeed, this theme is intimately related to our model of the Self as a centric duality: island within ocean matching crystal within aura. As in *The War and Culture* (1914), Powys is not really contrasting two peoples but two "Ideas" (*W*, II, 29) suggested by racial conflict.

How strong is the movement toward center? How far into the center can you move? Well, there is at first a sense of concrescence. The soul is established as a feeling of compression and condensation. Our conscious self is "the focus-point of a million rainbows of pain-rays and pleasure-rays" (*MS*, VII, 118). Again, *In Spite Of* outlines the ideal philosophy as "a gathering together and a focusing in one organic drive of all the most vital elements in our nature" (I, 10). The second cognitive zone—involving the Ego and therefore closely associated with the body—must be deliberately contracted. This will allow it to disappear into the infinitely receding interiority of the Self:

> A mind cannot exist without a body, nor thought without a thinker: to get rid of pride, therefore, we must constantly use our imagination to lessen the size and importance of our material envelope or inescapable embodiment. We must go on imagining it smaller and smaller till it is only a little more than a suppositional Euclidian point in an inescapable category of space. (III, 48)

This extreme interiority plunges the projected Self so far into inner space that it becomes a nothingness, an invisible centerpoint without substance or material form. Yet it is evident that the extreme inwardness of this innermost mental space is qualitatively the indrawn (spiritual) *equivalent* of the third cognitive zone. In the waxing and waning of the Self, its conquest of a double terrain may be sensed as an ambiguous hovering in midspace. But this is only an illusion. The Self does not inhabit an intermediary protectorate. This belongs exclusively to the Ego (see figure 6).

This fact that crystal is only another form of aura gives a special atmosphere to the loneliness of the contracted Self. The inner Self *is* withdrawal. But in the sterility of its onanism glimmers the hidden cosmogonic semen of an expanded fertility. The hard little crystal is always on the point of becoming a lustrous javelin, crossing "vast ethereal gulfs" to a domain free from tellurian restrictions:

Exulting in our loneliness, we have discovered the power of giving expression to the deeper loneliness—whereof we are a part—of the whole weight and mass of inorganic, primal "matter," erecting its vast world's-snake head, sullenly, from its orbic sleep, and turning its slant ambiguous eye upon the primal cause of its life! In this mood, and in the power of this experience, our lonely ego arrives at a very peculiar ecstasy of loneliness, for it draws into itself the loneliness of the vast ethereal gulfs between the heavenly bodies, and, as though it were itself *their* spirit, it hovers in mid-space, liberated from all the vexations and humiliations of its terrestrial life. (*DS,* I, 34)

Apart from "ecstasy of loneliness" and "hovers in mid-space," we notice in this passage that the Self becomes visible to itself in the prismatic tints of a primal slime: aboriginal matter made luminous by the Self. The Self has allowed its island fortress to expand infinitely so as to constitute the stellar bubble of the entire astronomical world. The first and third cognitive zones interpenetrate.

Such cosmic lovemaking acquires a human and personal form in the love between man qua Self and woman qua Self. At such moments, the solitary masculinity of the Powys hero may take pleasure in the mental trick of shifting from circumference to center at the most intense moment of erotic intimacy. While the Powysian woman seems to resist such a transition, the Powysian male actually delights in such cynical contractions. In *After My Fashion,* Richard Storm gets a "malicious satisfaction" (VIII, 118) from his ability to detach himself quickly from Nelly after their first embrace, and later, making love to Elise, he delights in withdrawing his soul "down some long corridor of reservation" (XVII, 222). Something rather different happens at the end of the *Brazen Head.* Peter Peregrinus suddenly feels a desperate longing to possess Lilith. All his life he has discovered his most intense mental thrills in solitude, so at this moment he cannot understand why he is risking his consolidated integrity. Here, the third cognitive zone seems to be pressing inward from the cosmic periphery. The middle belt (belonging to Ego) has been a kind of buffer zone, but now, with the intrusion of the outer Self, there is a "crack" or "crevice" in this field of awareness. The outer Self is visualized as a "sharp wedge" driving centripetally toward the inner Self—here no hard, little crystal but a vegetative embryo:

Is it perhaps that in the lives of all human beings there come moments when some particular desire . . . drives such a sharp wedge into the rocky substance of our animal nature that it goes clean through it, leaving a slit or crevice or crack in the mysterious thing that . . . the theologians declared to be the vegetative soul of the foetus developing a nutritive soul, which is thus laid open for "Something," we can call it a rational soul, to enter from the limitless Outside, when the infant is born? (XXII, 330)

This violent inward thrust "from the great 'Outside' of all our planetary struggles" (XXII, 331) is strong enough to reach the inmost center. We see this in the cosmic inflow described in *In Defence of Sensuality:* "I am conscious of the obscure weight of the whole stellar universe emanating from the 'first cause' and pressing in upon me from all sides" (I, 29). Again, in *In Spite Of,* the writer seems to share Kant's conception of a categorical imperative in the divided human mind "that shoots in upon us, like a spear of fire from a dimension totally outside this inescapable, temporal-spacious omnibus" (III, 67).

Although John Cowper Powys gradually drifts toward a more materialistic view in his later theoretical works, there is, sustained throughout his fiction, an ambiguity as to whether the "cosmic" feelings associated with the third cognitive zone actually denote the presence of a superhuman force or not. This agnosticism gives such works as *A Glastonbury Romance* a certain metaphysical resilience. The Powys novel at its best is a vision of a series of visions rather than just a single vision, the growth of a cartology rather than the unfolding of a ready-made map. Always, there is a centripetal pressure from a mysterious Outside. There is, to be sure, an outward radiation from inanimate objects in Glastonbury, but Sam Dekker nevertheless feels that buildings and places *move toward him* out of the inorganic surroundings (XXVIII, 936). At the drinking party in Mrs. Legge's front parlor, there is an ineffectual, subconscious presence "which they all felt pressing in upon them from that unearthly 'outside' " (XVI, 500). Sensing within her body the growing embryo, fathered by Sam, Nell Zoyland feels this supernatural presence as "something coming upon them all from outside—from *far* outside—coming over the wide-drenched moors, over the hissing muddy ditches, over the sobbing reeds, over the salt-marshes; coming from somewhere unearthly, somewhere beyond the natural" (XVI, 499). Having been brought to the verge of a supernatural Vision through acceptance of the challenge to spend a night in the eerie bedroom at Mark's Court, the intensely physical John Geard finally reaches a psychophysical conception of the Grail as "something that has been dropped upon our planet, dropped within the earthly atmosphere that surrounds Glastonbury, dropped from Somewhere Else" (XV, 456). As with Wolf Solent's "crystal" and "lake", the psychocosmic center is also the psychocosmic envelope. Revelation, incarnation, is the coming together of exteriority and interiority: the Grail "is a little nucleus of Eternity, dropped somehow from the outer spaces upon one particular spot" (XV, 458). When Sam Dekker finally sees the Grail, he is sitting on a coal sack at the stern of a barge floating on the Brue. As he sees a globular chalice, with a fish swimming in its blood-streaked water, "the earth and the water and the darkness *cracked*" (XXVIII, 938). We have already seen this motif in *The Brazen Head*: the "sharp wedge" going "clean through" our being, "leaving a slit or crevice or crack" (XXII, 330). Here in *A Glastonbury Romance*, the membrane encircling the inner Self is now rent. The circular outside invades Sam from above (the chalice in the sky) and from below (a spear striking him through the bowels). He becomes a bleeding mass of darkness. Something entirely new to human experience enters his being. The "gigantic spear" that tears him apart is the movement from periphery to center, the outer Self violently intruding upon the inner Self:

> The pain was so overwhelming that it was as if the whole of Sam's consciousness became the hidden darkness of his inmost organism; and when this darkness was split, and the whole atmosphere split, and the earth and the air split, what he felt to be a gigantic spear was struck into his bowels and struck *from below*. . . . He saw a globular chalice that had two circular handles. The substance it was made of was clearer than crystal; and within it there was dark water streaked with blood, and within the water was a shining fish. . . .
> *Is it a Tench?* Is there a fish of healing, one chance against all chances, at the bottom of the world-tank? *Is it a Tench?* Is cruelty always triumphant, or is there a hope beyond hope, a Something somewhere hid perhaps in the twisted heart of the cruel First Cause itself and able to break in *from outside* and smash to atoms this torturing chain of Cause and Effect? (XXVIII, 939–40)

Here, the hard little crystal (previously experienced by Wolf Solent) has been expanded from nucleus to envelope. The shining goblet is aura, "clearer than crystal." Passing through a dark, intervening fluidity, we find, at its center, the shining World Fish. This is crystal, come alive. Crystal swimming. This evanescent apparition seems to suggest a new symbolic complexity. The movement, from circumference to center, of a glistening projectile has become the contained swimming energy of a shimmering interiority. This means that the movement from circumference to center has *become* the center; the center as movement. The cosmic crack gives us a vertiginous glimpse of a world freed from duality and causality. The crystal nucleus has become a crystalline liquid in which navigation is the simultaneous presences of all directions, the eternal fluidity of an arrest. The fish is trapped, yet magical. Free as well as contained, it is relevant only as that mobile encapsulation.

4.2 Flow

In *The Art of Happiness*, John Cowper Powys brings the swimming Grail fish into the notion of an "Ichthian" act. This, he says, is one of his two psychological tricks, the other being the act of "de-carnation." The Ichthian act "bears a remote resemblance to the leap of a fish out of the water, into the air, and back again into the water" (I, 23). With this gesture, we arrive at Flow, the moment of Powysian enlargement.

The movement "from center to circumference" is crucial in Powys's thought.[1] In the Ichthian act described in *The Art of Happiness*, below, there is a centripetal "lumping together" of worldly paraphernalia; afterwards comes a "fierce leap" taking the circumscribed inner self into the "freer air" of the third cognitive zone. *De-carnation* is a weaker operation. Here the achievement of "hovering in the free air" still retains a suggestion of a connectedness with *"the centre of your awareness."* It is as if an invisible umbilical cord is there to remind the exterior Self of its aboriginal interiority:

> What I mean by the "Ichthian act" is a swift lumping together of all the evils of your life—as if you turned them into one element that completely surrounds you—followed by a fierce leap up of your inmost identity, a leap that takes you, if only for a second, into the freer air. . . .
>
> In no circumstance does [the] act of "de-carnation" help you more completely than when, confronted by some other person who is being a trial to you, you are tempted to pit your egoism, your desire for happiness at his or her expense, against the similar desire in this trying person. But when, hovering in the free air apart from both the self-asserting ones, you . . . are aloof from both, and, as it were, watching both from your airy vantage-ground [your] soul is still *the centre of your awareness,* but no longer the centre of your touchy animal identity. (I, 24–26)

These last lines suggest the difference between Ego-as-center (second cognitive zone) and Self-as-center (first cognitive zone). Wolf Solent lacked this ability to distinguish between *"the centre of your awareness"* (the inner Self) and *"the centre of your touchy animal identity"* (the Ego).

In Spite Of continues Powys's campaign against the psychologist's smug talk about developing an "integrated personality." We ought to strive instead for a disintegrated personality. This nonsensical statement is only valid if we understand by it a preference for the third cognitive zone over the second cognitive zone. In this third zone, consciousness is said to be like a flock of birds: by being scattered they have a good chance of survival even though some of them get killed (IX, 277). These "thought-birds" show a striking family resemblance to the colored "squadrons" of angels that Powys liked to imagine himself sending out in various directions (another centrifugalism) from his home in upstate New York (*A*, XII, 630–31). As from a mental control tower, his central consciousness monitors outward-flying subsystems of awareness.

At certain times, John Cowper feels that the activation of the third zone means the hollowing out of the first zone. He speaks of the Christian-Taoist trick that permits us to become nothing. We seem to pass across "the prison-walls of pride" (*DS*, VII, 220). The second zone (belonging to the Ego) is for the Self an intermediary no-man's-land. The Self must cross this limbo ("a gulf of intervening air"), if it is to expand from center to circumference. This psychic enlargement becomes a function of a central thinning out to a noncorporeal vacuum. We must try to

force this consciousness of ours . . . to cross a gulf of intervening air . . . But though we require our body as the reservoir from which to feed our consciousness, there is no reason why we should not have the power . . . of projecting our consciousness, from its base, or *point d'appui*, or jumping-off place in our body, till it stretches forth, like a quivering antenna or an elastic psychological navel-string, towards the particular object of its concentration. . . . The more depersonalized and de-subjectivized our consciousness becomes, and the more it becomes what might be called "pure and undiluted awareness," the further and faster it will be able to evolve, and the further from its base in our body and brain it will be able to carry its vibration. (*ISO*, IV, 108–10)

This centrifugal radiance creates the sensation of an aura: "a cloud of visible or invisible vapour" (IV, 121).

In *Autobiography*, the centrifugal is outlined as an early and integral aspect of the Cowperesque life design. The author describes the feeling with which he woke up every morning, a great life pulse flowing through him and giving him the feeling that he could move outward so as to flow through every inanimate object (II, 61). Here the self urge and the selfless urge are equally blended. The mood is selfish and unselfish. As we yield to it, a magnetic current from the center of our being is flung into space, where it reaches out to all our miserable fellow beings in the world (*AGO*, III, 55). So also, in *A Glastonbury Romance*, Mary Crow watches the processes of dawn from her window on Midsummer Day. The light seems dissociated from the sun, and something in the foliage, as well as in her inmost being, "flows forth" and "flows out" to greet this unreal luminosity (XIX, 554).

When Tom Barter's skull is cracked by a lethal blow at the end of *A*

Glastonbury Romance, his central "I" becomes "a released fountain-jet" shot into the periphery of an "invisible envelope." This process takes place as one mighty psychophysical spasm:

> His consciousness, the "I am I" of Tom Barter, shot up into the ether above them like a released fountain-jet and quivering there pulsed forth a spasm of feeling, in which outrage, ecstasy, indignation, recognition, pride, touched a dimension of Being more quick with cosmic life than Tom had ever reached before in his thirty-seven years of conscious existence. This heightened—nay! this quadrupled—awareness dissolved in a few seconds, after its escape from the broken cranium, but whether it passed, with its personal identity intact, into that invisible envelope of rarefied matter which surrounds our astronomical sphere or whether it perished irrecoverably, the present chronicler knows not. (XXIX, 1051)

This skull-crack corresponds to the "cosmic" crack releasing Sam's Grail vision. Ultimately, it stands for the mental ur-cleavage with which we are concerned in this book. In the novels, at some point, a cognitive slot is suddenly exposed, and there is unexpected release from quotidian reality. In *Owen Glendower,* the skull-crack has become an arrow-slit in the castle wall. Rhisiart first experiences pure lust with Luned in the Ladies' Tower, and he looks at this arrow-slit with the feeling that his soul has voyaged through it into space (IX, 306). His feeling approximates Wolf's feeling of shooting his soul "like a projectile" out of a closed window till it reached "the wind's home" (XXI, 477). To achieve such a violent release one must have "the power of *cracking* the wall of one dimension of life and passing through the crack into another" (O, XVII, 651).

This slit imagery easily evokes quasi-sexual inferences attendant on vulgar Freudianism. In fact, however, such slit imagery is something far more complex, interesting, and significant. It is related to one of the inherent imaginative ur-structures of the altered state of consciousness.[2] This imagery is given its most vital treatment in *Owen Glendower.* Rhisiart looks upon the prince's intense fits of ecstasy as "attacks." The narrator informs us, however, that they are really *"premeditated escapes of consciousness"* (XVI, 562). Owen flings his soul "into what [feels] like a vast cool empty space, an ethereal twilight of being." After his reconciliation with his wife, he keeps "flinging his soul—or, if you will, *imagining* that he flung his soul—far out to the horizon" (XIX, 769). To cope with seeing Tegolin married to Rhisiart, he goes through "the long-practised motion" of *"what felt to himself"* like flinging his soul through one of the open windows, out to the sea (XVIII, 713). There it floats detached and free,[3] lucidly monitoring his every movement. (Those quotations indicate Powys's refusal to be dogmatic on the question of transcendence. Such psychophysical sensations may be purely internal or they may not be.)

While there is no reason to believe that up-feelings and outward-feelings (or even slit-feelings) could not be generated by a mechanism of consciousness entirely independent of the sex drive, there are a number of passages where Powys deliberately connects the erotic with the transcendently ecstatic. In *A Glastonbury Romance*, Philip Crow illustrated our notion of the Ego as an interiority lacking the qualities of crystal. Yet in spite of this, or perhaps because of this, Philip can still achieve an ecstasy suggestive of aura rather than crystal. In emphasizing that the base of the second zone is phallic, Powys seems to suggest that the second zone is "closer" to this aura than is the first zone—for Philip, that is. Philip (the owner of a tin mine) walks to the exit of Wookey Hole Wood in a kind of *tin*-ecstasy. This is a strange trance, in which the industrial is mixed with the cosmic: so that while Wolf tended to hover as Kernel on the border between Ego and inner Self, Philip seems to hover in a hybrid ecstasy between Ego and outer Self. At this point there is an "orbic emanation from his body, projected like a moving nimbus round his figure as he moved" (*G*, XXI, 665). Stirred by a magnetism that seems to come from the ore in the mines, Philip feels "an excitement that was actually phallic." But here Powys does not see the "cosmic" feeling, in which the spirit seems to "mount up and radiate outward" (XXI, 666), as something generated by the stirring of the sex impulse. On the contrary, sex is seen as but one single aspect of a vast "cosmic ripple" running through the entire universe: "What mortals call Sex is only a manifestation in human life, and in animal and vegetable life, of a certain spasm, a certain delicious shudder, a certain *orgasm of a purely psychic nature*, which belongs to the Personality of the First Cause" (emphasis mine). We see this quasi-erotic sensation at work also in *Owen Glendower*, where *narrow slit* imagery and *up-feelings* are once more interrelated. Owen stretches his neck through a narrow slit in Harlech Castle to see a goosander floating on the waves beneath the moon. Even the seaweeds at the bottom of the ocean tremble upward. Their "oozy sap" is drawn with "maddeningly-sweet spasms upward" to the rippling surface of the moon sea (XVII, 645). The magnetism seems to initiate an involuntary, pseudocosmic response, emphasized by the moon being called "the great Whore of Eternity."

John Cowper Powys tends to polarize the microcosmic and the macrocosmic. The ultraphysical is made to face the supraphysical in what seems to be a very consciously developed strategy. The aim is to break down the reader's cautious attitude to the supranormal by giving an immediate feeling of naturalistically described sense impressions. In *A Glastonbury Romance*, we expect some awesome occult event to take place at Mark's Court when John Geard undertakes to brave the supernaturalism of the haunted chamber for a whole night. After a while, strange sounds are perceived. To our consternation, however, they turn out to be the noise of the servants below, making water into a metal chamber pot and breaking wind. Powys deliberately lingers over the event with an exaggerated, clinical interest, registering the divergence between the sounds of the man's urination and the more abruptly violent sounds of the female—as if that difference were weighted with the accumulated significance of esoteric wisdom, as if *this* were the ultimate key to the eternal World Riddle! Here the chamber pot becomes nucleus (first zone), the Milky Way, aura (third zone). Geard imagines an infinite centrifugal expansion of sound from human center to nonhuman periphery:

> A man making water. A woman making water. Every sound a vibration. Every vibration a radiation, a detonation. Every sound travelling from the earth outward into space. Will the sound of Mr. and Mrs. Bellamy making water in their room at Mark Court go on voyaging through space until it reaches the Milky Way? And not stop even then? No! No! Why should it stop then? Nothing once started can ever stop! It can come back perhaps, if space is round, but that's the best it can do. Here we go round Tom Tiddler's ground! The everlasting pissing of Mr. and Mrs. Bellamy. (XV, 445)

Later that night, John Geard contemplates the moon, like Owen Glendower at Harlech Castle, and like Owen he projects his consciousness centrifugally, "as if it had been a stone slung from a catapult . . . till it reached the unthinkable circumference of the astronomical universe. From this dizzy point he surveyed the whole sidereal world . . . the whole inconceivable ensemble of etheric and stellar and telluric Matter" (XV, 453). His thoughts parallel those of John Crow when his spirit, sensitized by lovemaking with Mary, experiences a sensation of endless expansion. His mind appears to travel over Norfolk. It sweeps over the pastures, fens, and dykes toward the North Sea. Here his spirit leaves the planet altogether. It shoots outward, through the atmosphere, until it reaches the soul of his dead mother in an invisible world beyond the entire stellar system (II, 73). Similarly, Owen Evans finds that he cannot share Persephone's erotic thrill when he hangs on the cross during the Glastonbury pageant. The quasi-lesbian magnetism between Persephone and Angela is based on an erotic current that is qualitatively alien to a dense, opaque, masculine eroticism. The wooden cross seems to absorb Persephone's psychophysical electricity instead of transferring it to Evans. *His* sexual impulses, by contrast, "shoot off, up, out, and away, into dimensions of non-natural existence, where the nerve-rays of women cannot follow" (XIX, 612). Later, still on the cross, Owen Evans feels that his soul is completely outside his body. Then he senses that, with pain, his body itself is expanding. It begins "to overbrim the confines of its human shape. His body projected itself under the pain in great waves of filmy chemical substance" (XIX, 614). His corporeal self then flings forth this semicorporeal aura in outward-moving streams and torrents. It merges with the surrounding landscape and finally with the round earth itself, swinging through space in its circular orbit (XIX, 615).

The way the mind travels elsewhere during the "prolonged reveries" of ecstasy (*O*, XII, 410) is not a process identical with the trick of "decarnation" described in *The Art of Happiness*. In *Maiden Castle*, for instance, Dud No-man finds himself outside the circus field with Thuella and suddenly feels as if a portion of his being is entirely detached from the fuss and bustle of the workaday world (II, 72). There is a crucial qualitative difference between this awareness of "the detached portion of his mind" (V, 211) and the "power of mental detachment" (*O*, XIX, 729) that the Powys hero uses in order to deliberately reduce the pressure of a crisis in daily survival operations. Dud No-man is suddenly disgusted with all the physical events that have taken place in Dorchester over the centuries, and to escape this gloomy feeling of historic tragedy, he makes an effort to conceive his consciousness as completely detached from matter (*MC*, III, 122).

Also, it may be useful to distinguish between the imagery connected with (1) the "jumping-off" place, (2) the flight itself, and (3) the "landing place" or "airfield" at the point of destination.

The same type of imagery may be used for all three categories. In *Owen Glendower*, the prince's thought-birds suggest the mental flight itself. It is a nervous habit of his to poke his head through every chamber window he comes close to. As he pushes his head through such a "narrow aperture," he begins to play his usual mental trick of letting his soul escape. It flies until it rests like "a ruffled starling" close to his son's bed in Pilleth (XVI, 574). A bit earlier, when Owen has to deal psychologically with a terrible and painful sight, crack and slit imagery appear once more. One of his men has been pierced from the rear, through the anus, with the sacred sword of Eliseg. At this point, the prince exteriorizes his consciousness till it crouches upon the handle of the bronze sword "like a small white bird" (XIV, 492). As with John Geard and the Bellamys in Mark's Court, the mental and the excremental are brought into violent collision. Powys brings the projected purity of an exploded whiteness into contact with the implosive filthiness of the smeared and dishonored sword.[4]

This thought-bird imagery may be compared with the corresponding imagery in *A Glastonbury Romance*. Here, Mary Crow experiences the most heightened moment of her conscious life when John takes her rowing on the big river. He picks her up at the New Inn. Bending over a brick wall on the other side of the road, Mary stares at a manure heap scratched by three black hens. The entire picture is suffused by a filmy opalescence suggestive of Mary's tranced state of mind. In this particular second of arrested time, the manure heap with the three black fowls becomes "a sort of extension of her own personality," and her soul seems only "scarcely attached" to her body (II, 68).

Most enigmatic of all, perhaps, are Owen Glendower's delicious reveries, eternally spawning new swirls and eddies. We have seen him split into a quaternity in a combined psychophysical gesture involving a synchronization of mirror gazing and "de-carnation." Owen manages to achieve a further cognitive quartering by deliberately involving another person (rather than his mirror self) in the act of mental expansion from inner zone to outer zone. In a rapturous daydream, he imagines himself "*whirled upwards*" with Tegolin until they are "*outside Space altogether*" (XIX, 722). At this point the prince looks at Rhisiart to see whether he has noticed that Tegolin is no longer in possession of her soul. He has now tried to do what he has never attempted so far: to exteriorize someone else's consciousness along with his own.

4.3 The Mind as Tide

Before considering the extent to which Powys's literary achievement provides us with a cartography of the ecstatic surpassing in range and richness of detail anything hitherto stated on this dimension of awareness, it may be appropriate to survey the various works chronologically in order to get an impression of how ecstatically *tidal* Powys's thought is.

Even in the first chapter of the first novel, *Wood and Stone* (1915), we encounter the intense sense of the centripetal. To be buried in Nevilton clay is not so much to be buried, it is to be "sucked in, drawn down, devoured, absorbed" (I, 6). It is this sense that turns the churchyard into "the very navel and centre of the village" (I, 7).

In *Rodmoor* (1916), most of the action takes place close to the North Sea. Here Powys analyzes "the action of that law which is perhaps the deepest in the universe, the law of *ebb and flow*" (XX, 301). In this bleak and desolate spot, the moon seems to draw not only the sea but also the air into its tidal suction: "The sky seemed to draw back, back and away, to some purer, clearer, more ethereal level" (XXIII, 356). "In its indrawings and outbreathings, in the ebb and flow of its fluctuating presence" (IV, 54), the darkness itself seems to participate in "the meeting of two infinite vistas of imaginative suggestion" (XV, 203).

In John Cowper's third novel,[5] *After My Fashion*, Richard Storm's brain contains an "observing demon" (II, 28). This "demon observer" (II, 38) views the center of the mind from a detached periphery. The motif of divided consciousness is perhaps at its strongest at the moment when the Reverend John Moreton dies in a state of terribly lucid intellection. In this clarity of vision, the crucifix he stares at becomes a butterfly. His death-ecstasy climaxes in the form of an intense curiosity about the name of this butterfly. The passage foreshadows the section in *A Glastonbury Romance* where Sam Dekker must at all costs determine the *specificity* ("Is it a Tench?") of the Grail Fish swimming in the Holy Grail. Thus, in both novels, the universality and generality of the symbol of Christ is at once undercut and reinforced, the implication being that only the fusion of ecstasy with personality can result in true release. Ecstasy has to marry personality; but, more significant, personality must marry ecstasy. Only in this way can the sacred become nonplatonic. Only in this way can that Crack open which allows the immaterial to pour into the material, the timeless (at the end of *A Glastonbury Romance*) to descend into time. In *After My Fashion*, ecstasy completely wipes out the theologian's doctrinal adherence to the specificity of knowledge. In ecstasy only insight matters, not knowledge. Therefore, the specificity of knowledge becomes generalized, while the nonspecificity of insight searches desperately for a specificity of its own. Knowledge can only exist as specificity: *this* collection of facts, theses, laws, definitions. Insight can only exist as generality: a universal formula evaporating as soon as it is formalized in symbolic form, whether mathematical or verbal. So at this moment of altered awareness, the cosmic situation is reversed. John Moreton's journey from knowledge to insight entails a transition from generality to specificity rather than vice versa:

> And in a flash he knew that this was his last moment of what is called life. . . .
> Yes, his brain was clearer than it had ever been in his life. The only thing that puzzled him was that the human arms of that crucifix which hovered just above poor Gracie's head were not fastened to anything but were waving in the air like the wings of a butterfly. What butterfly was it? That was the one thing that troubled him. He would like to know that, before darkness covered his eyes. . . .

Everything was growing smaller now, smaller and further away. And yet they were not leaving him. They were leaving themselves. He himself was getting further away—a stupid old man breathing like a cracked steam engine. He was *there,* and they were *there,* far off, far *away*—four unhappy people bending over a grotesque old entomologist stretched out on a bed. Why couldn't he communicate to them what a delicious thing it was to be fanned by butterfly wings?

Never had his brain been more clear. But it was annoying that he couldn't remember the name of that butterfly! And it was annoying that he couldn't remember what his opinions were about the immortality of the soul. He ought to be thinking about that now; not enjoying this unphilosophical happiness! . . .

The immortality of the soul? What *was* his view upon that problem? He hadn't the least idea. He had no idea of anything except of floating in a lovely blue space—a blue space that grew darker and darker. Then he recalled one single word out of a great many. It was the word *annihilation.* . . . But what was the connection between annihilation and the immortality of the soul? He wished he could remember what the immortality of the soul meant. It was a musical sentence. It must have meant something once to him when his brain was clouded. But his brain was clear now and it meant nothing at all! (X, 145–46)

This passage may help to suggest the distinction between an ecstatic reading and a nonecstatic reading. To view what is happening to John Moreton as a drifting away from reality into a purely emotional, nonrational, and "associative" mode of awareness is to misunderstand the passage. John Cowper is suggesting something quite different. First there is the intensified sense of a fall line, produced by ecstasy: he "was *there,* and they were *there.*" The fall line separates John from his nonecstatic fellow humans. This fall line also removes him from the understanding of life, the understanding of Being, that they represent. For them this understanding is knowledge, for him it is insight. Accordingly, he is removed from himself, from what he was moments earlier, before the ecstasy, before he crossed the fall line. He is moving toward a new understanding, toward the insight that will give him the butterfly as knowledge, the butterfly-ecstasy as knowledge, ecstasy as knowledge. He is groping for a new language, one that does not halt before ecstasy, one that is not silenced by ecstasy.

With this fall line in mind, it is quite logical for us to register the way in which John Moreton loses a sinistral understanding of the "immortality of the soul" at exactly the moment in his life which uniquely and directly gives him a dextral understanding of the "immortality of the soul." These two understandings exclude one another. This mutual exclusiveness is part of the same grand scheme that makes the word *annihilation* perfectly compatible with immortality. Death is ecstasy because ecstasy is death. Among other things it is the death of knowledge as knowledge is conceived by purely sinistral logic. But John Moreton can communicate this only to himself: not because the reality of ecstasy (reality as it is perceived in altered awareness) is illusion, while the reality of nonecstasy is nonillusion,[6] but because these two human modes of awareness convey realities that exclude one another. So the dying man shares his ecstasy only with the butterfly and with the reader: more precisely, with the reader who is open to the Powys ecstasy. Because death often triggers altered states of consciousness, and because literary creativity triggers frequent altered states of consciousness, we have in literature a vast number of penetrating and acute renderings of the death ecstasy. The writing and dying ecstasies communicate with one another for the simple reason that they are one and the same thing with one and the same background of available "information" and structural will-to-power. The various literary men that assembled to contemplate the death-countenance of Marcel Proust did so in order to study literature, not death, creation not annihilation, ecstasy, not the cessation of ecstasy.

The difference between the intelligence of the sinistral and the intelligence of the dextral is suggested in the last lines in the passage I have quoted. From the viewpoint of the dextral, John's sinistral awareness was "clouded." Far from being a moment in which logic is veiled by emotion, the death-ecstasy is a time when consciousness is cleared and *un*veiled. This new understanding is so deep that the words in which the sinistral knowledge of things was cloaked have become meaningless. The dextrality of the moment is also emphasized by the reference to the fact that "immortality of the soul" has now become "a musical sentence" for the dying man.[7] It is not that the merely euphonious has come to replace the intellectual substance of a sinistral awareness of the problem of immortality but, rather, that the achieved insight incorporates such musical qualities *in thought* that give a lasting poem on death an *intellectual* edge lacking in any nonlyrical statement about death. So, also, the limpidity of this dying man's mind is not a limpidity robbed of the critical quality; there is simply a new and different critical quality to his thinking, a quality that allows John Moreton not only to transcend the critical faculties that remove the nonecstatic entourage from ecstatic insight but also to evaluate critically the type of knowledge *they* sanctify. Their "opinions" about the immortality of the soul are worthless, because they are grounded on an epistemology that has ruthlessly excluded ecstatic awareness.

In *The Complex Vision* (1920), the analysis of death once more introduces what I have called the *tidal* qualities of the Cowperverse: inflow countering outflow and vice versa. In the final chapter, which is devoted to the idea of communism, John Cowper sees a crucial connection between the annihilation of life and the annihilation of identity: in other words, between the thrust of death and the thrust of possessive love. The latter desires a transformation of the loved one from autonomous individual into private property. Where love flows out in creative energy, the instinct to hold and possess relaxes. Love diffuses, expands, and projects itself. "The creative impulse is always centrifugal. The indrawing movement, the centripetal movement, is a sign of the presence of that inert malice which would reduce all life to nothingness" (XIV, 337). In *The Complex Vision*, Powys is still burdened by those dichotomies that spoil so much of his early writing, that also pervade *Ducdame* and much of *Wolf Solent*, and that only unfold into the satisfying trichotomies of the later works with time. Communism is thought to represent the outflowing, while private property represents the evil of inflow. The naïveté of this idea is largely derived from the mistaken notion of the unity of the center: Ego is center, Self circumference. According to this simplistic logic, the more you move outward, the more you become a loving Self, while the more you move inward, the more you become a hoarding Ego, accumulating property with selfish greed. This fundamental naïveté should not detract, however, from an appreciation of the validity of much of what John Cowper is saying. His critique of the possessive Ego is acute and penetrating: the lover destroying the identity of the loved one by wishing to merge with the other in an enlarged Ego-ism; the "possessive instinct in maternal love" (XIV, 336) making the same kind of war on life through subtle forms of self-deceit and pseudo-idealism.

The swing from communism to anticommunism (in the later works) can be clarified by a careful study of this fourteenth chapter in *The Complex Vision*. Although communism becomes a threat to the personality in the works of the ageing Powys because it is associated with an aggressive totalitarianism (Stalinism), in *The Complex Vision* it is a liberating force of the personality, since it declares war on personality's chief enemy: private property. This contempt for private property is an intense and authentic aspect of John Cowper's remarkable temperament, his somewhat careless extravagance in giving away money to random acquaintances being an integral element of his personality that came sometimes to annoy his family and inconvenience himself to no small degree. In *The Complex Vision*, private property comes to represent Evil-as-the-Inflowing, while communism is Good-as-the-Outflowing. Then, with the half-awareness of crystal as the Good-in-Inflowing, Powys writes *Wolf Solent*, arriving, in the works that follow, at a satisfying philosophy with a stable triadic conceptualization of inner complexity.

With this achievement, much of the false yearning of *The Complex Vision* evaporates. Because the center is no longer evil (being crystal rather than Ego), Powys no longer fears interiority. Therefore private property no longer looms as the monster it was, and the post-Wolfian Powys hero is no longer burdened by a sense of guilt and damnation. (I conjecture a parallel development in John Cowper himself.) In turn, the urgency of the outflowing into the communistic Self is now weakened, and with time the writer sees the communist system itself as a practical threat to the Self rather than as a vehicle for its liberation.

Ducdame (1925) is another work full of tidal imagery.[8] Powys's pre-triadic thinking is in this novel played out as a tension between the dualistic and the multiversal. Structurally, all of Powys's novels hover between duality and endless multiplicity: we need only think of *A Glastonbury Romance*, with its duality (the good/evil First Cause) subverted by the endlessly receding complexities of the individual moment of awareness or the individual moment of being—the cosmogonic Crack upsetting duality and collapsing it into the at-oneness of Grail ecstasy; the tiniest insect upsetting duality in the opposite way by being different from everything but itself, adding its tiny being, its tiny personality, to a cosmic conglomerate that is not reducible to any overall formula. But if this tension between the world as duality and the world as infinity survives as an integral aspect of the structure of the Powys novel, it does not survive within Powys's philosophy. (As we have seen, his philosophy after 1930 is consistently triadic.)

In *Ducdame*, Powys is still working out the duality/infinity polarity as a central philosophical and psychological problem not yet solved by the synthesis of a triadic paradigm (Self/Ego,/Self, or crystal/city/aura). Identified with his protagonist Rock Ashover, with whom he has so much in common, John Cowper turns the Vicar of Ashover, William Hastings, into a character who carries much of the dualistic philosophy that underlies his earlier metaphysical stance as it is elaborated, for instance, in the creative/destructive ur-structure of *Rodmoor*. This fictional mechanism allows Powys to distance himself from his earlier and less mature philosophical identity. This distancing is a later variant of the self-distancing performed throughout *Confessions*.

Hastings claims that there is an appalling struggle going on between two great powers in the cosmos. One of these powers is the life force, the other is the death force (*D*, XVIII, 286–87). This notion underlies the unfolding of ideas and events in *Rodmoor*, where the tossing violence of the sea comes to represent both cosmic thrusts, with a gloomy emphasis on the negative one. It is the central metaphysical poverty of this notion that cramps all of Powys's writing up to the time of *Wolf Solent*, a novel of crisis that offers catharsis for the writer, if not for Wolf himself. Put simply, Powys moves from this impoverishing duality to a conceptually rich triality and then, in his last works, on to pure multiplicity, anarchy.

But Rook is not all that impressed by Hastings's "two Powers." " 'All this sounds to me very like what I've heard in church' " (XVIII, 287). He then moves on toward that outline of a semi-chaotic multiverse which is given so much free play in the works beginning with *Porius* that the Cowperverse turns into a sphere of cosmogonic laissez-faire. In *Duc-dame*, however, this new vision of the order of things holds the promise of a luxuriance that has been denied by the crude duality of the writer's first phase:

> "I don't see why you should stop at this duality of yours. Why not take it for granted that the universe is crowded with levels, strata, planes, dimensions, altitudes, regions, all of them full of wretched sensitive beings like ourselves longing to escape?" . . .
> "You're not serious, Ashover," [Hastings] said. "No one who ana-lyses his own feelings can get away from *this great undertow of opposite tides*—the death urge and the life urge." . . .
> "I think nothing of these forces of yours, Hastings," he retorted. Why stop at life and death? Why not have a whole vortex of conflicting powers? Life and death are just words! All we know is a mad chaotic jumble of things that we call 'living' and things that we call 'dead.' What I feel is that the whole imbroglio may be a set of obscene dreams, a great concourse of phantasmagoric shadows, most of them disgust-ing; some of them magically lovely!" (XVIII, 288; emphasis mine)

While this infinitely extending concourse of "levels, strata, planes, di-mensions, altitudes, regions," and so on does illuminate the Cowper-verse with a glowing vitalism, it is a mistake to see this as a pantheistic world, for the very notion of pantheism springs from the idea of a seamless Block-Universe. To the extent that the Cowperverse is not sec-ularized or semi-secular, it is polytheistic rather than pantheistic. And if the writer surveys the entire volume of his pluralistic cosmos, he can do so not because he is all tissues, but because he is all seams.

Wolf Solent (1929) is as tidal as its predecessor, *Ducdame*. The butterfly/crucifix image in *After My Fashion* has now become a forked body stretching out fingertips rather than wings or arms: "Ah! His body and his soul were coming together again now! Emanating from his lean, striding form, from his spine, from his legs, from his finger-tips, his spirit extended outwards, dominating this forked 'animal-vegetable' which was himself" (XXV, 625). The "observing demon" in *After My Fashion* is here a "calculating demon perched on the top of his head" (XVIII, 394). The tidal imagery culminates after Wolf's retreat from Lenty Pond and the thought of suicide. He visualizes the cause of all life and of all death as a huge shellfish "placidly breathing in and breathing out on the floor of a sea-like infinity" (XXIII, 568).

The inner and outer forms of the Self are shown in a state of eerie interaction in chapter 8, when Darnley, Jason, Valley, and Wolf walk through the Blacksod streets on their way from the pub. In one of the small houses, Wolf notices an elderly woman reading by candlelight. He finds the situation strangely moving; or, rather, he finds the idea of the situation strangely moving. It is, so to speak, an emblematic representation of the inner Self. The reading woman is on the inside (inside her house), the men are on the outside. They have just come from the pub, from the noisy realm of the Ego where one enjoys the relativity of things. The woman is inside her book, within the ideational sphere of the absolute: writing, imagination, romance. But being inside this ideational sphere of the book also means moving outward to the great beyond (of romantic ideation) and not only moving into the halo of light produced by the two candles: the illuminated center of book and attentive mind. So, in this scene, the men in the street come to stand as intermediary observers caught midway between the inner zone of the reading Self and the outer zone of the Self waiting to be read (romance, story). As intermediary observer, Wolf intuitively resents this nontranscendent midspace, envying not only the illuminated interiority of romance (first cognitive zone) but also the fantasy-circumference into which the inward book-gaze of the old woman is ultimately transformed (third cognitive zone). Wolf resolves this double desire by allowing an idealized version of his own life and mythology to merge with the fictional projections of the reading woman and unfolding book. This etherealization of the Self into pure exteriority (aura) once more highlights the acute mental crisis produced by Wolf's inability to coordinate the sense of the outer Self with the sense of the inner Self. Unable to relate his outer Self to his own inner Self, he relates it to what is symbolically represented as the inner Self of another person. This is an inflowing motion: Wolf in the street identifying himself with the small circle of light around the book. Yet an equally pertinent countertide exists, and in this outflowing movement, the book moves outward to Wolf as its subject matter is imagined to be himself. The intermediary world of the Ego is represented by the prosaic streets of Blacksod as well as by materialist science, so that in a larger sense the chief polarization is one between art and science:

The book she read was obviously, from its shape and appearance, a cheap story; but as Wolf stared in upon her, sitting there in that commonplace room at midnight, an indescribable sense of the drama of human life passed through him. For leagues and leagues in every direction the great pastoral fields lay quiet in their muffled dew-drenched aloofness. But there, by those two pointed flames, one isolated consciousness kept up the old familiar interest, in love, in birth, in death, all the turbulent chances of mortal events. That simple, pallid, spectacled head became for him at that moment a little island of warm human awareness in the midst of the vast non-human night.

He thought to himself how, in some future time, when these formidable scientific inventions would have changed the face of the earth, some wayward philosopher like himself would still perhaps watch through a window a human head *reading by candlelight*, and find such a sight touching beyond words. Mentally he resolved once more, while to Mr Valley's surprise he still lingered, staring in at that candlelit window, that while he lived he would never allow the beauty of things of this sort to be overpowered for him by anything that science could do.

He submitted at last to his companion's uneasiness and walked on. But in his heart he thought: "That old woman in there might be reading a story about my own life! She might be reading about Shaftesbury town and yellow bracken and Gerda's whistling! She might be reading about Christie and the Malakite bookshop. . . .

"How unreal my life seems to be growing," he thought. "London seemed fantastic to me when I lived there, like a tissue of filmy threads; but . . . good Lord! . . . compared with this!—It would be curious if that old woman reading that book were really reading my history and has now perhaps come to my death. Well, as long as old women like that read books by candlelight there'll be *some* romance left!"

His mind withdrew into itself with a jerk at this point, trying to push away a certain image of things that rose discomfortably upon him—the image of a countryside covered from sea to sea by illuminated stations for airships, overspread from sea to sea by thousands of humming aeroplanes!

What would ever become of Tilly-Valley's religion in *that* world, with head-lights flashing along cemented highways, and all existence dominated by electricity? What would become of old women reading by candlelight? What would become of his own life-illusion, his secret 'mythology,' in such a world? . . .

And as he walked along, adapting his steps to his companion's shambling progress, he indulged in the fancy that his soul was like a vast cloudy serpent of writhing vapour that had the power of overreaching every kind of human invention. "All inventions," he thought, "come from man's brains. And man's soul can escape from them, and even while using them, treat them with contempt—treat them *as if they were not!* It can slip through them like a snake, float over them like a mist, burrow under them like a mole!" (VIII, 181–82)

In the transition from *Ducdame* to *Wolf Solent,* two remarkable things have happened. The first is that the Powys novel has suddenly acquired a totally different and infinitely more satisfying aesthetic dimension. The second is that the novels are henceforth dramatically propagandistic, advocating a counterculture similar in emotional-philosophical content to those later countercultural movements of the late sixties and early seventies.

In fact, I think that these two significant changes in the Powys novel are interrelated, a view that may seem surprising and controversial. How can the programmatic increase the aesthetic? Are these not antagonistic, if not mutually exclusive? Does not the stress on a "message" and on the materiality of propaganda lessen the aesthetic thrust of a work that ultimately must come to be evaluated as an artifact? There are two answers to this. The first is that the very intensity with which John Cowper plunged into the battle between the dextral and the sinistral allowed him to stop thinking consciously about achieving various aesthetic effects. All the pre-*Wolf Solent* works are basically dishonest and inauthentic, the writer always consciously manipulating the way things look, giving them the appearance that he thinks will guarantee their favorable reception. By this I do not mean that Powys became a less self-conscious writer. I mean that he shifted his attention, as it were, from form to content—and *because* of this shift, ironically, he finally achieved a satisfying form. Put bluntly, he finally had something to *say,* and the very heat generated by the urgency to convey his vision of things produced a certain aesthetic economy hitherto lacking in his writing.

The second answer to the problem of the compatibility of propaganda and aesthetic validity involves more complex lines of argument, all related to the relationship between writing and value judgments. There are levels of credibility for art, and there are additional complexities in these levels of credibility for novelistic art, since literature is art but also more than art—a fact that holds true especially for the novel. Furthermore, these levels of credibility are not unrelated to time: in other words, not unrelated to the time and age in which a novel or a work of criticism is written.

There are two very low levels of credibility: at one extreme, art for art's sake (literature as pure form); at the other extreme, literature as pure meaning, as a mere vehicle for sociopolitical "content." All higher levels of literary credibility involve complex, multidimensional interactions between these extremes. Yet, to come to terms with the unique achievement of John Cowper Powys, we must appreciate the particular nature of his message: that our society is moving toward a planetary situation in which civilization itself is threatened. No! not only civilization. Life! All life! The problem of whether literature should foreground value judgments or not is therefore largely a nonsensical question, since, with our progress through historical time into the nuclear age, literature has in itself come to *be* a value judgment. Literature, in the era of accelerating life-denial, is in itself a system of values through being a system of life. And although Powys wrote in a pre-atomic age, it is clear that all the various forces that have placed us where we are right now are forces he analyzed and feared, whether exteriorized in social malice and military science or primordially conceived as divided consciousness. By this line of argument, I am merely emphasizing that insofar as literature is a dimension of life, and insofar as the aesthetic is a dimension of being, the value judgments central to the Powys world are intrinsically of ultra-aesthetic significance. The idea that life is worth preserving is in itself aesthetic. It is aesthetic as value state-ment, but it is also aesthetic even as idea. This is one of the reasons why traditional ideas about literary-artistic "successfulness" cannot be applied to the Powys novel without radical qualifications. One implication of all this is of course that the reader unsympathetic to the intensity with which Powys battles on the side of life will largely miss the aesthetic dimension of the Powys novel, since that aesthetic dimension is inextricably fused with that battle. This is nowhere more apparent than in *Wolf Solent.*

From what has just been stated, it will readily be seen that value judg-ments are part of the present critical evaluation of Powys's achievement. If this seems strange, it is mainly so because we have become used to a standard of neutrality in criticism that is not only false but also at bottom theoretically hollow. There are reasons for sharing Edward W. Said's concern for this sudden silence in criticism. Is this silence perhaps an integral element of the cultural shift that John Cowper tried to define in *Wolf Solent* and in the works following it?

> Every great age of literature and criticism has had organic ties with a dominant value system of some sort. All critics of the past have held fairly explicit views of man, his destiny, his goods, goals, nature. In other words, literary criticism has always contained some sense of its place in the process of human history. For reasons I cannot quite articulate, this is not true of contemporary critical discourse. In most instances it is disturbingly quietistic. . . . That all this should be taking place as well in a world of exacerbated political and economic crisis increases one's wonderment at the ideological and evaluational silence of criticism today. What is the meaning of such silence? Need such silence be?[9]

In the nonfictional works of the 1930s, we see Powys elaborating the tidal element. In *The Meaning of Culture* (1929), he mentions the dangers involved in a unilateral development of either inflow or outflow. Only in conjunction can both movements give culture "its dynamic secret of growth" (VII, 129). It is dangerous always to bring mind and body into a too intimate relationship, for such intimacy may harden the Self into a solid nucleus. Often an entirely different gesture should be used, one that causes the Self "to dissolve into a floating vapour" (VII, 128):

> Such a *rapport* is invaluable only as long as we are banking up our identity against invasion; but when it becomes a matter of extending the circumference of our universe a completely opposite method is required. Then, as I have hinted, it is necessary to turn our inmost ego into a cloud,[10] a mist, a vapour, a nothingness, a pure receptivity. . . . There must, in fact, be always a systole and diastole in these mental movements. . . . Here . . . the great centripetal-centrifugal law of one's spiritual pulsebeat makes it inevitable that every rapture of humility shall be followed by a corresponding rapture of self-assertion. (VII, 129–30)

This emphasis on the double tidal nature of the moving Self is an equally prominent feature of *In Defence of Sensuality* (1930). Here the writer outlines a solitary stoicism that ironically undercuts the spectacular title. Again we notice how the stream of consciousness in the Ego is superceded by the pulsation in the Self. The ever-present thought of death is "a tide-pulse in the sea of eternal non-consciousness" (III, 100). The thought of death and nonbeing activates the Self both as inflow and outflow:

> It is as though . . . the icythyosaurus-ego on its mud-bed [the inner Self] . . . was diffused . . . far beyond the normal circumference of our awareness of place and hour. It is as though our consciousness could draw on the consciousness . . . of the great stellar system itself!—until we reach a point where the vast Not-Self is flung further back. We *are* the stellar "universe" when he draw on this magnetic power, and the "objective universe" of our defiance is compelled to withdraw itself to remoter coasts of existence. (I, 33)

The tidal theme is continued in *A Glastonbury Romance* (1932) as the novel moves toward its grand finale. It is the tidal expansion of the mighty Atlantic up along the Bristol Channel that eventually ends the direct and indirect operation of the Ego in Glastonbury. It ends all hopes of a capitalist, anarchist, communist, or mystical utopia as well. Yet the tidal patterning is also an inherent quality of things that unfold on a smaller scale in the novel. In Nell Zoyland, there is a tidal motion of the mind moving across "the ebb and the flow of her woman's moods" (XI, 300). Similar fluctuations sweep across Mary Crow. Walking with John on a sunny Saturday in August, after the Glastonbury pageant, Mary comes to question the enraptured man's claim that all happiness depends on contrasts. This world of contrasts and duality is perhaps still essentially the world of the Ego. The Self ought to be able to transcend such duality—both as inner Self and as outer Self. Thus Mary sometimes gets the feeling "that there's a world, just inside or just outside *this* world, where these opposites that are so hard to understand, lose their difference altogether" (XX, 628). The doubleness of this tidal possibility is also finely conveyed in Powys's fictional spatializations of pleasure and pain in *A Glastonbury Romance*. As John Crow limps across Salisbury Plain toward Stonehenge on his way from Norfolk to Glastonbury, the subjective phenomena of inner experience merge with the objective meteorological events in outer reality. Eventually it becomes impossible to know if mental patterns are being formed by electrophysiological brain events alone or by an unearthly interaction between mind and reality. In a suggestive treatment of this dualism, Powys evokes a complexity in which causal realities can be seen in operation from without as well as from within. As in *The Brazen Head,* a rusty brown color is associated with evil (*B*, IX, 120–21). The subjective world of pain now blends with the objective world of color, so that the exhausted traveler looks upon pain as color and upon color as pain. The radiating center of this color is the spot in the horizon where the sun has disappeared. This merges with the radiating center of pain, a spot in John's brain. As he appears to follow the sun westward into crepuscular extinction, John senses the spatial quality of this complex epiphenomenon as a centrifugal radiaton from inner Self to planetary circumference. But he also senses it as the centripetal suction of an antisun. This draws him cruelly toward a central nothingness where even color seems to collapse into murky dissolution:

The sky around those points of light was neither grey nor black. It was a colour for which there is no name among artists' pigments. But the man limping across Salisbury Plain gave this colour a name. He named it Pain. Where it reached the climax of appropriateness was in the west towards which the road was leading him. Here there was one fragment of sky, exactly where the sun had vanished, that to the neutrality of the rest added an obscure tinge—just the faintest dying tinge—of rusty brown. This low-lying wisp of rusty brown was like the throbbing pulse from the pressure of whose living centre pain spread through the firmament. Walking towards the West Country was like walking towards some mysterious celestial Fount wherein pain was transmuted into an unknown element. . . .

A dull, beating thud was proceeding from some portion of his body and travelling away from it into the darkness. He felt like a run-down clock which could not be hindered from a meaningless striking. Whether this thudding came from his heel, his heart, or his head he could not tell. It might, for all he knew, come from that rusty-brown place in the western sky. (III, 94–95)

The centripetal/centrifugal throbbing of this brownish anticolor is matched by the hypnotic expansion/contraction of an unearthly bluishness in Miss Elizabeth Crow's little house in Benedict Street. A massive conglomeration of bluebells seems to radiate a compact blueness. At the same time, the magnetic weight of this blueness appears to create a blue gravitation. In this implosive blueness, the spectator becomes drawn toward a compact center. The crystal/aura dichotomy can be seen in operation here in the tension between the translucent solidity of the glass bowl and the "opaque essence" of the blue "cloud." Like the Salisbury horizon, the bowl creates a typically Powysian geometricity through its rotundity:[11]

On this table was a huge glass bowl filled with an immense, tightly packed mass of bluebells. The gorgeous blueness, a deep Prussian blue mingled with blotches of purplish colour, rose up like a thickly packed cloud of almost opaque essence out of this bowl of heavy-drooping blooms and expanded and expanded till its richness of tint attracted towards it and seemed utterly to absorb all other coloured things in the room. (XVII, 507)

Moving on to consider Powysian tidalty as it comes over in *Autobiography* (1934), we find the author speaking in the very last pages about "the two great electric currents" of his life: "first the gradual discovering and the gradual strengthening of my inmost identity, till it can flow like water and petrify like a stone; and second the magic trick of losing myself in the continuity of the human generations (XII, 651–52).

This important statement clearly indicates the writer's consciousness of something not well understood in *The Complex Vision:* that it is necessary to develop the dual capacity of moving into the outer as well as the inner Self. Crystal is liquid transparency and diminutive solidity, which translates into the water/stone simile ("flow like water and petrify like a stone"). We glimpse the inner Self as crystal. At the same time, the words "flow" and "petrify" denote opposite inner processes: "flow" could mean inflow, but it seems rather to suggest the outflow into the "continuity of the human generations" that stands here for the outer Self.

Situated as it is by the sea, *Weymouth Sands* (1934) ought to be the tidal work par excellence within Powys's literary edifice.[12] And in some ways it is. There is an important set of macropolarities in this novel: wet sand versus dry sand, sand versus stone, and so on. All these tensions are conveyed as movements centrally related to the vital distinctions between inner Self and outer Self. The novel suggests a psychic synthesis enlarging our mental horizons by bringing aspects of our divided thought into vital interplay. The central contrast is that between Sand and Stone. Both of these can be either centre or circumference, the end product of the centripetal or the end product of the centrifugal. Stone is circumference as Portland stone, as geological ur-matter, Earth, Globe, the solid All. But stone is also center, the private crystal, the secret solidity, the pebble that Jobber Skald desperately holds on to. He clutches it in his pocket, and the pressure he exerts on it is the pressure needed to compress awareness into the integrality of identity when danger seems overwhelming. He can only do without the pebble when Perdita Wane becomes his for life. Then it is a woman, rather than stone, that becomes the tangible evidence of the reality of the inner Self. Before this consummation, the lovers are torn by the great cosmic tide. As they walk together along the gray wall of massive oolite, the reader is made to sense that its mass is "the weight of all the in-breathings and out-breathings of the orbic motion of the world, of the systole and diastole of space and time . . . of all the out-breath and the in-breath of the universe" (V, 163). Later, as Magnus Muir squats on a sleeper, staring at four lights, there is a centrifugal sense of the soul leaving the body, remaining connected only "by a leash" (IX, 312). But there is also an inward-moving quasi-physical feeling—the sensation of looking down and in toward the central point from which the eerie departure was originally made. As so often happens in the works of Powys, the polarization of the centrifugal and centripetal becomes a vehicle for a finely wrought antagonism between physicalism and mentalism. At mid-distance there are four lights: one from Curly's house, one from the Lodmoor hut, one from the White Nose, and one from a ship off Redcliff. Two main forces come into operation. The first emphasizes physicality. Squatting in a fetal position, Magnus is a "flesh-covered skeleton" crouching like a lean ape or self-absorbed Neanderthal man. He feels the "brittleness of his skull," "the bone-points of his buttocks," each "bony contour" and "fibrous hollow" in his biochemical structure (IX, 313). The second force works as "de-carnation." It does not take Magnus from this luminous mid-distance to a central nucleus, to a corporeal immobility, to a million-year-old ancestry suggesting primeval slime. Instead, this second force takes Magnus centrifugally out to a sense of aerial weightlessness. He becomes like a fifth point of light "travelling

through immeasurable gulfs of empty, black air." Thinned out, freed
from gravitation, he becomes a speck of matter journeying through eternity—perhaps even something lighter: the immaterial idea of such an
eternity, a winnowed self-awareness contemplating its own fleeting ideality.

This Powysian macropolarity between physicalism and mentalism is
given central significance in *A Philosophy of Solitude* (1933), a work
intimately affiliated with *The Art of Happiness* (1935) in its apprehension
of the gulf between happiness and unhappiness as the most significant of
dividing lines (*PS*, III, 80). In *The Art of Happiness*, Powys associates the
"Ichthian" act with the shuddering orgasms of sex and death: "there is the
same 'inbreathing' and 'outbreathing' . . . the same intensification of
identity and dispersing of identity . . . the same half-creation and half-
discovery of a cosmic focus-point" (I, 30). Here extreme compression *is*
extreme dispersal and vice versa. The periphery seems to be attainable
through an inward journey. This journey takes us into a central tunnel
that somehow fans out to circumference in four-dimensional space. Paradoxically, the spontaneous sense of floating out is to be achieved through
a self-induced contraction:

> But the point is that the relaxed and passive kind of happiness, when
> you float on the ocean of the exterior cosmos and allow its magical
> currents to flow through you, is a kind of happiness that can be reached
> deliberately and enjoyed deliberately when once you have acquired the
> trick of "pulling yourself together." (I, 12)

In other words: when you move from the second (cognitive) zone inward
to the first zone, you are already on your way to the third zone outside
both of them.[13]

As is suggested by its title, *A Philosophy of Solitude* wants to deal with
the first cognitive zone. Man must strip himself of superfluities (I, 26).
An "anti-social type of mystical thinker" like Laotze (I, 18), John Cowper believes it is necessary to develop the mental ability to escape from the
psychology of the Ego. This act of the mind depends on an effort corresponding to the effort required in learning a foreign language (V, 144). *A
Philosophy of Solitude* is tidal like all of Powys's works, emphasizing
outflow as a product of inflow. The writer does, to be sure, glorify
solitude, stating that a "happiness-barometer" would register greater happiness in the raptures of the solitary walker than in the merriment of the
lively gathering (V, 168). He claims to have seen a wounded kitten "gather
itself together to die with a dignity and decency worthy of the death of

Caesar" (III, 99)—an image that certainly suggests the first cognitive zone both in its emphasis on contraction and on animal primordia (recall the ichthyosaurus). With approval, Powys mentions Nietzsche's well-known thesis that most great human thinking comes into being through the process of walking in solitude (V, 147). These notions suggest mental contraction at first. On closer examination, however, they suggest an equal amount of expansion. Country solitude provides "a wide-open spacious gateway into the receding Unknown" (IV, 114). If solitude has given you the impression that you have shifted from sinistral to dextral awareness, then you can test this by asking yourself whether you are aware of the wind or not. If you are not aware of the wind it is because you are out of touch with the third cognitive zone, "the primeval grandeur of the world" (IV, 108). In other words, the first cognitive zone *is not* really the first cognitive zone if it is remote from any consciousness of the third zone. If "you take the wind for granted," you are alone with yourself in a false, uncreative, and sterile way. We can see this interdependence between the first and third zones even in the idea of Nietzsche's solitary walking. For the central sensation of this type of experience is an interaction between center and circumference, a "delicate adjustment of foreground and background" (V, 147). The magic of the walking process is not its linearity, as might be expected. At right angles to this linear progression (the paradigm, we may recall, for the motion of Ego) is the vaster and totally different movement between the first and third zones. This different movement comes about through the different relative speeds of foreground (first zone) and background (third zone): the latter changing so slowly as we walk that alteration is quite minute; the former being transformed every second we move.

The Powysian ecstasy, then, does not simply require soiltude as contraction but solitude as the first phase in a tidal motion bringing the ebb of personal solidity into vital contact with the flow toward "the great planetary processions and cycles." *A Philosophy of Solitude* wishes deliberately to move away from the intellectual structure of traditional philosophical investigations, since conventional philosophy has seldom, if ever, dealt with the interaction between ordinary consciousness and altered consciousness. No important metaphysical work has explored the nonecstasy/ecstasy interface, "the real crucial twinges of our daily endurances and the real delicious transports of our daily releases" (V, 135).

John Cowper Powys, in fact, is working toward a synthesis made significant by the manner in which Western culture has compartmentalized the two modes of awareness. Religion has looked upon ecstasy as its private domain, so that philosophy has come to concern itself with the other "half" of consciousness.

In *A Philosophy of Solitude,* therefore, Powys tries to articulate the experience produced when the contraction from second to first zone suddenly turns into an expansion from first to third zone. The first phase (ebb) becomes associated with physicalism: you become more acutely conscious of your personal solidity, as Magnus did squatting on the tracks in *Weymouth Sands* and sensing a skeletal concrescence. But the second phase (flow) is in some ways a more advanced form of selfsation, and it brings with it a sense of release from materiality. One can say that one of John Cowper's centermost ambitions was to articulate this vital phase of human awareness without employing the traditional rhetoric of church dogma. The conventional Western doctrines of established religion tend to be permeated by a quasi-platonic idealism that isolates the third cognitive zone in a psychological utopia where it is kept out of touch with the first cognitive zone. Therefore, it can be said that Powys's emphasis on physicality (we recall the enema immediately succeeding the Grail) and interiority does not primarily reflect a movement away from the "immateriality" of aura but, rather, a crucial concern for anchoring the sense of the beyond in the sense of the "in here": even making these two metaphysically coextensive.

A Philosophy of Solitude sports numerous passages that evoke quasi-religious feelings of moving out into an ethereal realm released from time, space, and materiality. In the moment of selfsation we can sense that our life is but one existence within a countless number of dimensions, and the circumference of the outer Self is felt to be a certainty expanded beyond the material rotundity of the entire astronomical universe (VI, 195). In this mood we feel that there are levels of being beyond visible reality (II, 46). This notion reflects the important motif of transcendence; but we are dealing with a double transcendence, implying a movement not only beyond the Ego but also beyond the inner Self. The crowd or social gathering in the Ego's City is too large for the Self. The pressure of the crowd throws the Self into an extreme seclusion. Yet, on the other hand, the crowd is also too small for the Self. In a romantic twilight mood, the Self expands to something more voluminous than the merry crowd, and this cosmic state of mind evokes the feeling that innumerable other humans are sharing this twilight-ecstasy. Thus its reality becomes not only something abstract, private, and ideational: the "strange blueness at the window" also signifies an enlargement of the human. The outer Self is now an "undulating sea of spaciousness," and far from being exclusive or contractive, this situation enables all individuals to move with it into the largest circumference, to escape "to the ocean-banks of its own widest horizons" (V, 170). Here Powys also points to the disuse of the word "soul" as a sign of mental fragmentation in the West (II, 48). This word has stood for dextral awareness, and this mode of awareness does not simply disappear from humanity because it has been inadequately replaced (through Freudianism, behaviorism, and so on) by a spurious set of pseudoscientific categories. Dextral awareness continues to be awareness, and as awareness it is reality, "the unity of this conscious spirit, which is at once the center and circumference of our whole being" (II, 49).

It is perhaps in *Owen Glendower* (1940) that Powys gives the outer Self its most exciting fictional representations. Owen is the Powys hero with the most finely developed ability to exteriorize consciousness as a means of enhancing self-control. His "unearthly self-conquest" (XVIII, 709) is matched by his wife's self-control (XIX, 744). The prince admires this quality in others, and he is astounded by Father Rheinalt's self-possession (XIX, 766). Occasionally, however, the outer Self seems to become governed by an autonomous will that pays little attention to the inner Self. Owen has broken Hywel Sele's back across a fallen tree after being ambushed by his gamekeepers, and he has buried the treacherous baron alive in a hollow trunk. Later, when he projects his consciousness centrifugally, so that it reaches the forests, he finds that there is a centripetal countermovement that speaks to his interior Self with the dark knowledge of its exteriority: "But the worst of having a soul like his which could *exteriorize* itself, or at least could imagine it could, was that . . . this wandering soul of his kept sending him messages from its perch on the hollow tree" (XIII, 440). Once again we notice the thought-bird imagery and how the narrator stresses his skepticism regarding the objective reality of such an externally projected aura.

Mortal Strife (1942) develops the notion of tidality by refining themes clarified in the nonfictional works of the 1930s. From these earlier works we recognize the rejection of the primacy of the idea of love in favor of the idea of the sensation of loneliness (IX, 151; I, 8–9). Each man lives in his "*separate* island fortress" (XIII, 227), and in the book's war propaganda this interior compactness is associated with the notion of Britain as an island fortress: a separate segment in the multiverse, a segment that will not only lose its identity and its status as the home of individualism in the case of a German victory but that will also surrender the overarching concept of the multiverse itself in that event by becoming absorbed into Hitler's Block-Universe. In *The War and Culture* (1914), we can see that Powys, even in his phase of open commitment to communism (I, 10), detests the idea of an all-powerful state erasing the colorful diversification of life (II, 24).

The idea of the multiverse is central to *Mortal Strife* (III, 41–42; V, 80;

X, 178). Despite the fact that Powys remains hostile to Ego-ism, which he calls "malicious individualism" (I, 16), despite his rejection of a competitive life-style (VIII, 131), and despite his contempt for a false Carlylian form of introversion, which he calls "auto-sadistic puritanism" (VII, 112), he eventually accepts capitalism as a tolerable alternative to the totally intolerable idea of totalitarianism. The ongoing war forces John Cowper to twist a number of his arguments and abandon some of the principles held high in *The Complex Vision* and elsewhere—and he is not unaware of this. How do his ideas of equality fit in with the idea of British capitalism? Indeed, how does the idea of noncompetition fit in with the idea of capitalism? Clearly they do not. This inconsistency is the weakness of *Mortal Strife*, but it is a weakness that should be seen in the light of the overtly propagandistic quality of the writing and in relation to the book's strength: its refinement of the description of the act of premeditated ecstasy.

Having to side with the established order of things (which is an extremely anti-Cowperesque state of affairs), Powys must find arguments to support a social system from which he had fled in his younger days and which he had refuted in his important writing. Thus the manner in which British capitalism suddenly emerges as something positive is somewhat arbitrary, if not dishonest. This shift is accomplished by Powys's device of linking the idea of the British with the idea of the individualistic, and the idea of capitalism with the idea of the multiverse. The British are "Pirate-Anarchists." If capitalism is the "daughter of Chaos" (I, 18), it nevertheless contains a recklessness that we have already seen positively evaluated in Richard Storm's confrontation with the rawness of New York in *After My Fashion*. Clearly, the archetypal Englishman in *Mortal Strife* is to a large extent a generalized projection of the personality of John Cowper himself: the war is fought for "the right to be careless and reckless and lazy and inefficient and solitary and absent-minded" (X, 171).

As I have already pointed out, communism is for Powys no longer the positive force it was back in *The War and Culture* and *The Complex Vision*. In *Mortal Strife*, it is on a par with capitalism: both are tolerable systems (until the war is over) simply because fascism is so much worse (X, 169). Powys can only give credibility to his argument by interrupting his antitotalitarian propaganda with asides informing the reader that he is well aware of the darker sides of laissez-faire economics. The first of these asides states his desire for a policy in support of poor ordinary people and against the wealthy few who should be "prodded and pruned and pinched" to the maximum (I, 10).

It is crucial to observe how Powys grounds his philosophy of equality on psychological introspection rather than on any preconceived prejudice or assimilated doctrine. In fact, the centermost portion of his philosophy has not changed in the least since the times of *The War and Culture* or *The Complex Vision:* what is new is his choice of political-metaphysical vehicles for his central ideas.

The major insight in *Mortal Strife* is that dextral awareness is something that a future society could place within the reach of most humans, while sinistral awareness (aspects of which we can measure in terms of IQ, for instance) varies from individual to individual. While each individual must enforce an extreme solitude in order to obtain the premeditated ecstasy, the actual experience of the ecstasy itself is supra-individual in its very being. In ecstasy there is a fullness that leaves an afterglow. This afterglow is a manifestation of excess, and in the richness of this excess, the very idea that some humans are to be enriched at the expense of others becomes sordid and trivial: "*All* souls contain *all*. And therefore all souls, because they contain all, are equal" (IV, 62). This, for Powys, is also the central idea of Christianity. Orwell's ironic tour de force in *Animal Farm* that all animals are equal, but that some animals are more equal than other animals, may be inverted into the Cowperism that all people are different, but some people are more different than others. Far from leading to any élitism, this truth results in an interpretation of that superfluous difference as an excess raising the lowest to a minimum level of respectability within the circle of the truly humane. In his excessive difference, Christ redeemed the most lowly: "Every soul is different from every other soul but in the aspect of it where the question of greatness lies there is no difference at all. . . . Below these outer qualities there is no difference. Everybody is a Nobody; and every Nobody is God" (IV, 63). Far from being nonsensical, this statement is in perfect alignment with the overall philosophy of the writer. Christ, for Powys, is part of ourselves (IV, 55). Christ is a sacred aspect of human consciousness, sacred because it removes us from other aspects of consciousness that contain evil and destruction. Because Christ is positive infinity, and because positive infinity is Christ, Christ is an equalizer. In ecstasy all humans are equal because full ecstasy removes relativity. In this way pain is also an equalizer, for pain is negative infinity (IV, 68). In the time of World War II, Powys saw the universalizing potency of pain as a factor that could make individuals aware of dimensions in being that are far removed from the sphere of the worldly and acquisitive.

There are strengths in *Mortal Strife* that sometimes make it seem Powys's most important extrafictional work. These surface when he brings the central ideas of *A Philosophy of Solitude, The Art of Happiness, The Meaning of Culture, The Complex Vision,* and *In Defence of Sensual-*

ity to their ultimate theoretical refinement by giving an ontological dimension to his psychological inquiry. There are, however, already signs of the intellectual sloppiness that blurs the later works, and *Mortal Strife* therefore holds an important position in the Powys oeuvre, being, as it were, both the end of the beginning and the beginning of the end. The intensity with which Powys illustrates the process of "de-carnation" and premeditated trance has a hypnotic quality. Four different objects anchor the minds of various war-harassed individuals: a familiar pattern on a carpet, a picture of a young man in uniform, a scrap of cloth caught flapping on some wire, the hairless belly of a dead dog bobbing up and down in the water in which it has drowned (IV, 57–58). These object have a significant psychological status—but also a crucial ontological vibrancy.

The chief achievement of *Mortal Strife* is its delineation of the limitations of sinistral awareness and of the superior quality of dextral awareness. In its extreme rationalism, sinistral thinking can never rid itself of duality: "Now what our rationalists are simple-minded enough to imagine as 'nothing' is a very different thing from the real and absolute nothing. The real and absolute nothing might be anything; that is the point" (VII, 113). The dextral capacities are just as intellectual as the sinistral capacities. Powys makes it clear "that in addition to our logical and scientific reason we possess other organ[s] of intelligence" (V, 85). Because dextral awareness opens up the humblest human being to the sense of the miraculous (through the altered state of consciousness), this mode of intellection is transcendental as well as egalitarian. Thus "the portion of our individual soul which is most common and most equal is the only portion that has a chance of surviving death" (VI, 94). Powys here makes a crucial connection between the idea of quality and equality (X, 168). The extraordinary quality of the dextral moment facilitates an appreciation of the ultimate equality of all organisms. Moreover, this transcendentalism is linked with the idea of the multiverse: the passage from one section of the multiverse to the next automatically implies some transcendence or other. Part of our life exists outside the present dimension (X, 169).

The difference between sinistral and dextral awareness is given its greatest significance in chapter 6. While sinistral intelligence is adapted "to the crudest, lowest, and most unimportant aspects of the Dimension which hems us in," dextral awareness is something more than merely the rationality of statistical man (VI, 95). Dextral intelligence does not contain the element of insanity and fanaticism present even in the most sober rationalism. The dextral faculties are holistic, activating "our whole nature," and they suggest the idea that a portion of our being may survive death (VI, 95). This idea is also connected with the notion that the dextral moment is one where we sense the supra-individual in the sense of race-sensation (IX, 142, 148). This holism can never mean pantheism, however, since pantheism implies the idea of a (spiritualized) Block-Universe, a seamless cosmos with no multiplicity of dimensions (XI, 199). Instead, this holism is connected with a centripetal act of the mind. In this act, which takes place in the altered state of consciousness, sense impressions and the different sensory channels themselves are brought within the unifying control of a complex, overarching system of awareness. The third cognitive zone is in operation in the sense that we have the feeling that the sensations "come from far away" (IX, 148). And this is essentially a situation of inflow, since, collected and synthesized in the first cognitive zone, the sensations are held present in the center, "all in one":

> I am speaking of those less obvious but not less transporting pleasures which have nothing to do with our erotic feelings or with satisfying hunger or thirst. I am speaking of those sensations that so often seem to reach us . . . through all our senses simultaneously, and that seem to be touch, taste, smell, hearing and seeing, *all in one*. These are the feelings that seem to pass through the very pores of our skin and *yet to come from far away*.
> *Inland* they are generally connected with the movements of the clouds or the wind or the feel of the air;[14] *on the coast* they are generally connected with the waves. But they reach us so indirectly that in the one case all the sensations of touch and smell and sight can be called up by the sound of a train's whistle, and in the other by the screaming of sea-gulls. (IX, 148)

In *Mortal Strife*, John Cowper Powys bases his polarization of the British and the German on the idea that British culture foregrounds the dextral, while German culture foregrounds the sinistral. Accordingly, the internal relationship between center and circumference is reversed as you move from one to the other. War is the sinistral versus the sinistral. Therefore, the British warrior fights with his circumference ("with our off-moments"; XI, 196), the German with his center. This difference works to the advantage of the British in Powys's view, because the constant centricity of the Continental fighter turns him into an individualized form of the Block-Universe. He becomes centralized and thus acquires the same limitations that centralized government imposes upon itself (IX, 158). In *The War and Culture*, Powys had already suggested that Nietzschean will-to-power is useless when limited to the Ego (I, 14).

Again, tidality is a central patterning device. In centralized man there is no movement, no adequate interchange between center and circumference; in centralized man there is no tide. Centralized man has lost the ability to keep in touch with the vital duality that shapes all life. Without this double movement, we die: "the ultimate life-trick, the ever-repeated life-leap, is to divide in order to rush together" (*MS*, IV, 60). The individual is dichotomous because the cosmos is a divine-diabolical duality. The spring of our life sensations flows "from within, and has to flow outward in order to return full-circle" (IX, 143). In *The Art of Growing Old* (1944), this mutualism of the first and third cognitive zones is described as "this leap-frog of self with self" (IV, 65), and in *Obstinate Cymric* (1947),[15] the cosmic flux is "the ceaseless flow of the vast centrifugal and centripetal currents of our corner of the multiverse" (X, 145). Here, as in *Rabelais* (1948), it is possible to trace a swing toward a less mentalistic and more electrophysiological concept of human awareness. There are now "inter-cosmic gulfs, full of nothing but the swaying backwards and forwards of soulless elements, forces, vibrations, currents, motions, of which we know not the purpose or cause or limit or aim or name" (*Ra*, X, 399).

Passing through the life-flow and "life-ebb" (*P*, VIII, 121) of *Porius* (1951), where the protagonist's second consciousness flaps its wings inside his body while analyzing his thoughts with detached curiosity (I, 14), we come to *The Inmates* (1952). Here numerous manias in the characters mirror some of John Cowper's own mental disturbances. There is here an "ebbing and flowing ocean" of thought always surrounding us (VII, 135), and one of the inmates, John Hush, is troubled by an imaginary difficulty in breathing. To counter this obsession he resorts to a special trick: he starts to breathe very consciously, "making each particular motion of inhaling and exhaling a separate undertaking . . . by continuing his monotone of vocal dichotomy, 'in-out, out-in, out-in, in-out' " (V, 83).

This passage suggests the intimate connection between Powys's awareness of internal, subjective phenomena and his metaphysical abstractions. The breathing of mind and body is the breathing of cosmos. Thus, when the writer turns in *In Spite Of* (1953) to "the tranquil in-breathing and out-breathing of universal nature," his concern with the necessity to blend consciousness with the "thinginess" of reality merely reflects this overall mutuality of the psychological and cosmological (VIII, 255). We are to gain access to our double Self by losing ourselves in trivial objects. This process is tidal, suggesting inflow as well as outflow. The thing must flow into the mind, but the mind must also flow out into the thing, saturating it with thought and subjectivity. To be vitally related to inanimate objects, we must develop the ability to "be absorbed by them, or to hug them to us and absorb them in ourselves" (IV, 108). This inflow/outflow interaction is repeated in *The Brazen Head* (1956), where

Ghosta tells Peleg that each individual soul is like a star. Any one of its radiating points may sooner or later turn into a "life-long road" of infinite interest. Yet there is an equally important inward motion that allows the lovers to exist at the heart of such a life-star. Here they can watch the shadows by their hearth and hear the wind in the chimney and the rain on the roof. In this existential nucleus, they "take to themselves the mystery of everything" (X, 151). Finally, in *All or Nothing* (1960), this inflow/ outflow motif is given its most extravagant cosmological representation in the description of how the lord of the house of Galligathol once directs his magic horn from outer space toward a "minute star." This minute star is the earth itself: " 'My supreme discovery was this power of *intake* in my horn parallel with its *outrush*. . . . What I came to feel was that there was a double energy . . . one of these energies flying outwards and the other diving inwards' " (XIV, 109).

From beginning to end, then, the Cowperverse is tidal. And it is this pervasive patterning that now brings us to consider the final significance of the dynamics of ecstasy.

5
VERTIGO

5.1 The Wheel of Fortune

In *Rodmoor*, Adriano Sorio annoys Baltazar Stork by pointing out how Dr. Raughty moves his head up and down while lighting his pipe. In Sorio's view, the doctor gets a "cosmic ecstasy" from this gesture. It makes him feel that he is "the centre of the universe" (V, 70). This up/down ecstasy is related to the inflow/outflow ecstasy.[1] In trying to establish that this is so, I hope to elucidate what I define as the end phase of Cowperesque will-to-ecstasy.

We have already come into brief contact with the up/down motif. We may recall the forest-of-Tywyn sections from *Owen Glendower* and also, for instance, the moment of Sam's Grail vision in *A Glastonbury Romance*. *In Defence of Sensuality* tells us that the organic urge of the life-sap is "like the thrust, both up and down, of a growing plant" (I, 27), and when Wolf Solent stretches himself out on a grassy slope, he enters "a world of leaves that fell and fell for ever, leaf upon leaf; a world where that which slowly mounted upwards endured eternally the eternal lapse of that which slowly settled downwards" (XVIII, 404).

As I have also suggested, there is no small significance in the interconnection between the post-Grail enema in *A Glastonbury Romance* and the painful sight of the anus-inserted sword in *Owen Glendower*. Both events concern the mutuality of pain and release within an overarching ecstasy. The sacred Welsh sword runs through rump into stomach, and it is this curious combination of the idea of slit/aperture with centrality and penetration that releases the most complex spatialization of altered awareness in the Cowperverse. An elusive or sacred wisdom seems latent in the idea of arriving at the center only by piercing a *hidden* part of the circumference. We arrive at the esoteric nucleus through the kitchen door of the cosmos (or the psyche), so to speak. One has to pass through the foulest of apertures, and the one most suggestive of the materiality of things, in order to rush to the transparent center where physicalism ceases to mean. We are told that "the whole atmosphere split," when Sam saw the sacred chalice (XXVIII, 939). I think the split and crack imagery in these passages suggests the intensity of the upward thrust of the ecstatic feeling. This thrust is so violent that it seems unlikely that it could have entered the body in a nonviolent manner or that it could be generated from an internal center of stillness. It seems as if some sharp weapon or instrument must have opened a rift. Sam Dekker feels that a gigantic spear is struck into his bowels from below. Consistent with this experience is also the opposite, centrifugal thrust creating *its* desire for aperture, but this time from within. Uncle Able is constipated, and this is no mere private matter—it is "the whole massed weight of the world's tormented flesh . . . labouring towards some release" (XXVIII, 948).

As pseudo-apertures, Mary Crow's nipples become similarly designated as strategic circumference-perforations in *A Glastonbury Romance*. When she suddenly finds herself alone with John, she feels an exultant shudder run quickly through her breasts. Something new and strange stirs in her, shivers "up from the centre of her being to the tips of her breasts" (I, 30). A bit later, when John is fondling her breasts, his wrists under her armpits, the flow of ecstasy is reversed. But instead of saying that it now flows inward rather than outward, the narrator informs us that the "up-flowing wave which she had felt before seemed now to encounter a down-flowing wave. Every conscious nerve of her body seemed to be responding to his hands" (I, 37). This is one of numerous significant passages suggesting that Powys is correct in assuming that ecstatic up-feelings and ecstatic out-feelings are basically one and the same mega-structure in the altered state of consciousness.

This fact becomes invested with special significance when we encounter the phenomenon to be discussed in the present chapter: eversion. Before considering this eversion in terms of the tidal polarities of inflow and outflow, we can examine several cases where the upward/downward tension clearly reveals how the three cognitive zones are involved in all ecstatic inversion. The moment of eversion is a moment when consciousness reaches a high-water mark or a low-water mark. Suddenly the centripetal has transformed itself into the centrifugal simply because it can no longer continue *as* the centripetal. The tide turns. This reversal of the ecstatic current is most suggestively outlined when John Crow contemplates the grin of a dead cat washed up on the muddy banks of the Brue. A descending vertical shaft pierces the planetary sphere. The compound imagery reflects the extraordinary spatial quality of Powysian thought.

The circular triad with the three cognitive zones is the implicit conceptualization underlying this curious cosmic image:

> Below the mud of the Brue there was a bed of clay; below the clay, the
> original granite of the planet's skeleton; below the granite an ocean of
> liquid rock upon which the granite floated; below this again, black
> gulfs of hollow emptiness full of smouldering gases, and down below
> these—as the plummet of John's mind dived and sank—this "down"
> became an "up," and the liquid rock-basis of the "antipodes" of Glas-
> tonbury . . . fumed and seethed and bubbled.
>   But . . . neither inwards nor outwards, from center to circumference
> . . . did the mind of the Earth grow aware of the existence of John
> Crow. (XIII, 358)

This passage finely illustrates how silly it is to take Powys's cosmic imagery at its surface value. While this "mind of the Earth" does contain a
very faint element of polytheism, its real meaning is something far more
complex; it is related in fact to all that has so far been said about interac-
tivity between antagonistic mental subsystems within divided consciousness. Such imagery taken in isolation and by itself looks adolescent
enough—yet when perceived within the integrative "mythology" of the
Cowperverse itself, it becomes quite sophisticated. Since Powys's cosmos
is essentially a vast projection of human consciousness and a vast projection of altered awareness, "the mind of the Earth" becomes a statement
about inner space rather than about outer space.

This cosmic passage is matched by an equally startling one in *The
Brazen Head*—a novel that, curiously, retains much of the crispness of
Powys's earlier imaginative work. In his spiritual intercourse with the
multiverse, Sir Mort tends to imagine that his consciousness is a flint-
arrowed spear. The head of this spear is a dozen times the size of an
ordinary arrowhead and shows an inversion of movement, from expansion to contraction, in its symmetrical outline. It grows wider and wider
for several inches, and then it narrows progressively for the same number
of inches. In this passage, there is no sudden supernatural illumination
that catches the individual off guard, as in the case of Sam's Grail vision
and attendant spear thrust. The spear movement, into the planet and out
from the planet, is conscious and deliberate. First, the centripetal act: Sir
Mort drives his spear consciousness through the planet's mossy surface.
As he descends through successive layers of earth, he sees roots and
worms and stones. Going deeper, he vividly apprehends "the variously
coloured veins of the different geological strata upon which his soul
impinged as it descended deeper and deeper into the hole it was making"

(III, 53). Finally, he listens to the animal-vegetable intercourse of various subterranean organisms. In the centrifugal countermovement, Sir Mort pulls himself out of the spear hole and shoots himself out into the planet's aerial envelope. His ingoing trajectory has brought him into intimate contact with the most minute aspects of organic life—he can understand a subhuman "earth-mould language." Now, in his outgoing voyage, he takes care to avoid every possible collision with the inorganic blocks and boulders of interstellar space, hoping to experience the ultimate sensation of pure nothingness.

At this point in our exploration of the Powys world, it becomes necessary to consider how the writer views the Ego/Self duality and the inner-Self/outer-Self dichotomy in relation to his ideas on human and planetary evolution.

We have already glimpsed this theme in the notion of the ichthyosaurus beast (subhumanity) and the ichthyosaurus god (superhumanity). In a sense, John Cowper Powys is an optimist in that he frequently advances the theory of the superman: according to this view, the present dilemmas and unhappinesses of mankind result from the transitional period that we are in. On the other hand, it is quite possible to argue that he is a pessimist. Somewhere way back in the primordial past of early man, something went wrong. From this viewpoint, the Ego/Self cleavage is an "error" in evolution. This notion reflects the ancient concept of the fall and of original sin. *In Defence of Sensuality* imagines the First Cause trying to put right its first "ghastly mistake" (I, 24). This is a more or less universal theme in Powys's writing. In *The Inmates*, this mistake is called "a ghastly cosmogonic blunder" (XI, 181), and in *Up and Out* he seems to be suggesting that the alleged early antagonism between Cro-Magnon man and Neanderthal man underlies a crucial evolutionary bifurcation in our species (12). Also, in *Owen Glendower*, Master Brut feels that the theological fall is

> "in reality simply a wrong turn taken by our remote ancestors. They weren't altogether to blame; for it was only the continuance on this earth of a crack in creation that had begun much earlier, had begun in fact in Heaven. It's because it goes so far back that we feel, as Saint Paul says, that all Nature shares it. Coming down the mountain this very day . . . I felt as I saw a mass of broken rocks and an old twisted thorn that they too were waiting and enduring. Enduring what?" He paused; then deepening his voice with intense conviction, "*Enduring Hell!*" he brought out. (XIII, 454–55)

The cosmos is cracked. It is "a System organised upon a mad substratum of monstrous duality" (*DS*, VIII, 252). Yes! The cosmos is cracked as mind, and the mind is cracked as cosmos. Small wonder, then, that the body itself is outlined as a duality in this vision of eternal difference. We have seen Owen Glendower's bifurcated beard, and to this we can add the recurrent descriptions of man as an "anthropoid biped" (*DS*, I, 57). In such "Forked Radishes" (II, 81), the loss of coordination between one foot and the other comes to suggest a loss of mental integration and a lack of spiritual coherence. Thus, when Rhisiart is shown the bronze sword of Eliseg, he finds that his "legs had suddenly begun to move, apparently of their own volition, and he was walking hurriedly towards the window" (*O*, VIII, 278). In *Rodmoor*, Adrian Sorio discovers that Brand Renshaw has made Linda pregnant and that Brand lacks the slightest feeling of remorse. Sorio strikes Renshaw furiously in a fever of passion. This leads to a nervous collapse in Sorio. He can no longer distinguish between the separate identities of the two important women in his life, Nancy and Philippa. At this moment he becomes divorced from himself—or, more accurately, the veil covering man's inherent dividedness is removed: "He staggered slowly now to one of the chairs, moving each foot as he did so with horrible deliberation as if nothing he did could be done naturally any more, or without conscious effort of will" (XXIV, 404). The action of the novel has moved toward a situation where it rehearses the initial notion of "the eternal barrier in whose isolating power lies all the tragedy and all the interest of life" (II, 25).

We now come to the *spiral*. The spiral is of course the idea of evolution fused with the idea of a circle. And since evolution can mean two things in Powys, we encounter two opposite types of spiral. When evolution means the negative process of merely expanding the cosmic ur-rift, there is a negative spiral. When, on the other hand, evolution means moving into a new phase transcending our present state of dividedness, there is a positive spiral. We are now concerned with "the whole great Spiral movement of civilization; that movement which is always *returning upon its advance*, but never quite back to its latest restart" (*AGO*, X, 188).

Our further analysis now requires a crucial understanding. In a situation of confluence, there are two entirely opposite possible outcomes. If there is to be continued evolution, man must discover "how to reconcile these two 'streams of tendency,' so that they shall intensify each other and not cancel or neutralize each other" (III, 53). If there is neutralization, Two will collapse into One. I shall call this *Whirlpool*. Whirlpool is the negative spiral. If, inversely, there is mutual reinforcement and intensification, Two will expand into Three. I shall call this *Gyration*. Gyration is the positive spiral.

The former process creates those "perpetual whirlpools of death" (*ISO*, I, 19) that lead through "this fissure" down to the underlying nothingness of existence, "the yawning void" (*WeS*, XIV, 519). The latter process shows that man is "a link in a long spiral ascent, not a finality" (*DS*, III, 94). Evolution is propelled by conflict. Such conflict has always "driven humanity forward on its long, spiral ascent" (*MS*, XI, 185). The positive spiral moves up into air rather than down into water. In that upstream, the mind spins like "a sort of spiritual helicopter" (*I*, VI, 111), freeing itself from dizzy whirls progressively discharged as its own superimposed aerial foundations. As in Yeats's "widening gyre," the heart of man must always recoil upon nature. This, we are told in *The Pleasures of Literature* (1938), is an absolute necessity, "lest in its struggle towards new points in the circumference it loses touch with the centre" (Introduction, 15).

Whirlpool and Gyration will be treated individually, each in a separate subsection. First, however, and by way of introduction, I would like to give some consideration to instances in Powys's fiction where the writer creates a *spiral equilibrium*. This is a poise achieved through a delicate balance between the centrifugal up-spiral and the centripetal down-spiral, between "the vortices and spirals of Nature's serpentine coils" (*MofC*, VII, 131).

In *Weymouth Sands*, Powys describes a rock platform at the extreme end of Portland Bill from which Jobber Skald and Perdita Wane contemplate the "endless whirlpools and revolving maelstroms of green water" (X, 348). Here the intensified circumfluence is clearly produced by the equal power of two opposite currents. Jobber Skald thinks of the dark, slippery undersea walls of this lethal sea-hole as revolving liquid death-sheets that would suspend their skeletons in a protracted circumrotation until the fishes had picked them clean. (X, 350) He gives Perdita a nautical account that defines the spot as the meeting place of far-drawn tides: one moving eastward, the other westward. Bending down so as to be able to stare right into the swirling vortex, he perceives the confluence of the two water courses, "the current that swept *in*, towards the inmost wall of this sea-level cave, and the opposing current that swept *out*, towards the whirlpools of foam" (X, 349).

The water spirals of this churning liquid expanse are matched in *A Glastonbury Romance* by the invisible air spirals of myth and faith. Glastonbury is one of those history-charged spots from which, in certain epochs, something at once psychic and material "whirls up" (XXIV, 779). Like a volcano, the place has its spasmodic eruptions when invisible forces "emanate from the soil." Here, the semi-erotic, semimystical frustrations of two thousand years that have "pulsed and jetted and spouted" are given a magical intermittent release (IV, 126). At the "brink" of this fount, at the "invisible rim" of this mystical circle, Mary and John feel the "gathering electric force out of the atomic air." Despite "sundering flesh" always striving outward and away toward autonomy, they succumb to this in-going magnetism. In this "etheric atmosphere," a balance is struck between Whirlpool and Gyration (IV, 125). There are "creative energies pouring into" Glastonbury from various cults, but these cults also "sucked their life-blood from its wind-blown, gossamer-light vortex." The electrophysiological eroticism between the Crow cousins becomes a personal love spiral that gathers momentum from the impersonal geopsychic myth spool of Glastonbury itself.

We see the same spiral equilibrium eroticized in *The Brazen Head.* The confluence of the masculine and feminine energy currents creates erotic tension. Out of such an iridescent catherine wheel is born the violent sexual confrontation between Peleg and Ghosta. The blood-shock of the ravishment and fury in Peleg's possessive onslaught sweeps them both "into a whirling vortex of rainbow-irradiated bubbles, tossed into space, as the confluent torrents of their two life-streams became one terrific river" (X, 147).

John Cowper looked upon Jonathan Swift as the greatest and most terrifying of the English writers (*AGO,* V, 88), and it is with his dark vision of humanity that the Powys hero ultimately comes to look at all spiral equilibriums. The most remarkable of these, and the most magnificent, is perhaps the eerie death-vortex in Morg ferch Lug's mill-pond in *Owen Glendower.* The towering circular structure of the immense millwheel creates a hollow gurgling that is neither a roar nor a murmur. Beneath the leprous whiteness of the waning moon and the drifting racks of unwholesome yellowish clouds, the elfish figure of Morg ferch Lug welcomes Owen to the spectral purlieus of Meifod mill. As the prince, accompanied by Rhisiart, approaches this huge rondure, the witchlike wife of Broch-o'-Meifod stops the wheel in order to lay the curse of the turning wheel, the curse of the water and the wind, on this man who is about to take her husband to battle and death. She speaks in old Welsh words, in the language of the old people who have held the land from the beginning before Owen introduced the dualistic metaphysics of good and evil. She tells Owen that the wheel has turned against him (XII, 432). The episode is poised as the centerpiece in the novel, at the halfway house of narrative development. Powys uses the ancient figure of the wheel of fortune to suggest the closing of a cycle of events: a turn for the worse that will have to be sustained until the wheel comes full circle in the phantom gyrations of time.

The wheel of fortune is the tenth card in the Tarot pack. When not reversed, it has secondary meanings beyond the divinatory one just offered above.[2] These secondary meanings are present also here in *Owen Glendower*. The wheel is a mandala suggestive of inner order and psychic wholeness, of interior peace and resolution of guilt. Owen is naturally shocked by the wheel and the curse. Yet at the same time his detached mind is at one with itself and with his fate. There may now be the commencement of a new cycle in his campaign. The knowledge that he is losing his personal control over events is somehow liberating rather than imprisoning; it allows him to stand further back from life, history, and himself, and to view the linear progression of worldly upheavals with serene acceptance. In esoteric phraseology, he is moving now from circumference to hub along the converging spokes that lead to the mystical center.

The Tarot card shows two strange beasts on the wheel of fortune: one descending (Ego), one ascending (Self). Owen now comes to a fuller acceptance of the wheel's motion, though he still shows a faint trace of redundant nonacceptance. Under the cloud-journeying deformity of the lunar disc, Owen pulls his green cloak around his trembling body. Morg ferch Lug has dropped her out-stretched hands after delivering the curse. She has turned away into the swallowing nocturnal hinterland. Left alone for a few seconds with himself, Owen suddenly slips back through the temporal axis of a magic turntable to a far-distant moment in his childhood. His younger brother, Tudor, had once leapt over a sandy tidal stream. Owen had been unable to overcome his fear at this moment, despite his father's encouragement. Now, tugging his bifurcated beard in the year 1400, he drifts far back into the fourteenth century. With hallucinatory intensity he sees what he saw in boyhood: a massive spar of timber from a ship riding on the in-coming tide *and* the out-flowing stream. The object is suspended in an aqueous limbo by this confluence. Like the Portland Bill maelstrom in *Weymouth Sands*, this hypnotic spot is formed by the meeting of two alien streams:

> For no reason, to no purpose, for no intelligible motive, this piece of timber endured the rush upon it from one side of the salt streams and from the other side of the fresh streams; and it was with this object that Owen has identified himself.
> In his boyish shame at not daring to jump, and at hearing his father say, "If you can't jump, Owen my boy, you'd better give it up," he had rather in the way he did still, tried to fling his soul into that ancient fragment. "It just follows the tide," he had said to himself. "For it *has* to float. *It can't jump.*" (XII, 434)

The passage shows Powys's understanding of the inherent interpretative duality in the wheel of fortune symbolism in the Tarot card. To accept the existential circumrotation is in a strange way to accept defeat but not

defeatism. *In* defeat there is victory. The ability to float is born out of the
inability to jump. In the Tarot card, the divine creature whose power
controls the wheel and makes it come full circle is only a squatting mon-
key. This is how we should perceive the Ego from the viewpoint of the
spiral divinity of a more complex understanding (Self).

The noncompleteness of the wheel-curse and of Owen Glendower's
wheel-acceptance is finely adumbrated at this point. Once more back in
his fifteenth-century present, the prince notices a piece of rotten wood
(foster child of that fourteenth-century spar of ship's timber) with a living
plant growing on it. It is being sucked toward the dark whirlpool under
the churning millwheel. Taking Rhisiart's sword, the Welsh prince now
bends over the pool and steers the floating object to their feet. As he
crosses the half open weirs and the treacherous water meadows during
their retreat, his pulse is quickened by the idea of this event. The wood-
plant now belongs to the category of minute organisms that John Cowper
enjoyed "saving" from imminent death on pavements and country lanes.
In its hyphenated organic-inorganic dichotomy, it also belongs to the
group of animate-inanimate entities archetypally represented by the sea-
weed-stone in *Weymouth Sands*. They all suggest a cryptic symbiosis at
the heart of the World Riddle.

5.2 Whirlpool

Morg ferch Lug refers to the prince as Owen the Destroyer. Her curse
outlines him as a conqueror who will succeed as long as he destroys, fail
as soon as he tries to rebuild (XII, 432–33). We see this inherent destruc-
tiveness in Owen once more in the following chapter, when his son
Griffith rushes in with half a dozen spearmen. Griffith hands over a
carefully sealed letter, and as his father proceeds to open the document,
breaking the seals one by one, he takes an evil and electric pleasure in the
actual destruction of sealing wax (XIII, 459). There is immense enjoyment in tearing asunder, *in reducing Two to One*. The exteriority/
interiority of envelope/document is reduced to pure content. The
suffering in the human condition grows out of duality. To escape the in-
dwelling pain of this duality, man may destroy it by foolishly conceiving
a simplistic, reductionist unity. This is Whirlpool, the negative spiral.

The negative spiral is a pervading Powysian concept. In *Atlantis* (1954),
the sea monster Keto is terrifying because of its "swirling whirlpool of
hair—the colour of the absolute void before there was any world at all"
(II, 64), and Nisos feels that Enorches is monstrous because of his enormous mouth with its "whirlpool-like suction" (IV, 124).

This is the physical whirlpool. The social whirlpool is the suicide toward which man is moving. In *The Art of Growing Old*, Powys speaks of the sustained conflict of World War II as "this confused vortex of swirling eddies" (VIII, 131). Almost two decades earlier, he foresees the sordid contemporary marriage of science and militarism that leads relentlessly on to some future "great war" (*DS*, IV, 148). From the viewpoint of our Ego/Self dichotomy, the human individual is *permanently* suicidal: the Ego always desiring the death of the Self, the Self always desiring the death of the Ego. Freud's "death wish" looks quite odd from this perspective. It is certainly clear from Powys's prefatory note to *The Inmates*, where he discusses the extravagance of Jung's followers, that the writer tends to look on the social dimension of the Ego as one of collective insanity. Compared with this disruption, the ultra-individualized world of the solitary madman is one of sanity.

Through the vision of a global holocaust, a scientifically realized lemming suicide, the social whirlpool becomes a cosmic whirlpool. The "lopsided mental activity" of man leads to the "*totalitarian ant-heap*" and the final "biological catastrophe" (*AGO*, X, 176–77). This is the central theme of *Up and Out*, where the notion of a cosmogonic end game and of apocalyptic darkness is the very starting place for the story's action.

This undertone of Hardyesque pessimism is sustained throughout. In *A Glastonbury Romance*, Sam Dekker arrives panting and elated to Whitelake Cottage. He knocks on the door and Nell Zoyland lets him in. He throws down his stick and hat, then hugs his mistress. At this moment, he comes to feel that his heart will burst if the ecstasy is maintained over an extended period of time. But this extended felicity is impossible: "The great suction-process of cosmogonic matter—always waiting to drain up in its huge, blind, clay belly, these rapturous overtones of its foster-children—was soon at work, sucking up the spilt drops of his happiness" (XI, 308).

From this it would appear that life is essentially painful and meaningless—unless of course we resort to some sly mental tricks. Time, then, in the sense of sustained human existence, is pain: the relativistic world of our daily routine is boring. The absolute and the timeless seem to offer the promise of ultimate release; but this, quite clearly, is not so for the author of *Up and Out*. Such a transition from the relative to the absolute and from time to eternity causes the fatal collapse of duality into monality. This, again, is Whirlpool, the negative spiral transforming Two into One. "The Absolute" is a meaningless expression: it can only signify empty space (85). The up-gyration that would turn us away from duality into the multiverse has become the metaphysical swirl reducing us to the universal blank. "How much better it would be," says Squeak in *All or Nothing*, "if our existing universe could be encouraged to grow larger and larger and larger, until the whole of Space was filled up" (IX, 66). But in fact this All would be the ultimate Nothing, as Powys points out in *Mortal Strife:* "The in-sucking vortex of this final development of the Hegelian Universe swallows every horizon, blots out every vista, nullifies every choice" (XIV, 231). In the perfection of this structurally rounded "Hegelian" Absolute, we have lost the cosmic element of surprise. The Block-Universe has no internal tension. There comes a terrible moment for Wolf Solent when he suddenly faces the collapse of Two into One. His erotic and supra-erotic fluctuation between Gerda and Christie seems for a long time to promise the birth of a kind of synthesis. But suddenly, as he watches a tiny beetle climbing up a bending stalk of grass, Wolf glimpses the cosmic indifference. By the field-path leading to Poll's Camp, he leans against a stile and contemplates the fierce sun sinking in the west, toward Glastonbury. The duality of father and mother now also dissolves into uniform indifference. There is no essential difference between "that paternal skull in the churchyard" mocking him cynically from under the plantains and the "iron-ribbed gaiety of his mother" (XI, 262). Made drowsy by the evening murmurs and the strong scent of herb-Robert, Wolf gropes for a single answer to his single life, suspended between the infinite blanks of prenatal and postmortal nonexistence. Christie seems to be the only possible solution, but like the beetle, Wolf will eventually turn back in resignation, only within an inch from the tip of the ur-stalk:

> "To the universe," he thought, "it matters no more whether I leave Gerda for Christie than whether that beetle reaches the top of that stalk! Gerda? . . . Christie? . . . What are they? Two skeletons covered with flesh; one richly and flexibly covered . . . one sparsely and meagrely covered! Two of them . . . that is all . . . just two of them!" (XI, 263)

Up and Out is a title that reflects the ascendental and centrifugal qualities of ecstatic tumescence discussed earlier. Here, time is Two and eternity is One. As the four space travelers move up and out toward the cosmic periphery, they first encounter the horrible duality of time. Then they face the yet more horrific monism of eternity. The section is one of the strangest in John Cowper Powys's writing. It has a negative, inverted Rabelaisian meatiness that is quite stunning in the abstract context of metaphysical categories like time and timelessness. The space ship, a disc of green earth-grass, makes "frantic circular cleavings" in the interstellar gulfs (35). As Time comes into view, it appears gradually, an enormous black slug. Piercing the heart of this Time-monster, the vessel runs through a swallowing central tunnel in its ugly body (36). In this intratemporal navigation, the craft bisects "a delicate, sensitive vital gland in the centre of the Time-slug's midriff, which now was floating, draggled and loose, and dripping with enormous drops of blood, completely clear of the diaphragm to which it had belonged" (37). The travelers, emerging on the other side of Time, are set free into the ultimate void. Yet in this void there is still Eternity. They have passed through the tremendous time tunnel only to encounter something worse.[3] Powys's hatred of such abstractions as Eternity results in a description that emphasizes the *physical* repulsiveness of this metaphysicality; rather, he stresses its physical insufficiency. Ecstasy is color. But this eternity is not color, not ecstasy. It is the static absolute of sinistral-mathematical thought. It is abstraction, not breathing. It is the absolute as Platonic inertia rather than as non-Platonic fluidity. The narrator finds Eternity to be beneath description, not beyond description. To say that (Platonic) Eternity is "colorless" is to flatter Eternity, for "colorlessness" somehow still suggests a certain pallid grayness that is not always aesthetically negative (39). So Powys gives Eternity a corpse-colored, yellowish tone—the color of dirty toilet paper (40).

The monster's aural impact is perhaps even more loathsome than its visual exudation: it produces a ravenous gulping and swallowing and digesting on a gigantic scale, suggesting eternity as an illusion concocted by priests and rhetoricians, feeding on human simple-mindedness (42). Such a Platonic Eternity contradicts the teaching of Jesus, and it has been used throughout history as an instrument of fear to enslave the ignorant (42–46).

The final metamorphosis in the Cowperverse now comes into operation. More than a movement of self-consciousness, it is perhaps rather a transition from self-self-consciousness to consciousness. It corresponds to the Einsteinian concepts of relativity in the realm of physics. In the spatialized psychology of John Cowper Powys, it takes the shape of a cosmic eversion:

> For no sooner were we all four clear of the unspeakable horror, than . . . [it] actually bent down, and after opening a hole in itself as wide as the Milky Way, it deliberately swallowed the dead body of Time! Yes, it swallowed it whole, just as the preachers had threatened us with being swallowed! And it was this swallowing of the corpse of Time that finished Eternity. The thing's whole vaporous covering turned in a second inside out. And beneath *that* covering another covering turned inside out. And after this process, which was desperately shocking to witness had gone on for several minutes—lo and behold! the thing had, so to speak, turned its very self inside out; in other words, *had swallowed itself.* And there before us, where Eternity had been, was simply

a hollow void. The big black hole between being and not-being was gone. (47)

This passage introduces an important motif in the Powys world: the idea of void. We also encounter the pervading concept of self-referentiality, a notion that always severely undercuts the intermittent transcendentalism. It is profitable to compare the time/eternity disembowelment of *Up and Out* with the time/timelessness analysis of *In Defence of Sensuality,* twenty-seven years earlier. In the third chapter, Powys discusses the way in which the altered state of consciousness gives us a feeling of some "overplane or super-dimension" (III, 92). But as so many writers have emphasized, the magic and beauty of this contact with the sense of the eternal acquires its impact through transitoriness. Soon quotidian time sweeps us away again into its master current. Powys therefore rejects the ancient oriental theosophies, since they sacrifice "the many to the one, the personal to the impersonal, the temporal to the timeless." The ecstatic moment of peak awareness actually does not emerge out of the timeless but "out of the conflict between Time and the Timeless." There must be no "obliteration of one side or the other of this perpetual antinomy." When eternity becomes purely self-referential, it is nonecstatic. Using the up/down continuum that we have already seen related to the tidal quality of the Cowperverse, Powys now moves on to contrast his premeditated ecstasy with the oriental manipulation of the altered state of consciousness—or, rather, the oriental failure to manipulate the altered state of consciousness. The eastern indifference to pleasure and pain comes precisely out of this passive encounter with ecstasy. Ecstasy rules man rather than vice versa (VI, 188–89). The consciously induced daydream is a "deliberate 'brown study,' " and as such it "is at the extreme opposite pole from what the Hindus call *Yogi*" (*AGO*, I, 33). Christ is now linked with the ascendental ecstasy, Buddha with the descendental ecstasy. The differentiation is not unrelated to our distinction between Gyration and Whirlpool:

> The ideas of Christ are like dew-wet, rain-drenched daffodil-shoots, of a pale, sickly, perilous green.[4] They have the sweet sharpness and deathly beauty of all young sprouting things pushing up *from* the cold earth. But the ideas of Buddha, with that monstrous life-blasphemy of being indifferent to both pain and pleasure, are like over-ripe medlars sinking, sinking, sinking down, full of the maggots of infinite dissolution, *into* the cold earth. The one set of ideas moves upwards, and their suffering is fecund, like that of women in travail;[5] whereas the other set moves downwards and their indifference is sterile, heavy with the gravitation-pull of death. (*DS*, VII, 219–20)

John Cowper Powys likes eversion. He admires the daring type of spirit that is "prepared to practise any number of *volte-faces*" (*AH*, I, 37). But at the same time he fears eversion, for *"at the back of the self . . . there is a terrifying void, a nothingness at which it is dangerous to stare"* (*ISO*, I, 20). It is quite clear that the later works reveal Powys's efforts to come to terms with the complex discoveries of physics and astronomy. The Einsteinian time-space curvature is a "tricky geometrical cul-de-sac" (II, 28), and the writer feels that a viable psychology-cosmology must somehow live up to the vertiginous implications of the physicist's finite infinity. Such a state of affairs seems to require a further understanding of the interrelationship between inner and outer Self. There is, we have just seen, a vital difference between the Buddhistic implosion and the Christian-Taoist explosion. When the latter is actualized, there is an obliteration of the first cognitive zone, the Self's central "field of operation" (*DS*, VII, 220). This gesture is the Christian "trick of *becoming nothing.*" But at the same time it is impossible to go on expanding forever even in the third cognitive zone. Man is dogged by "a mirror-trick at the circumference of our consciousness" (*AGO*, VI, 104). So, in a sense, there is merely a rebound effect. In a sense, even, the third cognitive zone collapses into the first zone, so that both ultimately merely refer to one another in a false metaphysics where man plays games with himself through the simple act of thought itself. The mouse runs round the conceptual cage and never gets out. The fact that consciousness thinks it understands the world "out there" by constructing a diagram of it only shows that it is the dupe of its own categories.[6] We are "arrested and stopped in our knowing by the very process of knowing, of the inherent nature of our consciousness" (*ISO*, I, 20). This is the problem of self-referentiality.

Yet the point about self-referentiality is that it can be seen in a positive as well as a negative sense. The metaphysical suggestiveness of the end of *A Glastonbury Romance* raises this point somewhat indirectly. It is advanced more drastically in the last sentence of *Autobiography.* Ultimately, man is spiritually self-sufficient. The human soul never really has to move out of itself: "what it finds is what it brings, and what it sees is what it is" (XII, 652). Write a biography of a personified cosmos, and what have you? An autobiography.

So, to advance is to recede. In the introduction to *The Pleasures of Literature*, we are told that the Millennium is essentially a reversion to the Golden Age (13). The Self cannot look forward to the future, for the future is itself. *"It looks forward to nothing"* (*DS*, VIII, 250). The Self's transcendence of time is not transcendence but, rather, merely the actualization of a special holistic temporality—the Self's integral sense of time, dextrotemporality: "Itself is its own Millennium. Its Eternity is its own

Past, its own Present, its own Future, even as it arbitrarily chooses to
decide how, in all three, it shall be." Thus the idea of eternity has to be
canceled—as illustrated by the swallowing of eternity in *Up and Out.*
Eternity is ecstasy provided that ecstasy is an internal reality in the dextral
here and now, not a metaphysical category Platonically beyond us in
suprasensory out-there-ness or theologically beyond us in paradisal
afterlife.

This modern anti-Platonic apprehension of temporality formalizes the
idea of the multiverse at the expense of the universe. Platonic timelessness
is a seamless *Above,* and oriental timelessness is a seamless *In Here.* But
by acknowledging the psychological truth that sinistral and dextral states
of awareness alternate in man, Powys arrives at a coherent vision based
first on the idea of ecstasy and second on the idea of difference between
ecstasy and nonecstasy. This vision sees a world illuminated by trances
rather than trance and a world crisscrossed by endless seams, rifts, com-
partments, canyons, gulfs, clefts, and segmentations. Powys's predilection for the diminutive grows naturally out of this notion of endless
diversification—the more divided a cosmos is, the smaller will be its
constituent elements. Hence his fascination with the very smallest in the
animal world—insects; the very smallest in humanity—the individual; the
very smallest in consciousness—a mood, a passing whim. Hence his
ideological rejection of mass production, big business, and state trusts
(*AGO,* XI, 194), the longing for small self-governing industries and
workshops over the entire world (XI, 199). Hence also the emphasis on
triviality in the sordid or obscure aspects of the workaday world. Seaminess is not only the recognition of the seam but also of the seamy. The
seamy is enclosure, a moment fenced off from everything else. As such it
is golden, open for ecstasy. Because it is enclosure rather than seaminess,
the seamy enclosure is a moment of truth in the Cowperverse. Proust's
madeleine gives an ecstasy through association, while Powys's pigsty
(*WoS,* XXIV, 586) gives ecstasy through dissociation, through being at
one with itself—defining difference and defying universality. At the horse
fair, Wolf Solent runs around among the tents looking for a place to make
water. When he reemerges into the sunshine, he finds himself in a state of
ecstasy. The ammoniacal smell of the place has reminded him of the acrid
smell in the public lavatory on the Weymouth esplanade (IX, 209). Even
the flight of spittle-stained steps is an image reinforcing the altered state
of consciousness. But the point, here, is that such an act of reminiscence
is in no way a prerequisite for trance in the Powys world. The public
lavatory is in itself a typical Powysian ecstasy trigger: it is pocket, cap-
sule, tank, cubic difference. Ecstasy opens the hermetic, while the open
never really lies in wait for ecstasy. The horse fair (IX, 209) represents the

unification of things within an overarching ideality, and Wolf escapes this to find identity in difference, however trivial and however different.

Whirlpool as the collapse of Two into One is also given an erotic dimension in Powys's writing. There are, to be sure, moments when what psychologists call "de-differentiation" acquires a positive sexual meaning.[7] The Grail Fish in *A Glastonbury Romance* is connected with the idea of the mythological Fisher-King. This being is guardian of the Grail by virtue of being a eunuch (*AGO*, XII, 207). Yet more significant—and especially in view of Powys's differentiation between "feminine intuition" and "the masculine logical formula" in *The Meaning of Culture* (VIII, 135)—is the meta-erotic polarization in *The Inmates*, where John Hush becomes obsessed by a single finger. This finger is Powys's intensest concretization of the transformation of Two into One. It suggests "the self-ravishing and self-impregnating sex-organ of some abysmal being in the process of whose eternal spawning the copulating opposites of mind and matter and male and female were as yet undifferentiated" (X, 174).[8]

The idea of Whirlpool as the descent from the vital tensionality of Two into the void of One is also, as I have intimated, an integral aspect of the writer's decline from literary potency in the last two decades of his life. It may be that the elderly John Cowper did achieve a state of fairly permanent mental bliss—a state in which he could enjoy himself by writing down whatever came into his mind. But it seems to me that this bliss has precisely those uniform oriental qualities so vehemently defied in *In Defence of Sensuality*. The writer, quite simply, has grown too comfortable—not too comfortable for life,[9] but too comfortable for literature. The great Powys novel is held together first and foremost by the alternation between ecstasy and nonecstasy. But this differentiation begins to dissolve from *Porius* onward, *The Brazen Head* being a rather remarkable exception. Suddenly, the dextral orgasm is absent, and one wonders whether the writer has actually ceased to have these epiphanies.[10] With this absence, much of the quasi-erotic thrust of the writing is gone. These last works are almost entirely devoid of the passionate preoccupation with woman and nature. The writing loses its sensuality, its mystique, its psychic nerve. There is no reader, no listener: just a voice enjoying itself in a vacuum . . . enjoying a vacuum. This is also Whirlpool.

That this problem of self-referentiality—whether in the writer or in his works—is centrally related to the idea of Whirlpool is very evident, as we see in *The Art of Growing Old*. When the mind flows centrifugally out to visualize the infinity of the astronomical universe, it comes to a dizzy point of intellection where it must suddenly turn itself inside out. But, then, on closer analysis, the inflowing infinity that succeeds this first phase is just as vertiginous. Somehow, man must come to terms with both these motions:

> Opposite to this atomic, or electronic, *false "infinite"* which outwardly surrounds us there is also on *"the other side"* of our conscious self an entirely empty darkness, wherein our thought returns upon itself in a complete void. . . .
>
> With one side of our consciousness we embrace the subtance of an astronomical world, a world which, whether in Space or in Time, or in any mingling of the two, we can neither think of as bounded or as boundless, while with the other side of our consciousness we are confronted by the void of our own thought contemplating itself in a closed circle.
>
> Here, then, is the conclusion of the whole matter. Here is the bedrock *basis* and the rock-bottom *basis* of the problem of Good and Evil. From the flow of the life-tides that culminate in this maelstrom what finally emerges is the *circular swirl* of the Self within the Not-Self, always creating its own private multiverse of world-bubbles, each single one of which reflects its creator. (VI, 104–5)

5.3 Gyration

In *After My Fashion*, the Reverend John Moreton has structured his life around a good/evil, Christ/God duality. In his view, the great cosmic struggle involves a tension between two forces. Richard Storm questions the validity of this belief. He feels that the human mind has not been striving for the victory of one force over the other but, rather, for some reconciliation between the two antagonistic streams. There must, he feels, be "some fundamental unity in things" (V, 76). At this juncture, some plovers, "wheeling in circles" round a neighboring field, make an insistent noise suggesting a suprahuman transcendence of dualistic metaphysics:

> "To my mind the world is an arena of perpetual conflict between these two forces, one of which I renounce and defy; the other I worship in the Mass."
>
> "Pee-wit! pee-wit!" cried the plovers over the old man's head as he concluded this strange statement of heresy; and Richard thought to himself—*On which side would he put the cry of that bird?* (V, 76)

This passage contains a crucial implication because the bird has the same animal neutrality as the tench that Sam Dekker sees glimmering in the Grail chalice. Indeed, it has the same animal neutrality as the butterfly that John Moreton sees in his own death-ecstasy. The Grail itself is the ideal, the quasi-Platonic. Synthesis as idea. But this animal neutrality seems to imply that the transformation from Two to Three may be derived from something implicit in nature itself—from something already "here," in the tissues of the planetary, and not from some act of the mind, some conscious trick that we play on our own soul so as to free it from matter into an elaborate ideality. We shall find that insofar as Gyration is a positive rather than a negative transcendence of cyclicity, it can involve both these radically diverging sources of liberation.

But let us look, first, at John Crow's swirl-ecstasy in *A Glastonbury Romance.* We have already seen several examples of the use of the image of a crack. In this novel, it will be remembered, the crack signifies the collapse of duality. It moves in at right angles to the polarity between the two sides of the First Cause. In this way the power of the First Cause is canceled. A new power takes over, a third force, that is linked up with the idea of Christ. Christ, put simply, becomes Three, and God becomes Two. We have also seen how the motif of the asexual, antisexual, or bisexual sometimes comes to be connected with the idea of this third force: we have the Fisher-King as eunuch, and we have the personal development of Sam Dekker—he gives up his sexual life in order to arrive at the Grail vision through chastity, purification, and asceticism. However, things are somewhat more complicated than this. First, crack imagery and phallic imagery are one and the same (being merely inversions of one another—the crack as invagination); and second, there is an enormous erotic quality to the whole Grail experience. In a sense, Sam has not abstained from the erotic, he has only intensified it. Now I do not intend to give this phenomenon the Freudian label of "sublimation." Sublimation would be a false notion here, because it implies that copulation is a kind of original naturality, and that everything different from that sexual naturality is essentially eccentric, if not perverse. Within such a vision as Powys's, however, the mystical is not a divergent form of the sexual. On the contrary: sexual intercourse is merely a halfway stage on the road to optimal eroticization. *In Defence of Sensuality* tells us that "the whole 'square of love' " (Ego/Self plus Self/Ego) perfects the erotic in the full encounter between lovers (IV, 145). But this "final completion of the planetary quincunx" is equally an integral part of the pure nature ecstasy. The Self has, so to speak, sexual organs of its own, a fact that is clarified in the inversion of crack imagery. In its most magnetic awareness, the Self is conscious of "what might be described as a quick silver-soul of electrified vitality, a torpedo-shaped slippery *life-fish*" (*AGO*, XII, 209). In alignment with this imagery, there is a great curving alder root in *Wolf Solent* that comes to an intimate correspondence with the willow shoot in

John's swirl-ecstasy. After a long amorous reverie, taking him to the "celestial Toll-Pike of the Infinite" (VII, 151) through a turquoise gap in the overcast sky, Wolf evokes this "smooth phallic serpent of vegetation" (VII, 152). The leap from the serpentine flexibility of Wolf's alder root curving over the banks of the Lunt to John's willow shoot in *A Glaston-bury Romance* is small indeed. John has been carried into a vortex of erotic passion through inlets into the humanity of Mary. Yet, entirely distinct from this ecstasy produced by the erotically *human*, there is an ecstatic quality in the nonhuman that is equally intense and equally erotic—whether this nonhumanity is the mineral, the vegetable, or even the purely abstract. The willow shoot is seen trailing here into a tinkling rivulet:

> Every now and then . . . he saw a drooping willow shoot trailing in the ditch beside him. Its extremity seen through the water was different from the upper part of it seen through the air . . . There was an imperative upon him to remember his vow about "competing." This "never competing" became identified with the slow swirl of the ditch stream as it made tiny ripples round the suspended shoot. He was *allowed*, he dimly felt, to enjoy his paradisiac lassitude, as long as he, this being who was partly John Crow and partly a willow shoot, kept these ripples in mind. All these phenomena made up a complete world, and in this world he was fulfilling all his moral obligations and fulfilling them with a delicious sense of virtue merely by keeping these ripples in mind; and the drip-drop, drip-drop of the tinkling rivulet at his elbow was the voice of the queer imperative which he obeyed. (II, 84–85)

I think the peculiar significance of this passage is the connection made between spiral and duality: between the idea of the "slow swirl" and the double bipartition—the air part of the shoot separated from the water part of the shoot; the intracorporeal John Crow separated from the ex-tracorporeal John Crow that is "partly a willow shoot."

The general idea behind this passage may serve to introduce what I view as the vital paradigm underlying Gyration. To begin with, it may be necessary to recall our previous discrimination between macropolarity and subpolarity (figure 7). If there is a crack in duality, or a phallic penetration of duality, then that is not difference—it is difference within difference (or on top of difference). This is so because duality is in itself difference (the difference between Good and Evil, competition and non-competition, Ego and Self, and so on).

So duality is Two. And Two is difference. Then this difference becomes different from itself either by becoming One (Whirlpool) or by becoming Three (Gyration). I mention this idea once more, by way of clarification, in order to prevent the extremely common conceptual confusion of this first primordial difference with the secondary overarching difference. The difference between these two differences is clearly outlined in *A Glastonbury Romance.* The "third pulse" suggests a differentiation not originally present in an initial difference *(one-two):*

> The first motive of every living creature must be to realize its own identity—to fight for itself against the cruelty of life, while the second motive of all conscious souls turned about towards the others.
> *One-two . . . One-two . . .* went the heartbeat of the world! Was there a third pulse there that no one could yet hear? (XXVIII, 937)

As I have mentioned, also, there is a crucial interplay between the number Two and the number Three in the Cowperverse. And this complex interaction is ultimately related to the central rift between sinistral and dextral awareness. In fact, my intention now is to demonstrate how the positive transcendence of duality in the Cowperverse can come about only through dextral awareness and as dextral awareness.

I will explain the basic paradigm naively first. Schematically, and with full knowledge of the enormous complexity of brain processes, let us imagine a crude compartmentalization within the skull. In the left lobe of the brain I insert the cipher 2. In the right lobe of the brain I insert the cipher 1 but also the cipher 3. This model of paradigmatic differentiation in the Powys world appears in figure 11.

Sinistral awareness is represented by the cipher 2, since it is essentially a binary mode of intellection—similar to that used in computer systems—and socially it is enhanced through the dualistic metaphysical schemes of established philosophy, established religion, established ideology, estab-

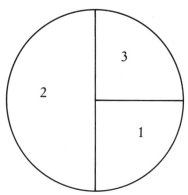

Figure 11. The structure of difference.

lished criticism, and so on. It underlies all those sterile categories with which we are so familiar: reality versus illusion, logic versus intuition, masculine versus feminine, classicism versus romanticism, exteriority versus interiority, and so on. Significantly, Powys turns for metaphysical validity to the pre-Socratic philosophers: Democritus, Pythagoras, Empedocles, and Heraclitus. These philosophers are "amphibiums" (DS, IV, 144), not because they understand duality, but because they have a double understanding of duality (he thinks). They understand 2, but also the tension between 2 and that which is not 2. They are concerned, in other words, not with difference so much as with the interplay between different differences.

Dextral awareness is the very nerve and fiber of the Powys world. And dextral awareness is not Two; that is—it *is* Two in the sense that duality and polarity shape difference. But it is not Two in the way that sinistral awareness is Two, because sinistral awareness is Two only on a single plane and only in a rather simplistic sense. Recent metaphysical thinking (Nietzsche, Derrida) includes traits that may set it off from the dualistic post-Platonic tradition. Strongly influenced by Nietzsche, and well acquainted with most of the great philosophers, Powys moved toward a complex relation to the idea of duality and difference. It is important to grasp this metaphysical complexity in nondualistic terms for the simple reason that a novel like *A Glastonbury Romance* begins by cosmogonizing a paradigm of differences such as that simplified in figure 11. The very fact that Powys speaks of polarity and duality is in itself a trap for the reader-critic, just as the idea of the dual First Cause is a trap for man in *A Glastonbury Romance*. There is a third factor (the Grail). This third factor is dextral awareness. More intelligently: dextral awareness is awareness of this third factor. Therefore the dextral (as in figure 11) is 1 or 3. But then, again, this is not quite so. The Grail is not *added* to duality. The Grail is not simply the progression from Two to Three. The Grail is not triality. The Grail is the addition of Difference to Difference. *The Grail is a double difference.* And this is why the ur-structure of the novels is not polarity but a double polarity. *A Glastonbury Romance* ends in three words, "Never or Always." Never/Always is duality. Yet Never/Always is also more than duality, since Never implies Whirlpool, the collapse into nonduality as uniformity, blankness, and since Always implies Gyration, transcendence. To the facticity of duality is therefore added the uncertainty of duality. This hesitation—as it is conveyed in the last pages of the novel—is not made into the hesitation *of* Two (Evil or Good?). Instead this hesitation is itself apotheosis. So that in "Never or Always," there exists the One of *Never,* the Two of *or* and the Three of *Always.*

I said that the Grail was a double difference. But I do not quite mean that. I mean that the Grail, insofar as it is *"outside"* (XXVIII, 940) us, is difference, and that it is a double difference insofar as it magically becomes an integral part of us—for then it adds itself as difference to the difference already in us.

It may be asked then, how this notion fits into the present argument. If the world of John Cowper Powys is so antidualistic, then why are we using a critical duality (Ego/Self) to come to terms with it? Because Ego/ Self is a double duality and not a duality! As we have seen, Ego in itself is duality (interpreting life as contest, dividing the weak from the strong), and Self is the positive or negative transcendence of that duality—in the numerical symbolism of Three and One.

In *Owen Glendower*, Dennis Burnell radiates a strange inner alienation, so that Rhisiart feels that his mind is "forever functioning on two levels" (X, 325). The main rift in Dennis Burnell is that between his identity as a man of swift action in the practical world and a man of profound inner vision. In this particular type of spatialization, that which looks outward is the pragmatic, self-asserting portion of our personality, while that which looks inward is more sensitive and less futile. In *The Art of Growing Old*, this spatialization leads to a curious inversion of the normal way in which we look upon egoism as centripetal and altruism as centrifugal. The outward-moving gesture is here said to be a motion that "represents only *one side*" of our living identity (VI, 103). There is another side, *"the inner side."* The chief imperative of our conscience *"looking outwards"* is to enjoy everything; but the "second half" of this imperative faces the "interior Void," and *"looking inwards,"* it commands us to be kind to all. Free from this absurd inversion of the altruism/ egoism antinomy, *The Meaning of Culture* highlights the difference between the confluence of Two into One and the confluence of Two into Three. A crossmodal synthesis is the foundation of dextral thought. This synthesis serves "to orientate the two parallel methods of approach" (VIII, 134), so that dextral being is interiority-as-femininity:

> It must be remembered that the problem confronting us here is not the purely scientific one of the worth of any particular pragmatic hypothesis, but the subtler human one of personal growth in general planetary wisdom. A richly cultured mind, like that of Goethe, can fall into many specific errors, just because of its refusal to harden itself against a certain feminism in its own being (such as eternally rebels against the dry assumption that the mathematical laws of cause and effect can deal adequately with the mystery of life) and yet, in spite of such specific errors, can steadily grow more formidable in massive adjustment to the pulse-beat of the universe. (VIII, 134)

In John Cowper Powys's concept of evolution, the deciding factor in determining the future of humanity is the choice between sinistral thinking and dextral thinking. Sinistral thinking will lead us to destruction. Dextral thinking will lead us to a new phase of evolution.

This idea is linked to the discrimination between Whirlpool and Gyration. In *The Meaning of Culture*, "the combined vision" (VIII, 135) energizing Gyration comes from an uplifting intensification rather than from "any toning down of the two extremes," or from any "insipid compromise between exciting opposites." This "vapid neutrality between living intensities" is Whirlpool—the collapse of Two into One. The metamorphosis from Two to Three, on the other hand, is a "clairvoyant synthesis," in which "each of these distinct visions is heightened separately to the limit of its own orientation" (VIII, 139).

Gyration, it will be seen, is essentially an intellectual achievement. By this I do not mean that it is an intellectual state but that it is initiated by and through the intellect. In his introduction to *The Pleasures of Literature*, John Cowper writes that all "progress in ideas is spiral, forever returning upon itself. Every revolution is a reaction, every leap-forward a renaissance, every new thought a returning to a spring that has been choked up" (12). There is of course nothing new in this insight, yet it is significant within the overall presence of Powysian spiral imagery as this is related to the sinistral/dextral antimony. When the evolutionary pressure is focused on the human race, "its apex-point of advance" runs *"through the human intelligence"* (*AH,* I, 21). From dextral to sinistral and then back to dextral—numerically from One to Two to Three in our paradigm of differential interplay (figure 11)—evolution moves through a set of "threefold spiral curves" in a quasi-Hegelian fashion (I, 13). The fall line is crossed twice: first, from right to left (this is the development from the fantasies of childhood to the ratiocinations of adulthood), then from left to right, if the individual is to transcend adulthood and be able to anticipate the next phase of evolution. The return to the dextral is no real return, however, since one returns to the dextral as Three and not to the dextral as One. The new dextrality (dextrality-as-Three) retains an assimilated awareness of the potentials of sinistral logic. These are not abandoned, they are simply automatized and transcended (*aufgehoben*, in Hegel's terminology), just as the elementary physical capacities that enrapture the child become automatized and surmounted in adulthood without being "lost." These concepts link up with Powys's sustained preoccupation with the idea of second childhood in his later works and letters. The general theory also acquires a deepening intimacy with his advocation of conscious retardation of intellectual development (*AGO,* Introduction, 11).[11] Children who put off learning to talk for as long as possible may have a subtle form of intelligence (*MS,* VII, 102).[12]

Far from being intellectually sloppy, John Cowper Powys refuses to embrace that facile psychological and ideological reductionism which in recent times has monitored the revolt against sinistral power structures. I am thinking of the sentimental and weak-minded aspects of the counter-culture movement in the sixties and seventies. The alternative to rational-ism and commonsensicalism is not to accept the other extreme—for that would only be possible in a situation of polarity, and not in a situation of a double polarity. Because, like Nietzsche, he resents *all* forms of vulgar duality-thinking, John Cowper will always demystify the mystique in his novels and always rationalize their mystique. He gives a complex coher-ence to his world of ideas by rejecting the purely sinistral as well as the purely antisinistral. He can do this because the dextral is not just the antisinistral. The dextral is something more—always something more coming from within and without, like the Grail. The dextral suggests a kind of crystallization. It is only with our whole nature that we may intelligently question the "reality-revealing power of *logic* as *logic*" (*AGO*, VII, 108). Logic as logic is useless. Indeed, it is the most danger-ous thing in the world (a fact overwhelmingly clear in this nuclear age). Pure reason is always *"a little mad"* when left to herself (*MS*, VI, 95). But then again, the fashionable rationalistic explanations of the world riddle (*MofC*, I, 17) cannot be viably subverted by a mode of intellection that is only the opposite extreme on the same level of understanding. And so John Cowper looks upon the mania for the occult and the so-called psychic as a form of modern hysteria (*ISO*, VIII, 238). This, in turn, is also why the psychic and occult elements in *A Glastonbury Romance* (and elsewhere) are introduced in such a way that they in fact cannot be seen as "elements" but only as integral subunits of a higher order of understand-ing—higher than logic but also higher than occultism. The truly complex mode of ideal being "is no more and no less 'spiritual' than the in-breathing and the out-breathing of a minnow in a stream" (*DS*, V, 170).

Man as a minnow-in-a-stream is not, as we have seen, man-as-stream. Man-as-stream is pure consciousness, and pure, fluid consciousness is really only animal awareness. What we need is pure *self*-consciousness, and this means that the normal stream of consciousness must be "actually superseded by a totally different 'stream'" (*ISO*, IV, 100). After a period of evolution in which our species has lived in a state of half-intelligence and half-stupidity, lasting only "a miserable twenty thousand years" (*DS*, III, 122), we are now "waking slowly into the consciousness of being conscious" (*UO*, 86). Sinistral awareness is "mechanical logic" (*DS*, III, 95), and this cannot take man further on the road of evolution. If man continues to uphold this aspect of consciousness as the apex of the mind, evolution will come to an abrupt halt. Sinistral logic, in and by itself, is

"an altogether misleading and quite paltry by-alley of modern thought."
As pure sinistrality, "the Intellect is constitutionally unsuited to deal with
Life" (*MS*, XII, 214).

Let us look, then, at Gyration and at dextrality, so that we understand
exactly what this force consists of and why it is sufficiently strong to shift
humanity into a dramatically novel phase of evolution. To begin with,
perhaps, there should be an understanding of how delicate the balance
between Gyration and Whirlpool really is. As the number Two, we are as
close to One as to Three:

> Every individual personality is like a vast cavern with endless ave-
> nues and stairways, leading up and down, leading north, south, east,
> and west. All have *that* in them which belongs to the vegetable world.
> All have *that* in them which belongs to a still earlier world of inorganic
> stellar nebulae. And we also have moods of strange prophetic premoni-
> tion in which we anticipate in our feelings the feelings of those mysteri-
> ous superhuman beings who in the process of time will take the place of
> humanity. (*DS*, III, 95–96)

Far from being an isolated caprice of the writer's mind, this idea is a
pervasive one in Powys's writing. The passage just quoted is from *In
Defence of Sensuality*. In *The Art of Growing Old*, he considers the way
in which humanity is waiting for something. We are waiting for "*the next
transformation*" (IV, 74). We do not know exactly what this transformation will be, but in *The Inmates* Powys suggests that in "our human
mental world it's like splitting the atom" (VI, 115). *In Spite Of* describes
it as a "leap forward in planetary evolution" (IV, 113) that will give birth
to "a new self-created self" (V, 130). This phrasing suggests that John
Cowper looks upon his struggles with his own consciousness as
significant events in man's efforts to approach this new evolutionary
threshold. The act of selfsation, giving access, as it does, to the premeditated ecstasy, is an "evolutionary experiment" (IV, 111; IX, 293).
Thus the altered state of consciousness and the alteration of consciousness—through an internal act of the mind rather than through narcotics—
hold key positions in the overall strategy for a leap beyond the present
order of things. Eventually, we will come to "a particular moment in our
history when, to speak roughly and crudely, a living human consciousness 'jumps out of its own skin' " (IV, 114). Such an "evolutionary gesture" (IV, 10) would bring us to the actualization of the calm superman, a
creature already being formed in the future (*DS*, V, 163; VI, 201–2; VII,
213):

We human beings suffer so miserably, both in our daily work and in our passive moments, because we represent a transitional period—God knows it is a long enough period!—between the happy half-consciousness of animals and the full self-consciousness of the super-men of the future.

In this transitional epoch our minds are conscious, but we have not trained ourselves to regulate the thoughts *of which* they are conscious. We resemble therefore conscious automata; and this resemblance is increased by the accursed false philosophy of . . . behaviouristic determinism, which has so grossly discredited the power of the human soul. (*AH*, V, 207–8)

A spirit can stand on the rim of the ocean and feel within itself a tumult and a serenity belonging to a prehuman time (*DS*, III, 100). But there is a corresponding sense of existing in an evolutionary beyond. As we evolve "a completely new psycho-physical power" out of ourselves, we actually initiate a process that is as significant to our evolution and history as the emergence of living organisms from the sea to the sand or of our more recent ancestors from the trees to the ground (*ISO*, IV, 106). Ultimately, therefore, the emancipation of the human mind does not come from myth, scientism, or social revolution but, rather, from an act of the mind itself. Our ordinary perceptions and our ordinary mode of awareness are quite limited. We really only use a tiny portion of our cognitive capacities. This gives hope:

For our conscience itself develops! Here and nowhere else lies the true hope of our earthquake-shaken world. And the majestic irony of the situation lies in the fact that the very organism upon whose solitude-in-the-dark priests and messiahs and medicine-men have for so long played is now *itself* the one grand engine of retort that has the power to blow them all sky-high! (*AGO*, VI, 96)

But why does increased self-consciousness involve a shift from sinistral to dextral thinking? As I have already said, sinistral thought is in the long run incommensurable with ecstatic self-consciousness, because it is essentially lineal, affirmative, and positivistic. When it is critical, moving often into the hypercritical, it is still positivistic, *for it is never critical of itself.* How could it be? Then it would have to stop, look around, reconsider the world, and by then it would have already vanished—as that which it is: uninterrupted line, sequence. Sinistral awareness thinks; it does not stop to think. So this planet, as a collective thought, is not at present an inverted thought but only an ongoing thinking. Humanity, strictly speaking, has never seen itself.

In contradistinction to sinistral thinking, which only grasps the lowest, crudest, and most insignificant features of reality (*MS*, VI, 95), dextral awareness is holistic. Central to this holism is the actualization of self-consciousness. This self-consciousness informs the individual observing his own thinking that a large proportion of the waking life is spent in reverie. That is to say; it *was* reverie, but now that there is consciousness of it, it turns out to be something radically different from what the sinistral intellect had contemptuously dismissed as "daydreaming." Dextral thinking should reverse the established order by giving a negative and belittling label to the *anti*daydreaming faculties. In the first and more primitive situation, the sinistral thinker finds "daydreaming" to be an essentially irritating interruption of his linear thinking (which he calls "concentration") and of his linear workaday routines (which are all task oriented, pointing to a goal; it does not really matter *which* goal, but it certainly must be *a* goal). In the more complex situation of Powysian awareness, however, the situation is reversed. Now it is sinistral thinking that is interrupting dextral awareness rather than vice versa. The sinistral thoughts must be brushed aside. They are "like mosquitoes troubling a sleeper" (*DS*, III, 104).

The "daydream" seems to be a blank—at least when it is over, probably because of the fall line and the amnesic barrier. But perhaps it is no blank. No philosophy seems to have bothered to center the daydream: "These moments of day-dreaming have not been sufficiently considered by philosophic writers" (*ISO*, VIII, 249). So perhaps, metaphorically, "daydreaming" is a kind of four-dimensional thinking, in which a dimension is added rather than subtracted:

> The whole problem of the nature and quality of the human consciousness in quiescence, whether in fact this function that we feel working within us when we use the phrase "my mind" is to be praised or blamed when it falls into absent-mindedness or a "brown study," is one of the most important of all human questions. And it has been strongly neglected by both metaphysicians and psychologists! (*AGO*, I, 33)

Powys thinks that it is necessary to interrupt the ordinary processes of linear thinking (*DS*, V, 162), because by doing so the individual comes into contact with creativity. This creativity is not only human-artistic creativity, it is the very life-thrust that is the intellectual driving force of "original Creation" (III, 91). It is not necessary to resort to LSD; *Wolf Solent* ends with *tea*—the very last word of the novel, and *In Defence of Sensuality* tells us that coffee is sufficient to change a man's universe:

"Something inside a person swings slowly round upon a mystical pivot" (I, 54). This is the swing taking us across the fall line in the manner outlined in the first chapter of this book. In *Atlantis*, Nisos Naubolides becomes aware of the structure of dextral consciousness in one of "these interruptions of our ordinary consciousness" (III, 90). Now "there was permitted to him what is permitted to few among us mortals during our lifetime, namely the realization of what actually happens to us when we fall, as we all do, into these day-dreams" (III, 91). Through such "brooding trances," we learn in *Atlantis*, man is "without knowing it, living a double life." In the average human mind today, there is no real dextral consciousness. The moments of ecstasy and reverie come and go like "random thoughts" (*AH*, II, 65). They are rarely observed, hardly ever tied together. Life, therefore, misses its integrative dimension, since this complex vision of the dextrotemporal mood is in itself integrative and holistic (*DS*, I, 12).

The extraordinary significance that John Cowper Powys attached to his developing model of the universe may occasionally be glimpsed in *Autobiography* and *Confessions*. But it is perhaps at its clearest in *Rodmoor*. Powys obviously considers himself to be if not in possession then on the threshold of a unique apprehension of the structure of cosmos and consciousness. He is, in fact, enormously pretentious, and his later humility is really only an inversion of his fundamental intellectual arrogance. He operates in a curious, fertile no-man's-land, thus acquiring a centermost strategic position in the cultural terrain. He knows philosophy, but he is not *in* philosophy; he knows psychology, but he is no psychologist. Also, in an odd way, he is a man of letters without really existing in literature. He does sometimes *become* literature, but this is essentially so mainly in the way that he magically choses to become anything he wants to become. By this I do not mean to belittle his literary achievement—that should be clear by now. On the contrary. He somehow has the ability to force literature to transcend itself, making it conform to the idiosyncrasy of his own recklessly systematic "mythology." I have the feeling that John Cowper Powys interrupts literature, and that he (and sometimes literature) enjoys this.

I also think it is a misunderstanding, and no small misunderstanding, to look upon this quality of his textual being as "amateurishness." Clearly, this writer chooses very deliberately, indeed programmatically, to stay clear of the established forms of philosophy, psychology, sociology, and art. He did this in the belief that he could use his unique insights as the basis for his work, making raids into the various disciplines or genres as these came naturally into communion with his intellectual development. In all his attitudes there is an electric self-confidence, the kind of ruthless

self-assertion that has always characterized the highly individualized human who prefers to follow the voice of his inner convictions rather than
to accept current doctrinal fads. Even when it seems necessary to challenge the long-standing value systems of an entire culture, even when it
seems necessary to defy the species itself, Powys retains his authority.
You cannot quarrel with humanity Baltazar tells Adrian in *Rodmoor*. The
answer is unmistakably suggestive of the personal arrogance of John
Cowper himself:

> Adrian turned fiercely round on him. "Can't I?" he exclaimed.
> "Can't I quarrel with humanity? You wait, my friend, till I've got my
> book published. Then you'll see! I tell you I'll strike this cursed human
> race of yours such a blow that they'll wish they'd treated a poor wan-
> derer on the face of the earth a little better." (XX, 289)

In view of our model of a fall line, it is interesting to compare Powys's
cool and remote way of writing about his son in a letter to G. Wilson
Knight, dated 6 January 1957,[13] and the touching emotional immediacy in
the description in *Rodmoor* of how the protagonist endures his separation
from a son. (In both cases, the Atlantic separates the two.) In my view,
the former attitude is unauthentic; this dishonesty is not the result of a
deliberate downgrading of bygone emotional realities; we have simply a
case of state dependent retrieval. Here, the letter-writing Powys just does
not have access to the emotional reality that he does have access to in his
fiction-writing mode of awareness. It is totally unthinkable that a man of
such enormous receptivity and such reverberating sympathy for the
humane should be lacking in emotional intensity vis-à-vis *anyone*. It is
not totally unthinkable that a man of such overdeveloped sensibility
should gradually evolve a technique of self-removal that permits him to
continue functioning normally without having to be scorched from
within by an excessively passionate disposition (*AFU*, 9). In *Rodmoor*,
Sorio's situation is really quite desperate. Only his son understands what
he is "trying to do in the darkness" (XV, 210). As Sorio proceeds to reveal
his emotions to his mistress Philippa, we are for a moment allowed to
glimpse the human vulnerability that Powys spent most of his life
fighting. We glimpse also the underlying pessimism and gloom from
which the writer escaped only through his philosophy of cheerfulness.
We observe the stark misanthropy from which he evolved the exaggerated, ultraphilanthropical stance of his later life, the diabolical defiance
that ironically came to spawn his mystical quietism:

> "They'd be a bit surprised, wouldn't they," he burst out, "if they
> knew about the manuscripts *he*"—he uttered this last word with con-
> centrated reverence,—"is guarding for me over there? *He* understands

me, Phil, and not a living person except him. Listen, Phil! Since I've known you I've been able to breathe—just able to breathe—in this damned England. Before that—God! I shudder to think of it—I was dumb, strangled, suffocated, paralyzed, dead. Even now—even with you, Phil,—I'm still fumbling and groping after it—after what I have to say to the world, after my secret, my idea!" . . .

He pulled out of his pocket a small thick notebook closely written, blurred with erasures and insertions, stained with salt-water. . . . "I *know* I've got it in me to give to the world something it's never dreamed of—something with a real madness of truth in it—something with a bite that gets to the very bone of things. I know I've got that in me." (VIII, 105–6)

An immense yearning for his son took possession of him and he set himself to recall every precise incident of their separation. He saw himself standing at the side of the crowded liner. He saw the people waving and shouting from the wooden jetty of the great dock. He saw Baptiste, standing a little apart from the rest, motionless, not raising even a hand, paralyzed by the misery of his departure. He too was sick with misery then. He remembered the exact sensation of it and how he envied the sea-gulls who never knew these human sufferings and the gay people on the ship who seemed to have all they loved with them at their side.

"Oh, God," he muttered to himself, "give me back my son and you may take everything—my book, my pride, my brain—everything! everything!" (XXI, 329–30)

The strong Powys-hermit lives archetypally within an aerial helix: "The loneliness of such a being extends itself around him like a spiral windstorm" (*DS*, III, 131). But if this gyrational envelope protects the individual from a too intimate confrontation with the brutalities of the modern world, there is also, as in *Wolf Solent*, a cosmic consciousness that is the sensation of the World-Spirit as the widest of circumferences. Wolf sees a field of buttercups, and in the aureate ecstasy that follows, the yellowness of the flowers changes from Byzantine to Cimmerian gold, giving him the feeling that that entire segment of West Country landscape is a living god, immanent and actual (*WoS*, XXV, 632). The earlier yellow infinity in Wolf's vaporous primrose-cloud-ecstasy seems to promise a pure happiness that is attained neither through asceticism nor through epicureanism (VII, 151–52). The blue immensity within a sky-gap opens Wolf's consciousness to a more profound recognition of some elemental force that can be directly extracted from nature. The ecstasy he is looking for is not just the happiness of loving Gerda. It cannot be called love, for it is much more than love. His mind becomes a vortex with a revolving wheel that churns out the terrifying image of the poor, forsaken human being that Wolf had seen at the London station before coming out to the West Country. As with John Crow's willow-swirl-ecstasy in *A Glastonbury Romance*, there is a strong confluence of ethics and sensuality that removes the traditional polarization of self-enjoyment and self-transcendence. Wolf Solent's morality becomes an inversion of Jason Otter's traditional morality, because, unlike Jason, Wolf can transcend a simplistic conception of duality and a simplistic conception of difference. The insight underlying these lines alienates the Powys hero from his fellow beings, yet at the same time it brings him into immediate, almost physical contact with the very texture of their being. The movement is neither in-and-towards or from-and-away, but a curious double movement that ultimately relies on a reversal of culturally ingrained habits of thought:

> And then, like an automatic wheel that revolved in his brain, a wheel from one of whose spokes hung a bodiless human head, his thoughts brought him back to that Living Despair on the Waterloo steps. And he recalled what Jason Otter had said about pity: how if you had pity and there was one miserable consciousness left in the universe, you had no right to be happy. Oh, that was a wicked thought! You had, on the contrary, a desperately punctilious reason to be happy.
>
> That face upon the Waterloo steps *gave* you your happiness. It was the only gift it could give. Between your happiness and that face there was an umbilical cord. (VII, 153)

From *In Spite Of,* we learn that John Cowper Powys acknowledges ignorance as to what "lobes or cells in our brain" are involved in *"the feeling of selfness"* (VIII, 252). So also, in my differentiation between sinistral and dextral thinking, I really claim no access to any conclusive theory about neurophysiological patternings: I have not imagined some ecstatic rash or titillation in the right brain during ecstatic reverie, with a left lobe kept numb and uninvolved. There are complex changes of balance from left to right that are quite measurable in physiological terms; yet even so, my main purpose has been to get away from the conscious/subconscious duality that has been misused in all fields.

The idea of a fall line, and the idea of a central cleavage in mind and brain, may perhaps finally be (somewhat ironically) related to that dramatic dilemma in *Rodmoor* where Hamish Traherne has to decide what to do with Baltazar's body after the man's suicide. The sexton is inebriated and absent, so Traherne consults various ancient scholastic authorities before deciding whether to place the corpse inside or outside the holy area of the churchyard. His final decision involves a metaphysical bisec-

224 THE ECSTATIC WORLD OF JOHN COWPER POWYS

tion of the dead man's brain and being. Profoundly heretical and profoundly orthodox, like John Cowper himself, Traherne comes to a somewhat startling heathen-Christian compromise. It dooms the main part of the buried man while saving only "the posterior lobes of the human skull." Man ends, as he has begun, as a self-divided enigma:

> In the end, what he did, with a whimsical prayer to Providence to forgive him, was to *begin* digging the hole just outside the consecrated area, but by means of a slight northward *excavation*, when he got a few feet down, to arrange the completed orifice in such a way that, while Baltazar's body remained in common earth, his head was lodged safe and secure, under soil blessed by Holy Church. (XXVI, 431)

It is perhaps unwise to remove oneself too far from the fall line; perhaps it transects also the present work. It is perhaps unwise to favor a definitive resolution, stating that Gyration always triumphs over Whirlpool, or even Self always over Ego. Things hang very much in the balance, and there they must no doubt go on hanging for some time. Thus our final mood may fall into agreement with that of the majestic ending to *Owen Glendower.* With the collapse of his struggle in time and with the collapse of his cremated skeleton, the material-spiritual presence of the prince retreats into the ruins of Mathrafal, into the central forest mysteries of Wales and its druidic ur-void. "*Nis gwn!* I don't know! *Nis gwn!*" one old raven croaks to the other. The heavy-flapping fowls move diagonally eastward, mounting up in huge spiral circles, higher and higher. In that final croak, there is, or there is not, some elusive promise of release.

Nis gwn.

NOTES

Chapter 1. The Cowperverse

1. See for instance Roger Sperry, *Science and Moral Priority: Merging Mind, Brain, and Human Values* (New York: Columbia University Press, 1983), pp. 77–103.

2. See Ernest R. Hilgard, *Divided Consciousness: Multiple Controls in Human Thought and Action* (New York: John Wiley and Sons, 1977), p. 248. This, to my knowledge, is the most satisfying scientific work on multiple personality, split consciousness, and the entire area of internal dislocations with which we will be concerned. Hilgard's neodissociative theory is a modern version of Janet's dissociation theory. The disruptions can be studied in hypnotized humans and are not to be confused with Freudian stratifications or with mental aberrations.

3. This approximates the enlarged concept of the unconscious developed by Jacques Lacan. See his *Écrits: A Selection*, trans. Alan Sheridan (London: Tavistock, 1980). Original French publication, 1966.

4. A significant comment on Freud's attitude to daydreaming will be found in Jerome L. Singer, *Daydreaming and Fantasy* (London: George Allen and Unwin, 1976), p. 103.

5. This is the central thesis in Colin Martindale's *Romantic Progression: The Psychology of Literary History* (New York: John Wiley and Sons, 1975).

6. This is Arnold M. Ludwig's argument in *Altered States of Consciousness: A Book of Readings*, ed. C. T. Tart (New York: John Wiley and Sons, 1969), p. 18: "[The] very presence and prevalence of these states in man . . . attests to their importance in his everyday functioning. I find it difficult to accept, for example, that man's ability to lapse into trance has been evolved just so he can be hypnotized on stage or in a clinical or laboratory setting."

7. In this I am merely following up the semi-ironic conceptualizations initiated by Powys in *Autobiography* (XII, 626).

8. See Arnold M. Ludwig's reference to reading ecstasies in *Altered States of Consciousness*, p. 12. For a literary-critical discussion of daydreaming, see Gaston Bachelard's brilliant work, *La Poétique de la rêverie* (Paris: Presses Universitaires de France, 1960). The phenomenology of daydreaming is of course not unrelated to Jung's differentiation between animus and anima.

9. See Claude Lévi-Strauss, *Myth and Meaning* (London: Routledge and Kegan Paul, 1978), pp. 5–6.

10. See Sperry, *Science and Moral Priority*, p. 84.

11. See, for instance, H. P. Collins, *John Cowper Powys: Old Earth-Man* (London: Barrie and Rockliff, 1966), p. 89.

12. This is well worked into Morine Krissdottir's discrimination between the psychologi-

cal novel and the visionary novel in her *John Cowper Powys and the Magical Quest* (London: Macdonald and Jane's, 1980), p. 52.

13. Two significant works on altered awareness should be mentioned. There is the dense volume edited by C. T. Tart entitled *Altered States of Consciousness* (see n. 6), and there is Marghanita Laski's rather less scholarly but very well-documented inquiry, *Ecstasy: A Study of Some Secular and Religious Experiences* (London: The Cresset Press, 1961). The most startling phenomenon uncovered in these investigations is perhaps the similarity between the accounts of ecstasy given by different individuals. From such concordance, a quite stable pattern of altered awareness emerges. In all major respects, the Powys ecstasy fits very well into this overall picture.

14. See also Powys's *Psychoanalysis and Morality* (1923).

15. See Powys's acceptance of the finality of death in his 1960 preface to a new edition of *Wolf Solent:* p. 11 (Macdonald, 1961; Penguin, 1964).

16. *Ineffability* is one of the nine major operative categories listed by Walter N. Pahnke and William A. Richards as being principal features of ecstatic awareness. See their essay "Implications of LSD and Experimental Mysticism," in *Altered States of Consciousness,* ed. C. T. Tart (New York: John Wiley and Sons, 1969) pp. 401–7. In the psychedelic experience of mystical consciousness (to use the term chosen by the authors), the other main aspects of ecstasy are the sense of *unity,* the sense of *reality* or objectivity, the sense of *timelessness and spacelessness,* the sense of *sacredness,* the sense of *joy,* the sense of *paradoxicality,* the sense of *transience*—and, in addition, sometimes the sense of an *attitudinal shift* involving a subsequent change of attitudes toward oneself, toward others, and toward the phenomenon of mystical consciousness. These concomitant changes (all related to the central propaganda in Powys's nonfictional works, as are the nine operative categories themselves) are reported to be linked to the sense of increased personality integration, "including a renewed sense of personal worth coupled with a relaxation of habitual mechanisms of ego defense" (p. 406). The universally experienced sense of ego-dissolution in ecstasy is particularly significant within the context of our formulation of an Ego-versus-Self-theory. This is so not only because of the dissolution of this ego but, primarily, because somehow a crystalline form of consciousness takes its place, implying some new observer, some different cogito: The "empirical ego (i.e., the usual sense of individuality) seems to die or fade away while pure consciousness of what is being experienced paradoxically remains and seems to expand as a vaster inner world is encountered" (p. 401). This remarkable affinity between Powys's nondrug-induced awareness and drug-induced awareness as it has been studied clinically is sensed by Jean-Jacques Mayoux in his interesting essay "L'Extase et la sensualité: John Cowper Powys et *Wolf Solent,*" *Critique,* vol. 24, no. 252 (May 1968): 462–74. "*Lorsqu'on connaîtra mieux la chimie de la penseé, on saura pourquoi certains d'entre nous . . . sont des drogués naturels*" (p. 462).

17. This is a reference to the work of Ernest Hilgard; see n. 2.

18. See Roland Fischer, "A Cartography of the Ecstatic and Meditative States," *Science 4012 (1971): 897–904.*

19. *Stan Gooch, The Double Helix of the Mind,* (London: Wildwood House, 1980). This book is a mixture of the most brilliant insights and the most extravagant speculations. I have found its chief value in the delineation of the fear of the Ego vis-à-vis the Self. Gooch also clarifies the existence of a pseudo-Self (p. 126).

20. Relevant documentation will be found in my *Timescapes of John Fowles* (Rutherford, N.J.: Fairleigh Dickinson University Press; London and Toronto: Associated University Presses, 1984).

21. Fischer, "Cartography," p. 902. See also Pahnke and Richards, "Experimental Mysticism," p. 402.

22. See Howard R. Pollio, "Intuitive Thinking," in *Aspects of Consciousness*, vol. 1, ed. Geoffrey Underwood and Robin Stevens (New York: Academic Press, 1979), p. 33.

23. The connection between altered awareness and literary creativity is extensively documented in Rosamund Harding's *Anatomy of Inspiration* (Cambridge: W. Heffer and Sons, 1942).

24. See, in particular, P. D. Ouspensky, *The Fourth Way* (London: Routledge and Kegan Paul, 1957).

25. See Singer, *Daydreaming and Fantasy*.

26. In Jerome Singer's body of research, reviewed in *Daydreaming and Fantasy*, there is nothing to support the view that any significant variations exist between the sexes with respect to the extent of daydreaming. The content of daydreaming, on the other hand, differs substantially with gender.

27. See Heinrich Klüver, *Mescal, and Mechanism of Hallucinations* (Chicago: Chicago University Press, 1966). In view of the extraordinary *visual* bias of Powys's art, commented on by himself, it is interesting to consider the hallucinatory quality of many of his visions (whether of landscape or still life) in significant relation to the way in which the laboratory psychologist records changes in spatial perception in persons that have ingested a psychedelic drug. Pahnke and Richards report how the attendant changes in the nervous system increase the subject's sensitivity to color and form. Colors deepen with an enriched intensity, while contours of objects seem to stand out in sharper relief: "The whole environment may seem to come into sharper focus, as though the person had just discarded a dirty, incorrectly ground pair of glasses for a clean, perfectly ground pair." Geometric patterns of a visionary nature are likely to be perceived in multicolored abstract lines, three-dimensionally projected, and changing constantly in a steady, rhythmic flow ("Experimental Mysticism," pp. 407–8). An awareness of these mechanisms may be fruitful for Powys criticism in suggesting that far from being quasi-metaphysical abstractions of a logical-mathematical kind, the various geometric configurations with which we shall be concerned in this study are actually epiphenomena of the ecstatic. They are not tokens of a cerebral, intellectualizing type of formalization but, rather, of an opposite bias.

28. On color and ecstasy, see Klüver, *Mescal*, and Pahnke and Richards, "Experimental Mysticism."

29. See Richard A. Block, "Time and Consciousness," in *Aspects of Consciousness*, p. 201.

30. Non-rapid-eye-movement-sleep.

31. Block, "Time and Consciousness," p. 201.

32. See Ernest R. Hilgard, "Neodissociation Theory of Multiple Cognitive Control Systems," in *Consciousness and Self-Regulation*, vol. 1, ed. Gary E. Schwartz and David Shapiro (New York and London: Plenum Press, 1976).

33. See Fischer's intelligent discussion of this mechanism in "Cartography," p. 903.

34. See Pollio, "Intuitive Thinking," p. 32.

35. Fischer, "Cartography," p. 903.

36. See Sperry, *Science and Moral Priority*, p. 94.

37. Fischer, "Cartography," p. 903.

38. For an account of the amnesic barrier, see Hilgard, "Neodissociation Theory," pp. 142–43.

39. See Fischer, "Cartography," p. 903.

40. The state of ecstatic joy has an overall erotic quality as a result of the intensity of the experience—an intensity only reached outside altered awareness through sexual excitation. Pahnke and Richards define this ecstatic joy as "a state resembling prolonged intense sexual orgasm. The latter degree of intensity is generally dissociated from any stimulation or

excitation of the sexual organs, being 'spiritual' rather than 'erotic' in nature" ("Experimental Mysticism," p. 404).

41. Paradoxicality is in itself one of the main operative categories of altered awareness (see n. 16). Intrinsically, ecstatic consciousness violates the laws of Aristotelian logic. I think most of these paradoxes are precisely to be understood in terms of a model of divided consciousness. The subject claims to have ceased to exist, yet enthusiastically describes the intensity of a new set of experiences. He claims to dwell in a void, yet this void is said to contain all reality. He speaks of non-being as something more ontologically tangible than being. He is no longer in the body, yet he clearly still is *of* the body. See "Experimental Mysticism," pp. 404–5.

Chapter 2. The Interior Distance

1. See Hilgard, *Divided Consciousness*, pp. 1–16.
2. This is a typical example of what Hilgard defines in "Neodissociation Theory" as the activity of the "hidden observer" (pp. 144–45).
3. See Gooch, *The Double Helix of the Mind*, p. 83.
4. See my *Timescapes*, pp. 144–61. My theory of a delinearized temporality *(dextrotemporality)* is anticipated by Jacques Derrida's analogous mode of thinking in *Of Grammatology*, trans. Gayatri Chakravorty Spivak (Baltimore and London: John Hopkins University Press, 1976), pp. 85–87.
5. This, clearly, is also a master concept in *Ducdame*. It is with the writing of *Wolf Solent* that John Cowper Powys transcends this crude philosophy, moving from a theory of opposites to a theory of double opposites.
6. Rock Ashover has a striking resemblance to John Cowper himself, just as his brother, Lexie, has a striking resemblance to Llewelyn Powys. As is well-known also, the Rook-Lexie relationship is suggestive of the John-Llewelyn relationship.
7. John Cowper was never happily married, and there are strong autobiographical elements also in this aspect of *Ducdame*.
8. Jeremy Hooker, *John Cowper Powys* (Cardiff: University of Wales Press, 1973), p. 36.
9. *Levotemporality* and *dextrotemporality*. See my *Timescapes*, p. 148.
10. It is this "life illusion" (echoing Ibsen) that foreshadows the "mythology" in *Wolf Solent*.
11. John Cowper was himself a stone worshiper (*LNR*, 107).

Chapter 3. Crystal and Aura

1. See *Timescapes*, pp. 89–107.
2. I am using the field-of-consciousness concept in a manner radically different from that developed by Wilhelm Wundt in *Grundzüge der Physiologischen Psychologie* (Leipzig: Engelmann, 1874). Wundt's *central focal level* and *peripheral, diffuse level* do not correspond to the *crystal* versus *aura* antinomy elaborated here. I am suggesting an expansion of the cognitive field *without loss of intensity*. See Arthur L. Blumenthal, *The Process of Cognition* (Englewood Cliffs, N.J.: Prentice-Hall, 1977), p. 16.
3. John Donne, "A Valediction: Forbidding Mourning."
4. Published first as *Jobber Skald*. This novel appears as *Weymouth Sands* in the 1963 Macdonald edition (London).

5. See Hilgard, "Neodissociation Theory," pp. 144–45, on the "hidden observer."

6. John Cowper Powys never traveled by air. He was hostile to a number of modern inventions; he considered television to be harmful to human intelligence (*LNR*, 145).

7. Henri Bergson, *Essai sur les données immédiates de la conscience* (Paris: Librairie Félix Alcan, 1914), p. 180. See also p. 183.

8. There are of course pre-Joycean trends in literature foreshadowing this phenomenon: one need only consider Alfred Jingle's steno-language in *Pickwick Papers* and how it anticipates more extensive uses of stream of consciousness.

9. Blumenthal, *Process of Cognition*, pp. 19–21.

10. See *LWK*, pp. 20, 69.

11. John Cowper Powys often lived in extreme solitude during the time of his most intense literary creativity in the 1930s.

12. Psychologists speak nowadays of the *cocktail party phenomenon* (Blumenthal, *Process of Cognition*, p. 14). This is a reference to the way in which an individual must focus first on one conversation, then on another, in order to make sense out of what would otherwise be a word-soup. But, archetypally, the Powys hero *would automatize that selection process too.* He would transcend not only the word-soup but also the lineal awarenesses in that word-soup. Through a concentrated reverie, he has access to a complex, multimodal form of consciousness which is neither chaos nor linearity, neither the unconcentrated nor the "concentrated": it is the hyperconcentrated.

13. See *LWK*, p. 63.

14. See ibid., p. 34.

Chapter 4. Ebb and Flow

1. In *The Meaning of Culture*, Powys discusses erotic love in relation to personality. It is obvious, he writes, that sex love "should affect it from centre to circumference" (VIII, 136). In *Mortal Strife* it is pain, not pleasure, that receives his chief attention, yet here again the mind is subject to a centrifugal motion: "The great circle of the soul is not reduced to smaller size, but it is cleansed of its duskiness and its opacity. From centre to circumference the microcosm is washed clean" (IV, 68).

2. See Laski, *Ecstasy*, p. 82.

3. In *The Origin of Consciousness in the Breakdown of the Bicameral Mind* (Boston: Houghton Mifflin, 1976), Julian Jaynes gives an important discussion of the localization of consciousness. His analysis would have fascinated John Cowper Powys. The everyman theory of consciousness locates awareness inside our own heads. We are always assuming a space behind our companion's eyes into which we are talking. This resembles the space we imagine inside our heads as the place that we are talking from (pp. 44–45). But this idea about locating consciousness in the head is really only a deeply ingrained habit. It is almost impossible for us to think exosomatically because of this automatization. But, in fact, consciousness could be located by the "I" on a wall or on the floor, or even somewhere far away (p. 46). In the altered state of consciousness there is a de-automatization of this habit of thought. Above all, such experiences illustrate the arbitrariness of the localization of consciousness.

4. See Laski, *Ecstasy*, p. 72, n. 1. Laski states that the Welsh word *gwyn* signifies white but also *fair, happy, holy, blessed.* To be white is to be ecstatic; to be ecstatic is to be white.

5. *After My Fashion* was published posthumously, as late as 1980, by Picador/Pan Books (London).

6. A common fallacy in the lower reaches of the intelligentsia is the one connecting

altered states of consciousness with individuals who lack training in critical-academic awareness and who do not have rigorously analytic powers of mind. It is significant, in this context, that the majority of the U.S. astronauts with extraterrestrial experience have vivid and intense moments of altered awareness in space. For these highly intelligent men, the sudden experience of the noncompatibility of the sinistral and the dextral often leads to a dramatic intellectual reorientation.

7. This is an interesting image, since the right hemisphere of the brain is generally involved with the musical awareness of most humans (the hemisphericity of professional musicians is, however, somewhat more complexly defined).

8. By "tidal imagery," I mean an intense preoccupation with outflowings and inflowings of various kinds.

9. Edward W. Said, "Roads Taken and Not Taken in Contemporary Criticism," *Directions for Criticism: Structuralism and Its Alternatives,* ed. Murray Krieger and L. S. Dembo (Madison: University of Wisconsin Press, 1977), p. 54.

10. This is one of the occasions on which Powys is using "ego" to refer to what is being defined in this study as "Self."

11. Powys's tendency toward an elaboration of the spatio-geometric is in itself typical of so-called right hemisphere thinking, while an elaboration of time patternings in terms of causation and complexity of plot would have been a significantly more "sinistral" activity.

12. See chap. 3, n. 4.

13. The effect is structurally related to what is known as *trophotropic rebound:* see Fischer, "Cartography," p. 902. Ecstasy can be achieved by an intense speeding up of psychic excitement or by a slowing down into an absolute calm, a meditative serenity. Trophotropic rebound is the sudden switch from the excited Self to the meditative Self: Fischer believes that these two Selves form one and the same subpersonality.

14. The inland/on-the-coast duality is in itself suggestive of the zonal interaction, Britain being an island, an earth-zone entirely surrounded by a sea-zone.

15. This is a collection of essays from 1935 to 1947 that deal with Wales.

Chapter 5. Vertigo

1. See Laski, *Ecstasy,* p. 67. Laski observes that up-feelings are the most common of the quasi-physical sensations reported in descriptions of ecstatic rapture. She refers here to a sense of exaltation, elevation, soaring weightlessness, and so on. In Powys's writing, the feeling of expansion is far more frequent than the purely vertical sense of an upward thrust. I believe that the two are variants of a single ecstatic megastructure, the reference to upward movement merely being more descriptively primitive.

2. See Alfred Douglas, *The Tarot* (Harmondsworth: Penguin Books, 1982), pp. 74–76.

3. The morbid imagery reflects the thought patterns of a man overfamiliar both with extended death-expectancy and intestinal disruptions.

4. I find this peculiarly interesting color imagery suggestive in the context of John Cowper's change of color preferences around 1948. Before this, his favorite color is purple. After 1948 his favorite color is "a peculiar mixture of yellow and green that I find on all the rocks and stones and old walls about here [Corwen, Wales]. . . . It's more yellow than green. It's a mineral yellow, a hard hard opaque yellow-green, very MECHANICAL: a verdigris-gamboge sort of hard factory, artificial un-organic, ungrassy, unleafy HARD metallic YELLOW-GREEN" (*LNR,* 103–4).

5. Laski has a special chapter on ecstasy and childbirth (*Ecstasy,* pp. 138–44). While childbirth is of course a pain-saturated event for most women, there are numerous cases

where childbirth becomes the person's first experience of the altered state of consciousness. Significantly, in the Powys world, pain and ecstasy are never far removed from one another—the enema and the painful constipation attending the Grail vision are pressured tortures closely related to the sensory dynamics of childbirth.

6. In *Mind and Matter* (Cambridge: Cambridge University Press, 1958), Erwin Schrödinger has quite courageously tried to demonstrate how on the one hand all our knowledge about reality (whether inside or outside the laboratory) rests entirely on immediate sense perception, while this knowledge, on the other hand, completely fails to reveal the relations of these sense perceptions to outer reality (p. 88).

7. See Martindale, *Romantic Progression* (pp. 13ff.) for a discussion of "de-differentiation."

8. The masturbatory element is not insignificant in the erotic Powys world: see chap. 3, n. 10.

9. I refer, here, to psychic comfort, not material well-being. The close of John Cowper's life was spent in quite humble circumstances.

10. It is curious to observe Powys's definitive statement about the vanishing of all orgastic possibilities within the *physical* sphere (*LWK*, 68).

11. This notion of retardation is in alignment with what we know about creative-dextral thinking in general. Deferment is a crucial phase in the creative process, and it is likely also to be an integral aspect of vaster ontogenetic patterns. Generally speaking, organisms with higher intelligence spend a longer relative time span in maturation compared with less intelligent creatures. These latter beings have a short period of childhood. Within the overall evolutionary hierarchy, long childhood results in complex systems of intelligence. On creativity and deferment, see William J. J. Gordon, *Synectics: The Development of Creative Capacity* (New York: Harper and Bros., 1961), p. 18.

12. This is a curious reflection, perhaps more whimsical than profound. It is suggestive in the context of the right hemisphere being called the "mute" hemisphere, but there is little scientific evidence to support Powys's view.

13. *LWK*, 63.

BIBLIOGRAPHY

Works by John Cowper Powys

After My Fashion. London: Pan Books/Picador, 1980.

All or Nothing. London: Macdonald, 1960; Village Press, 1973.

The Art of Forgetting the Unpleasant. Girard, Kan.: Haldeman-Julius, 1928; London: Village Press, 1974.

The Art of Growing Old. London: Jonathan Cape, 1944.

The Art of Happiness. New York: Simon and Schuster; London: John Lane, The Bodley Head, 1935; Village Press 1975.

"The Art of Happiness." [Booklet] Girard: Haldeman-Julius, 1923; London: Village Press, 1974.

Atlantis. London: Macdonald, 1954.

Autobiography. New York: Simon and Schuster; London: John Lane, The Bodley Head, 1934; Macdonald, 1967; Pan Books/Picador, 1982.

The Brazen Head. London: Macdonald, 1956; Pan Books/Picador, 1978.

The Complex Vision. New York: Dodd, Mead, 1920; London: Village Press, 1975.

Confessions of Two Brothers (with Llewelyn Powys). Rochester: Manas Press, 1916; London: Sinclair Browne, 1982.

Debate! Is Modern Marriage a Failure? New York: The Discussion Guild, 1930.

Dorothy M. Richardson. London: Joiner and Steele, 1931; Village Press, 1974.

Dostoievsky. London: John Lane, The Bodley Head, 1946.

Ducdame. New York: Doubleday, Page,; London: Grant Richards, 1925; Village Press, 1974.

An Englishman Upstate. London: Village Press, 1974.

The Enjoyment of Literature. New York: Simon and Schuster, 1938.

A Glastonbury Romance. New York: Simon and Schuster, 1932; London: John Lane, The Bodley Head, 1933; Macdonald, 1955; Pan Books/Picador, 1975.

Homer and the Aether. London: Macdonald, 1959.

In Defence of Sensuality. New York: Simon and Schuster; London: Victor Gollancz, 1930; Village Press, 1974.

The Inmates. New York: Philosophical Library; London: Macdonald, 1952.

In Spite Of: A Philosophy for Everyman. New York: Philosophical Library; London: Macdonald, 1953; Village Press, 1974.

James Joyce's Ulysses: An Appreciation. London: Village Press, 1975.

Letters 1937–54. Edited by Iorwerth Peate. Cardiff: University of Wales Press, 1974.

Letters from John Cowper Powys to C. Benson Roberts. Edited by C. Benson Roberts. London: Village Press, 1975.

The Letters of John Cowper Powys to G. R. Wilson Knight. Edited by Robert Blackmore. London: Cecil Woolf, 1983.

Letters of John Cowper Powys to His Brother Llewelyn. Vol. 1. Edited by Malcolm Elwin. London: Village Press, 1975.

Letters of John Cowper Powys to Louis Wilkinson: 1935–1956. Edited by Louis Wilkinson. London: Macdonald, 1958.

Letters of John Cowper Powys to Sven-Erik Täckmark. Edited by Cedric Hentschel. London: Cecil Woolf, 1983.

Letters to Clifford Tolchard from John Cowper Powys. Edited by Clifford Tolchard. London: Village Press, 1975.

Letters to Glyn Hughes. Edited by Bernard Jones. Stevenage: Ore Publications, 1971.

Letters to Nicholas Ross. Selected by Nicholas and Adelaide Ross. Edited by Arthur Uphill. London: Bertram Rota, 1971.

Lucifer: A Poem. London: Macdonald, 1956; Village Press, 1974.

Maiden Castle. New York: Simon and Schuster, 1936; London: Cassell, 1937; Macdonald, 1966; Pan Books/Picador, 1979.

Mandragora: Poems. New York: G. Arnold Shaw, 1917; London: Village Press, 1975.

The Meaning of Culture. New York: W. W. Norton, 1929; London: Jonathan Cape, 1930 and 1940. Village Press, 1974.

The Menace of German Culture: A Reply to Professor Münsterberg. London: Rider, 1915.

Mortal Strife. London: Jonathan Cape, 1942; Village Press, 1974.

Morwyn, or The Vengeance of God. London: Cassell, 1937; Village Press, 1974; Sphere Books, 1977.

Obstinate Cymric: Essays 1935–1947. Carmarthen: Druid Press, 1947; London: Village Press, 1973.

Odes and Other Poems. London: W. Rider and Sons, 1896; Village Press, 1975.

One Hundred Best Books, with Commentary and an Essay on Books and Reading. New York: G. Arnold Shaw, 1916; London: Village Press, 1975.

Owen Glendower: An Historical Novel. New York: Simon and Schuster, 1940; London: John Lane, The Bodley Head, 1942; Pan Books/Picador, 1978.

The Owl, the Duck, and—Miss Rowe! Miss Rowe! Chicago: William Targ, 1930; London: Village Press, 1975.

Paddock Calls. London: Greymitre Books, 1984.

A Philosophy of Solitude. New York: Simon and Schuster; London: Jonathan Cape, 1933.

The Pleasures of Literature. London: Cassell, 1938; Village Press, 1975.

Poems. London: Rider, 1899; Village Press, 1975.

Poems: A Selection. Edited by Kenneth Hopkins. Hamilton, N.Y.: Colgate University Press; London: Macdonalds, 1964.

Porius: A Romance of the Dark Ages. New York: Philosophical Library, 1952; London: Macdonald, 1951; Village Press, 1974.

Psychoanalysis and Morality. San Francisco: Jessica Colbert, 1923; London Village Press, 1975.

Rabelais. New York: Philosophical Library, 1951; London: John Lane, The Bodley Head, 1948; Village Press, 1974.

Real Wraiths. London: Village Press, 1974.

The Religion of a Sceptic. New York: Dodd, Mead, 1925; London: Village Press, 1975.

Rodmoor: A Romance. New York: G. Arnold Shaw, 1916; Hamilton, N.Y.: Colgate University Press; London: Macdonald, 1973.

Romer Mowl and Other Stories. St. Peter Port, Guernsey: Toucan Press, 1974.

Samphire: Poems. New York: Thomas Seltzer, 1922; London: Village Press, 1975.

The Secret of Self-Development. Girard, Kans.: Haldeman-Julius, 1926; London: Village Press, 1974.

Suspended Judgments: Essays on Books and Sensations. New York: G. Arnold Shaw, 1916; London: Village Press, 1975.

Three Fantasies. Manchester: Carcanet Press, 1985.

Two and Two. London: Village Press, 1974.

Up and Out. London: Macdonald, 1957; Village Press, 1974.

Uriah on the Hill. Cambridge: Minority Press, 1930.

Visions and Revisions: A Book of Literary Devotions. New York: G. Arnold Shaw, 1915; London: Macdonald, 1955; Village Press, 1974.

The War and Culture: A Reply to Professor Münsterberg. New York: G. Arnold Shaw, 1914; London: Village Press, 1975.

Weymouth Sands. New York: Simon and Schuster, 1934; Harper Colophon, 1984; London: Macdonald, 1963 (first published as *Jobber Skald,* London: John Lane, The Bodley Head, 1935); Pan Books/Picador, 1980.

Wolf's-Bane: Rhymes. New York: G. Arnold Shaw, 1916; London: Village Press, 1975.

Wolf Solent. New York: Simon and Schuster, 1929; Harper Colophon, 1984; London: Jonathan Cape, 1929; Macdonald, 1961; Harmondsworth: Penguin, 1964, 1978.

Wood and Stone: A Romance. New York: G. Arnold Shaw, 1915; London: Heineman, 1917; Village Press, 1974.

You and Me. London: Village Press, 1975.

Other Works

Ardrey, Robert, *The Hunting Hypothesis.* London: Collins, 1976.

Bachelard, Gaston. *La Poétique de la rêverie.* Paris: Presses Universitaires de France, 1960.

Bakan, Paul. "Dreaming, REM Sleep and the Right Hemisphere." *Journal of Altered States of Consciousness* 3 (1977–78): 285–307.

Beierwaltes, Werner. *Identität und Differenz.* Frankfurt am Main: Vittorio Klostermann, 1980.

Berger. Peter L., and Luckman, Thomas. *The Social Construction of Reality.* London: Allen Tate, The Penguin Press, 1967.

Bergson, Henri. *Duration and Simultaneity.* Indianapolis: Bobbs-Merrill, 1965.

————. *Essai sur les données immédiates de la conscience.* Paris: Librairie Félix Alcan, 1914.

Bennett, J. F. *Kant's Dialectic.* Cambridge: Cambridge University Press, 1974.

Besant, Annie. *The Seven Principles of Man.* Adyar, Madras: The Theosophical Publishing House, 1979.

Blackmur, Richard P. *Eleven Essays in the European Novel.* New York: Harcourt, Brace and World, 1964.

Block, Richard A. "Time and Consciousness." In *Aspects of Consciousness,* volume 1, edited by Geoffrey Underwood and Robin Stevens. London and New York: Academic Press, 1979.

Blumenthal, Arthur L. *The Process of Cognition.* Englewood Cliffs, N.J.: Prentice-Hall, 1977.

————. "A Reappraisal of Wilhelm Wundt." *American Psychologist* 30 (1975): 1081–88.

Brebner, John A. *The Demon Within.* London: Macdonald, 1973.

Bruner, Jerome S. *The Process of Education.* Cambridge: Harvard University Press, 1960.

Cavaliero, Glen. *John Cowper Powys: Novelist.* Oxford: Oxford University Press, 1973.

Collins, H. P. *John Cowper Powys: Old Earth-Man.* London: Barrie and Rockliff, 1966.

Coates, C. A. *John Cowper Powys in Search of a Landscape.* London: Macmillan, 1982.

Corballis, Michael, and Beale, Ivan. *The Psychology of Left and Right.* Hillsdale, N.J.: Lawrence Erlbaum Associates, 1976.

Culler, Jonathan. *On Deconstruction: Theory and Criticism after Structuralism.* London: Routledge and Kegan Paul, 1983.

Derrida, Jacques. *Of Grammatology.* Translated by Gayatri Chakravorty Spivak. Baltimore and London: John Hopkins University Press, 1976.

Dimond, S. J., and Beaumont, J. G. *Hemisphere Function in the Human Brain.* London: Elek Science, 1974.

Douglas, Alfred. *The Tarot.* Harmondsworth: Penguin Books, 1982.

Efron, Robert. "Temporal Perception, Aphasia, and Déjà Vu." *Brain* 86 (1965): 420–23.

Fawkner, H. W. *The Timescapes of John Fowles.* Rutherford, N.J.: Fairleigh Dickinson University Press; London and Toronto: Associated University Presses, 1984.

Fischer, Roland. "A Cartography of the Ecstatic and Meditative States." *Science* 4012 (1971): 897–904.

———. "The Making of Reality." *Journal of Altered States of Consciousness* 3 (1977–78): 371–89.

Fromm, Erich. *Greatness and Limitations of Freud's Thought.* New York: Mentor, 1980.

Fubek, John, ed. *Sensory Deprivation: Fifteen Years of Research.* New York: Appleton-Century-Crofts, 1969.

Gazzaniga, Michael S., and LeDoux, Joseph E. *The Integrated Mind.* New York: Plenum Press, 1978.

Gooch, Stan. *The Double Helix of the Mind.* London: Wildwood House, 1980.

Gordon, J. J. *Synectics: The Development of Creative Capacity.* New York: Harper and Bros., 1961.

Graff, Gerald. *Literature against Itself: Literary Ideas in Modern Society.* Chicago and London: University of Chicago Press, 1979.

Graves, Richard Perceval. *The Brothers Powys.* London: Routledge and Kegan Paul, 1983.

Graves, Robert. *The White Goddess.* London: Faber and Faber, 1961.

Gurdjieff, G. I. *Meetings with Remarkable Men.* Translated by A. R. Orage. London: Routledge and Kegan Paul, 1963.

Harding, Rosamund. *The Anatomy of Inspiration.* Cambridge: W. Heffer and Sons, 1942.

Hegel, G. W. F. *Phenomenology of Spirit.* Translated by A. V. Miller. Oxford and New York: Oxford University Press, 1977.

Hilgard, Ernest R. *Divided Consciousness: Multiple Controls in Human Thought and Action.* New York: John Wiley and Sons, 1977.

———. "Neodissociation Theory of Multiple Cognitive Control Systems." In *Consciousness and Self-Regulation,* volume 1, edited by Gary E. Schwartz and David Shapiro, pp. 137–71. New York and London: Plenum Press, 1976.

Hooker, Jeremy. *John Cowper Powys.* Cardiff: University of Wales Press, 1973.

Hopkins, Kenneth. *The Powys Brothers.* London: Phoenix House, 1967.

Humfrey, Belinda, ed. *Essays on John Cowper Powys.* Cardiff: University of Wales Press, 1972.

————, ed. *Recollections of the Powys Brothers: Llewelyn, Theodore and John Cowper.* London: Peter Owen, 1980.

Inwood, M. J. *Hegel.* London and Boston: Routledge and Kegan Paul, 1983.

James, William. *The Principles of Psychology.* Vol. 1. New York: Henry Holt, 1890.

Jaynes, Julian. *The Origin of Consciousness in the Breakdown of the Bicameral Mind.* Boston: Houghton Mifflin, 1976.

Keup, Wolfram, ed. *Origin and Mechanisms of Hallucinations.* New York: Plenum Press, 1970.

Klüver, Heinrich. *Mescal, and Mechanism of Hallucinations.* Chicago: Chicago University Press, 1966.

Knight, Wilson G. *Neglected Powers: Essays on Nineteenth and Twentieth Century Literature.* London: Routledge and Kegan Paul, 1971.

————. *The Saturnian Quest.* London: Methuen, 1964; Atlantic Highlands, N.J.: Humanities Press, 1978.

Kockelmans, Joseph J. *Edmund Husserl's Phenomenological Psychology: A Historico-Critical Study.* Atlantic Highlands, N.J.: Humanities Press, 1978. First published in 1967.

Krieger, Murray and Dembo, L. S., eds. *Directions for Criticism: Structuralism and Its Alternatives.* Madison: University of Wisconsin Press, 1977.

Krissdottir, Morine. *John Cowper Powys and the Magical Quest.* London: Macdonald and Jane's, 1980.

Lacan, Jacques. *Écrits: A Selection.* Translated by Alan Sheridan. London: Tavistock, 1980.

Langridge, Derek. *John Cowper Powys: A Record of Achievement.* London: The Library Association, 1966.

Laski, Marghanita. *Ecstasy: A Study of Some Secular and Religious Experiences.* London: The Cresset Press, 1961.

LeDoux, Joseph E. "Neuroevolutionary Mechanisms of Cerebral Asymmetry in Man." *Brain, Behavior, and Evolution* 20 (1982): 196–212.

Lévi-Strauss, Claude. *Myth and Meaning.* London: Routledge and Kegan Paul, 1978.

Lindsay R., and Norman D. *Psychology: An Information Processing Approach.* New York: Academic Press, 1972.

Lorenz, Konrad. *On Aggression.* London: University Paperbacks, 1967.

Ludwig, Arnold M. "Altered States of Consciousness." In *Altered States of Consciousness,* edited by C. T. Tart, pp. 9–22. New York: John Wiley and Sons, 1969.

Martindale, Colin. *Romantic Progression: The Psychology of Literary History.* New York: John Wiley and Sons, 1975.

Maslow, Abraham. *The Psychology of Science: A Reconnaissance.* Chicago: Henry Regnery, 1969.

Mayoux, Jean-Jacques. "L'Extase et la sensualité: John Cowper Powys et *Wolf Solent.*" *Critique,* vol. 24, no. 252 (May 1968): 462–74.

Melzack, R. *The Puzzle of Pain.* New York: Basic Books, 1973.

Mookerjee, Ajit. *Tantra Art: Its Philosophy and Physics.* New Delhi: Ravi Kumar, 1966.

Nelson, R. J. *The Logic of Mind.* London and Boston: D. Reidel, 1982.

Nietzsche, Friedrich. *Beyond Good and Evil: Prelude to a Philosophy of the Future.* Translated by R. J. Hillingdale. Harmondsworth: Penguin Books, 1973.

———. *The Birth of Tragedy.* Translated by Walter Kaufmann. New York: Vintage Books, 1967.

———. *On the Genealogy of Morals.* Translated by Walter Kaufmann and R. J. Hollingdale. New York: Vintage Books, 1969.

Oppenheimer, J. Robert. *Science and the Human Understanding.* New York: Simon and Schuster, 1966.

Orme, John Edward. *Time, Experience and Behavior.* New York: American Elsevier Publishing; London: Iliffe Books, 1969.

Ouspensky, P. D. *The Fourth Way.* London: Routledge and Kegan Paul, 1957.

———. *In Search of the Miraculous: Fragments of an Unknown Teaching.* New York: Harcourt Brace Jovanovich, 1949.

Pahnke, Walter N., and Richards, William A. "Implications of LSD and Experimental Mysticism." In *Altered States of Consciousness,* edited by C. T. Tart, pp. 399–428. New York: John Wiley and Sons, 1969.

Pollio, Howard R. "Intuitive Thinking." In *Aspects of Consciousness,* vol. 1, edited by Geoffrey Underwood and Robin Stevens. New York: Academic Press, 1979.

Polzella, Donald J.; DaPolito, Frank; and Hinsman, M. Christine. "Cerebral Asymmetry in Time Perception." *Perception and Psycophysics* 21 (1977): 187–92.

Popper, Karl. *Conjectures and Refutations: The Growth of Scientific Knowledge.* New York: Basic Books, 1962.

———, and Eccles, John C. *The Self and Its Brain: An Argument for Interactionism.* New York: Springer, 1977.

Powys, Littleton. *The Joy of It.* London: Chapman and Hall, 1937.

Powys, Llewelyn. *A Pagan's Pilgrimage.* London: Longman and Green, 1931.

Powys, Theodore Francis. *Soliloquies of a Hermit.* London: Village Press, 1975.

Ricoeur, Paul. *The Conflict of Interpretations; Essays in Hermeneutics.* Edited by Don Ihde. Evanston: Northwestern University Press, 1974.

Said, Edward W. "Roads Taken and Not Taken in Contemporary Criticism." In *Directions for Criticism,* edited by Murray Krieger and L. S. Dembo. Madison: University of Wisconsin Press, 1977.

Schrödinger, Erwin. *Mind and Matter.* Cambridge: Cambridge University Press, 1958.

Schwartz, Gary E. and Shapiro, David, eds. *Consciousness and Self-Regulation,* volume 1. New York and London: Plenum Press. 1976.

Shah, Idries. *The Way of the Sufi.* New York: E. P. Dutton, 1970.

Singer, Jerome L. *Daydreaming and Fantasy.* London: George Allen and Unwin, 1976.

Sinnett, A. P. *Esoteric Buddhism.* Boston: Houghton, Mifflin, 1887.

Sperry, Roger. *Science and Moral Priority: Merging Mind, Brain, and Human Values.* New York: Columbia University Press, 1983.

————. "Some Effects of Disconnecting the Cerebral Hemispheres." *Science* 217 (1982): 1223–26.

Tart, C. T., ed. *Altered States of Consciousness: A Book of Readings.* New York: John Wiley and Sons, 1969.

Underhill, Evelyn. *Mysticism: A Study in the Nature and Development of Man's Spiritual Consciousness.* London: Methuen, 1911; reprinted in 1919.

Underwood, Geoffrey, and Stevens, Robin, eds. *Aspects of Consciousness.* Vol. 1. New York: Academic Press, 1979.

Ward, Richard Heron. *The Powys Brothers.* London: The Bodley Head, 1935.

Weston, Jessie. *From Ritual to Romance.* Garden City, N.Y.: Doubleday, 1957.

Wilkinson, Louis [Louis Marlow, pseud.]. *Swan's Milk.* London: Faber and Faber, 1934.

————. *Welsh Ambassadors.* London: Chapman and Hall, 1936; Village Press, 1975.

Wittgenstein, Ludwig. *Remarks on Colour.* Edited by G. E. M. Anscombe. Translated by Linda L. McAlister and Margarete Schättle. Oxford: Basil Blackwell, 1977.

Wundt, Wilhelm. *Grundzüge der Physiologischen Psychologie.* Leipzig: Engelmann, 1874.

INDEX

Absentmindedness, 187, 219

Absolute, metaphysical, 20, 22, 96, 189, 203–4. *See also* Hegel; Platonism

Acausal thinking, 39

Aestheticism, 16, 33, 177. *See also* Criticism

Aesthetics: ascetic, 16; and bisexuality, 40; and color, 52; and geometric figuration, 50; and positivism, 32–33; and rhythm, 150; and "stream" theories, 147. *See also* Criticism

Affectation. *See* Sincerity

Aftereffects, from ecstasy, 55

After my Fashion: and art/science, 40; and death ecstasy, 169–71; and determinism, 55–56; and dextral center, 70; and doppelgänger phenomenon, 85; and duality, 209; and Ego/Self, 92–93; and fall line, 59; and hidden observer, 169, 174; and ineffability, 38; and love of America, 72; and malicious erotic detachment, 159; and masculinity, 72; and raw elementalism, 72, 187; and time, 97; and universality of ecstasy, 35–36

Ageing. *See* Degeneration

Agnosticism, 160

Air fighting. *See* German/British antagonism

Air travel, 229

Alienation. *See* Fall line; Objectification

All or Nothing, 192, 202–3

Allusions, historical, 32

Altered states of consciousness. *See* Fall line

Amateurishness, 220. *See also* Charlatanism

Ambidextrous consciousness. *See* Fall line

America, love of, 72

Amnesia, multiple, 63–64, 108. *See also* Amnesic barrier; Fall line; Memory

Amnesic barrier, 64, 68, 153, 219

Amphibiousness, 211, 213

Anarchism, 74, 179, 187

Androgyny, 68, 77, 210

Animal Farm, 188

Animate/inanimate interface, 49–51, 59, 117, 119

Anticolor, 181, 201, 204

Anti-intellectualism, 17, 36

Antisystematism, 19

Aperture. *See* Crack imagery; Enema

Apex, cognitive. See *Complex Vision, The;* Control; Demonism; Fall line; Hidden observer; Scanner; Willpower

Aristotle, 17, 31, 39, 228

Arousal, cognitive. *See* Fall line

Arrogance. *See* Pretentiousness

Arrow-slit. *See* Crack imagery

Art for art, 177

Art of Forgetting the Unpleasant, The, 21, 76, 88, 221

Art of Growing Old, The: and altruism/egoism, 163, 214; and capitalism, 207; and centripetalism/centrifugalism, 191, 214; and circular triad, 129; and the Ego, 142; and evolutionary optimism, 217, 218; and Fisher-King, 208; and global suicide, 202; and Grail, 208; and intellectual retardation, 215; and interior void, 153, 208–9; position of, in oeuvre, 41; and pseudologic, 216; and scientific neglect of daydreaming, 219; and "selfsation," 139; and

240

Pain: and cancer, 88, 111; and childbirth, 205; and color, 180–81; and ecstatic verticalism, 193; and equality, 189; existential, 202; and heartlessness, 142; and inflow/outflow, 158, 161, 229; ontological, 201; and orientalism, 37, 205; and Schopenhauer, 87–88. *See also* Stoicism

Painting, 52, 92

Pantheism, 174, 190

Paradoxicality. See Hegel; Ontology; Self-contradiction

Parallel processing, 39, 148. *See also* Fall line

Paranormalism. *See* Supernaturalism

Participation. *See* Criticism; Empathy; "Selfsation"

Paul, Saint, 196

Peak awareness. *See* Fall line

Pedantry, 31

Penetration, 50, 159, 161, 167, 193–94, 210–11. *See also* Crack imagery; Eroticism; Verticalism

Perception. *See* Fall line; Scanner; "Selfsation," Sensory deprivation; Sensory overload

Perfection, artistic. *See* Aesthetics; Criticism; Successfulness

Periphery. *See* Fall line

Perversion. *See* Eversion; Inversion; Inverted world; Sadomasochism

Pessimism, 196, 202, 221. *See also* Skepticism; Stoicism; "Whirlpool"

Phase, evolutionary. *See* Evolution

Phenomenology of Spirit, 16, 19, 20, 22

Philanthropy. *See* Communism; Fall line: and individualism/collectivism; Generosity; Oceanic feeling

Philistinism, 31–32

Philosophy of Solitude, A: and centripetalism/centrifugalism, 183–86; and circular triad, 125–29, 134; and evolution, 47; and false pleasure, 55; and mental health, 76; and mental inversion, 66; and physicalism/mentalism, 183; position of, in oeuvre, 41, 45; and solitude, 99, 149; and sustaining the Self, 54–55

Physics, 204, 206

Pickwick Papers, 229

Piracy, 187. *See also* Recklessness

Plato, 20, 36, 101. *See also* Platonism

Platonism, 18–23, 74, 146, 202–7, 213

Pleasure. *See* Epicureanism; Eroticism; Orgasm; "Selfsation"; Stream of ecstasy

Pleasures of Literature, The, 32, 198, 206, 215

Plovers, 209

Pluralism, 70, 72–75. *See also* Multiverse/universe; Ontology; Polytheism

Poems, first collection of, 78

Politics. *See* Capitalism; Communism; Fall line: and individualism/collectivism

Pollio, Howard R., 227

Polytheism, 174, 195

Pool. *See* Suicide; Wheel of Fortune; "Whirlpool"

Popes, 105

Porius: and centripetalism/centrifugalism, 151, 191; and ecstatic-narrative thrust, 151, 208; and loss of structure, 174, 208; position of, in oeuvre, 14, 151, 174

Pornograpy, 75. *See also* Eroticism; Sadomasochism; Sincerity

Positivism, logical, 31, 218. *See also* Atomism; Cartesianism; Commonsensicalism; Conformism; Materialism; Realism; Sense-certainty

Possessiveness, 172–73. *See also* Capitalism; Eroticism; Private property

Poststructuralism, 19, 32, 73–75

Power. *See* Capitalism; Demonism; Fall line: and individualism/collectivism; German/British antagonism; Willpower

Powys, Llewelyn, 228

Powys criticism. *See* Criticism

Pragmatism: as egotism, 214; as the less-than-ecstatic, 44–45; versus mysticism, 60. *See also* Commonsensicality; Criticism

Prayer, 94. *See also* Etherealization

Preconscious thinking, 39

Presence, metaphysics of, 18

Pre-Socratic philosophy, 213

Pretentiousness, 19, 220–22

Pride, 163. *See also* Demonism; Pretentiousness

Primary-process thinking, 30

Private property, 102, 172–73

Privatism. *See* Capitalism; Fall line: and individualism/collectivism; Narcissism; Self-referentiality

Propaganda, 41, 186